RAISING
GOVERNMENT
CHILDREN

RAISING GOVERNMENT CHILDREN

A HISTORY OF FOSTER CARE
AND THE AMERICAN WELFARE STATE

Catherine E. Rymph

The University of North Carolina Press
Chapel Hill

This book was published with the assistance of the
Anniversary Fund of the University of North Carolina Press and
a subvention from the University of Missouri Research Council.

© 2017 The University of North Carolina Press
All rights reserved
Manufactured in the United States of America

Designed by April Leidig
Set in Arno by Copperline Book Services, Inc.

The University of North Carolina Press has been a member
of the Green Press Initiative since 2003.

Cover illustration: From the United Home Finding Campaign
(Chicago), "*Help Me* and You Help America!," ca. 1943,
National Archives, College Park, Md.

Library of Congress Cataloging-in-Publication Data
Names: Rymph, Catherine E., author.
Title: Raising government children : a history of foster care
and the American welfare state / Catherine E. Rymph.
Description: Chapel Hill : University of North Carolina Press, [2017] |
Includes bibliographical references and index.
Identifiers: LCCN 2017015700| ISBN 9781469635637 (cloth : alk. paper) |
ISBN 9781469635644 (pbk : alk. paper) | ISBN 9781469635651 (ebook)
Subjects: LCSH: Foster home care — United States — History — 20th
century. | Foster home care — Government policy — United States. |
Foster parents — United States. | Public welfare — United States.
Classification: LCC HV881 .R95 2017 | DDC 362.73/309730904 — dc23
LC record available at https://lccn.loc.gov/2017015700

Parts of chapter 2 and chapter 4 appeared previously in somewhat
different form, respectively, in Catherine E. Rymph, "From
'Economic Want' to 'Family Pathology': Foster Family Care, the New
Deal, and the Emergence of a Public Child Welfare System," *Journal
of Policy History* 24, no. 1 (2012): 7–25; and Catherine E. Rymph,
"Looking for Fathers in the Postwar U.S. Foster Care System," in
*Inventing the Modern Family: Family Values and Social Change in
20th Century United States*, ed. Isabel Heinemann, 177–95
(Frankfurt and New York: Campus Verlag, 2012).

To D-D and to Polly

CONTENTS

Acknowledgments ix

Abbreviations xv

Introduction 1

CHAPTER 1
Into the Family Life of Strangers:
The Origins of Foster Family Care 17

CHAPTER 2
The New Deal, Family Security, and the Emergence
of a Public Child Welfare System 43

CHAPTER 3
Helping America's Orphans of War 66

CHAPTER 4
Providing Love and Care:
Foster Parents as Parents 91

CHAPTER 5
The Hard-to-Place Child:
Family Pathology, Race, and Poverty 113

CHAPTER 6
Compensated Motherhood and the State:
Foster Parents as Workers 135

CHAPTER 7
Poverty, Punishment, and Public Assistance:
Reorienting Foster Family Care 157

Conclusion 177

Appendix 187

Notes 189

Bibliography 227

Index 243

ILLUSTRATIONS

"Board Wanted" 79

"A War Job for You in Your Own Home!" 83

"*Help Me* and You Help America" 84

Joy and cash 85

"We Need Homes" 128

"Surprise Your Husband with a Child That Isn't His" 153

Foster fathers 155

ACKNOWLEDGMENTS

It is striking the number of people I know, from different parts of my life, who feel some personal connection to the subject of foster care. Three aspects of this book in particular seem to resonate deeply and broadly — defining the meaning of family, locating the line between labor and love, and assessing the way society values children. Indeed, in my many conversations about this project over the years — be they with friends, acquaintances, historians and other scholars, or nonacademics — scholarly discussions easily morphed into the personal, and personal conversations readily produced insights that followed me into my writing. Thus I have a lot of people to thank.

First on the list, though, are institutions. I have received funding for this project from the Social Welfare History Archives, University of Minnesota; the University of Missouri–Columbia Research Council, the University of Missouri System Research Board, and the University of Missouri–Columbia's Department of Women's and Gender Studies. That funding has made it possible for me to do my research, which involved, above all, traveling to archives. The work of historians would not be possible without archives and archivists. I am grateful for staff at the Library of Congress, the Butler Rare Book and Manuscript Room of Columbia University, the National Archives, and the Social Welfare History Archives at the University of Minnesota, especially Dave Klaassen. Anyone who works on the subject of child welfare passes through this archive at some point, and if they did so before Dave's retirement, they benefited from his copious knowledge of the SWHA's holdings and of the field of child welfare history and from his engaging conversation. Thanks also are due Sally Kenney and Norman Foster, who kindly provided me with a place to stay while in Minneapolis. Most of the archives I worked at are public institutions, and thus I want to acknowledge the taxpayers who enable these fine organizations to collect and preserve our past and make documents available to researchers like me. They are a precious resource.

Chuck Grench, Jad Adkins, and the staff at the University of North Carolina Press believed in this project and shepherded it expertly through the final stages of publication. Two extraordinary historians, Ellen Herman and Eileen Boris, have supported this project for many years. They have written me letters of recommendation, commented on conference papers, and read the manuscript in its entirety. "Thank you" only scratches the surface. Scott Southwick, of course, is always my first editor and has watched every part of this story unfold. I wish that I wrote with half of his wit, elegance, and craft, but he is always generous and gracious in his criticism. I am very lucky to have him.

Over the years, I have had the opportunity to present parts of this project at a number of conferences and have benefited from the wise comments of Wayne Carp, Sara Feldman, Colin Gordon, Isabel Heinemann, Linda Kerber, Molly Ladd-Taylor, the late Paul Longmore, and Michael Willrich. This book has also been enriched by ongoing informal conference conversations with Karen Balcom, Julie Berebitsky, Eileen Boris, Dianne Creagh, Laura Curran, Claire Halstead, Ellen Herman, Marjorie Levine-Clark, Andrew Morris, Kim Nielsen, Ethan Sribnick, Emilie Stoltzfus, Sandy Suffian, and Teresa Toguchi Swartz.

I continue to be sustained, both intellectually and personally, by friendships that first began in graduate school at the University of Iowa. In particular, I thank Sierra Bruckner, Charles Hawley, Marjorie Levine-Clark, Kim Nielsen, and Amy Petersen. Although I doubt he even remembers anymore, it was Chris Gerteis who first encouraged me to pursue a project on foster care, years ago now. I completed many of the final revisions for this project while staying with Sierra Bruckner and Rudi Kräuter. Indeed, I only wish I could do more of my writing at their breakfast table in Moabit. Thank you also to Kathleen Mills, who isn't a grad school buddy but who has been a sounding board for most of my adult life.

My splendid writing group of University of Missouri colleagues has been an anchor during the completion of this book. Elizabeth Chang, Keona Ervin, Emma Lipton, and Robert Smale have been appropriately supportive and irreverent as the occasion required, even if they sometimes talked too much about youth soccer. I would be at sea without them. We come from different disciplines and different fields. What we share is a desire to finish our current book projects. I just hope they will let me stay in the group now that I have completed this one. I must also thank profusely the good folks at Café Berlin, Kaldi's Coffee, and Uprise Bakery who graciously put up with us week after week.

I am fortunate to be a member of a department as collegial as mine. It makes a big difference. Special thanks are due Jonathan Sperber, Russ Zguta, and

John Wigger, who, as department chairs, have supported me in obtaining the time and resources needed to complete this project. My tenacious colleague Michelle Morris deserves special mention for graciously and enthusiastically tracking down the "real" Benjamin Eaton and for helping me with all things seventeenth century. Anyone in my department will happily sing the praises of our exemplary staff. I want to especially thank Lyn Summers, who has a miraculous gift for finding me resources when I most need them, and Melinda Lockwood, who has helped me not only with copying, printing, formatting, and general computer support but also with her genuine enthusiasm for my project. Ph.D. students Sean Rost and Chris Deutsch provided valuable research assistance. Sarah Lirely McCune helped me with the bibliography. I want to also thank Cassie Yacovazzi for her assistance with my index and LeRoy Rowe, whose own work on black girls and out-of-home care in Missouri taught me much.

The outstanding group of engaged students over the years who have taken my History of Adoption, Child Welfare and the Family course gave me the opportunity early on to think through many of my ideas. I learned a great deal from them. One semester I had the opportunity to team-teach the course with Ann Breidenbach. Ann brought her own perspectives as a scholar, a parent, and a writer to that course and helped me wrestle with a number of knotty issues.

My thinking about foster care has benefited from the local child welfare community in Boone County, Missouri, including foster parents, social workers, and legal advocates, especially Karen Anderson, Pam Brendler, Joan Hermsen, Sue Jones, Karen Kelley, Wendy Libey, Anna Lingo, Amy Merkel, and Francine Roling. And many, many people have shared with me over the years their stories of adoption, foster care, and family, including Karen Anderson, Tiffany Borst, Ann Breidenbach, the late Jan Colbert, Tina Drury, Sara Evans, Sara Gable, Sandy Hodge, Sandy Kietzman, Ted Koditschek, Jackie Litt, Linda Little, Nicole Monnier, and Cindy Robinette. Above all, Kerri Urban and Mike Urban have been there almost from the beginning with their enormous hearts and their powerful intellects. Thank you, friends.

Two amazing individuals died too young and did not live to see this book. Ken Cmiel was an exceptional historian who himself wrote a book on child welfare but whom I remember more for his compassion and wisdom about the historical profession shared over drinks at George's Bar in Iowa City. About my brother Georg Rymph, there are no words. I hope he would have liked this book and been proud of me.

I am lucky to have a quirky, challenging, loving family, and I thank them all: Scott Southwick, Polly Southwick, Linus Southwick, Raymond Rymph, and D-D Rymph. I am also deeply grateful to the newest extensions of our family, Josh Baker and Christine Baker and their sons, Holden and Greysen. It is to Polly and D-D, my daughter and my mother, whose own stories of foster care couldn't be more different, that I dedicate this book.

ABBREVIATIONS

ADC	Aid to Dependent Children
AFDC	Aid to Families with Dependent Children
ASFA	Adoption and Safe Families Act
FERA	Federal Emergency Relief Act
NFPA	National Foster Parent Association
RFC	Reconstruction Finance Corporation
TPR	termination of parental rights
USCOM	U.S. Committee for the Care of European Children

RAISING GOVERNMENT CHILDREN

INTRODUCTION

In December 2012, the *Los Angeles Times* ran a moving human-interest story about a young woman named Meredith Kensington. When she had been a child, both of Meredith's parents had struggled with substance abuse, and she was placed in a foster home. Two younger siblings lived for a time with their grandmother, but Meredith was unable to maintain contact with them once they, too, entered foster care. Meredith recounted her own experiences with foster parents who committed fraud, her appeals to social workers who seemed indifferent, and her fears that her younger siblings might have ended up in homes "as bad as hers had been." She eventually ran away from her foster home, leaving behind four half-siblings. Two of them ended up in prison; another was homeless. Now at Christmastime, the *Los Angeles Times* reporter focused on Meredith's desire to spend the holidays with the younger siblings she had lost track of fifteen years earlier when they "entered the byzantine bureaucracy of the Los Angeles County foster care system."[1]

Today, we (like that *Los Angeles Times* reporter) speak of the "foster care system," a system intended to serve dependent, neglected, and abused children who need to be, at least temporarily, removed from their families of origin.[2] Children are removed, characteristically, under the authority of a local court, but their cases are managed by a local child welfare agency, which places a child in a licensed, out-of-home environment, preferably with a family. Public agencies often contract with private agencies (a number of which are sectarian) to provide and monitor foster family care. Some foster youth also end up in group homes or institutions, typically because they have severe behavioral issues or because, for whatever reason, a suitable foster family is not available. When most people think of foster care, however, they are probably thinking not of group homes or institutions but of family placements — what mid-twentieth-century experts called "foster family care."

Foster care is a "system" in which state authorities intervene in family life (occasionally at the request of parents themselves) to fulfill the public's duty to protect children. It is a system with all the negative, bureaucratic meanings that word can contain (particularly for those parents and children, like Meredith, who have suffered under it). What the *Los Angeles Times* reporter refers to as a "byzantine bureaucracy," one advocacy group has taken to calling the "foster care industrial complex."[3] The foster care system today includes thousands of genuinely caring and committed foster parents and social workers who devote their lives to the low-prestige work of serving foster children. Yet the system is widely criticized for failing the children and families it is intended to help. "Statistics Suggest Bleak Futures for Children Who Grow Up in Foster Care" is a typical headline.[4] A number of local and state studies have found higher rates of physical and sexual abuse in foster care than in the general population.[5] Some 30 percent of the nation's homeless population has spent time in foster care.[6] The same is true for 20 percent of the adult prison population under age thirty.[7] Foster children in 2008 were prescribed psychotropic medications at rates two and a half to four and a half times higher than poor children who were not in foster care.[8] By age twenty-four, only 6 percent have completed a two-year or four-year degree.[9] And African American children (like Meredith Kensington and her siblings) are overrepresented among foster children.[10] When I selected Meredith's story to open these pages — essentially at random — I had plenty to choose from. Heartbreaking stories like hers appear regularly in the nation's newspapers. Professional and scholarly writing on foster care, too, is marked by deep pessimism.[11]

Sixty or seventy years ago, child welfare reformers were far more hopeful that they could formalize, rationalize, and modernize existing child welfare practices and provide appropriate services that would truly help children and families. They did not imagine themselves to be setting up a heartless bureaucracy but rather believed they were developing a therapeutic service, one tailored to the individual needs of children that would be delivered in part through professional casework but more importantly through the loving care of temporary substitute families. Reformers' optimism was buoyed by faith in the efficiencies promised by bureaucratization; by the quality of services believed to accompany child welfare professionalization, standardization, and regulation; and by the humane potential of the nascent New Deal welfare state. Foster care services as they existed in the 1930s did not yet constitute a "system," neither a professional, efficient, caring one nor an anonymous, heartless, dysfunctional one. Foster care was instead provided haphazardly through a tangle of practices with roots in much earlier efforts of public authorities, charities, entrepreneurs, and private families.

When parents are poor, or ill, or overwhelmed, or neglectful, or powerless, they often lack the resources, the ability, or the legal right to hold onto their children. The alternatives have not always been particularly nurturing. Foster family care developed in the United States as one of a number of ways of dealing with the problem of dependent children. Indeed, when one examines late nineteenth- and early twentieth-century discussions of foster care, the attentive researcher must bear in mind that the term "foster care" was used much more capaciously than is common today. Foster care once referred to a variety of out-of-home placements for dependent children — boarding homes (where receiving families received minimal board payments), free homes (where no board was paid), and work homes (where children worked in exchange for their support). Indenture laws (under which children could be bound out for a fixed term) still remained in the statutes of some states, although they were rarely used.[12] Many of these "foster" arrangements were actually sought by (rather than imposed on) desperate parents who lacked the resources to care for their children and had no other options.

Particularly vexing for the modern reader, foster care also referred to the placement of children in formal adoptive homes and orphanages, practices usually thought of today as decidedly distinct from foster care.[13] In the early decades of the twentieth century, approximately 1,500–1,600 orphanages were serving between 140,000 and 143,000 children.[14] Adoption, still a relatively new practice in the late nineteenth century, differed from other systems of caring for dependent children because it severed completely and forever all bonds created by birth and replaced them with new, legally binding ties. By contrast, parents placing children in orphanages (for, indeed, most of these children had at least one living parent) retained legal ties to their children.[15]

All of these arrangements were efforts to address some fundamental questions concerning the public's responsibility to ensure the welfare of children. When parents could not or would not care for their offspring — or cared for them in a way the public deemed inadequate or unacceptable — what was to become of those children? What options (and rights) did parents have? In what ways could outsiders concerned with child welfare assist children they believed to be neglected? In what circumstances were biological families worth preserving? What were the responsibilities of public authorities toward such children and their families? Which children fell altogether outside the boundaries of a community's concern or of its responsibility?

This book examines the evolving system of American foster family care from the 1930s, when the Social Security Act first established the basic federal programs of the American welfare state, to the 1970s, by which point it was clear that the vision embraced by New Deal–era reformers was not going to come to pass. I focus on the ideas, debates, and policies surrounding foster care, foster parents, and foster parenting and their relationship to public welfare. Foster care was never and still is not a "national system." Although there are some federal laws that govern it and some federal programs that fund it indirectly, foster care developed at the state and local level, with practices that varied, sometimes considerably.

I think of my approach to exploring foster care as a social history of public policy. According to Margot Canaday and others, the state is "what officials do," including not only "top decision-makers but bureaucrats at all levels," from heads of federal agencies to the person who happens to be working at the desk of a small government office on a particular day.[16] Foster care — which has always been more of a state program than a federal one — has been crafted in part by those "bureaucrats at all levels." Also important have been social workers and professional child welfare experts employed not only by public entities but also by private agencies and university schools of social work. Indeed, such nongovernmental bodies have been crucial to both developing and implementing foster care practices, a "fluid" relationship between state and society that Brian Balogh urges historians to take more seriously.[17] In addition — and this should not be overlooked — foster parents themselves have helped craft our system of foster care, through their frontline work as practitioners and through their individual (and sometimes collective) negotiations with agencies and courts. Thus twentieth-century foster family care was created through interactions among law, policy, elite professionals, social workers in the field, and families themselves. This is a diffuse picture of policy making but one I find most helpful in understanding the way policy is made, practiced, and experienced.

By the mid-twentieth century, there was something akin to a "national conversation" (albeit one initially geared more to the Northeast and Midwest) about foster care that took place among schools of social work, the Child Welfare League of America, the Children's Bureau, and professionals working on the ground. In exploring that conversation and considering more broadly the meanings and practices of mid-twentieth-century foster care, I juggle three overlapping ways of understanding it: (1) as a *public obligation*—foster care as a means for society to fulfill its responsibilities (moral and legal) to ensure the welfare of dependent children; (2) as a component of *household economy*—foster care as a strategy used by families (both families of birth and foster families) to address the logic and realities of their own economic circumstances; and (3) as a type of *family*—foster care as a practice that created alternative family forms, relationships, and even bonds of love. That these three themes are so entwined in foster care reveals an American form of welfare provision that is necessarily buttressed by the sometimes messy work—paid labor, emotional labor, and care work—of private families.

To some extent, that "national" conversation was also international, through the inclusion of some Canadian child welfare agencies among the Child Welfare League's membership, as well as some international connections between individuals through the League of Nations and United Nations. And, to be sure, in Canada, Australia, and a few other countries, modern foster care developed out of earlier practices in ways somewhat similar to what occurred in the United States.[18] Yet rates of industrialization and state formation, different conceptions of the state and its responsibilities for public welfare, experiences of colonialism for many countries, and diverse notions of kinship, community, and secularization (among other factors) have meant that foster care has looked quite different around the world.[19]

In the United States, when other systems designed to help poor families have failed, often all that remains is foster care. Despite the importance of foster care to contemporary welfare policy, historians have done little to explore the origins and development of this perplexing form of social provision.[20] As a form of assistance to dependent children, foster families are not entirely part of the state (and are understudied in scholarship on the welfare state), nor do foster homes truly constitute families in a legal sense (and are understudied in scholarship on substitute caregiving such as adoption). Foster family care is significant for these histories, however, as a site where state policies concerning assistance to dependent children are implemented through and sustained by one of society's most private and intimate institutions and where oblique conversations about what constitutes a "real" family take place. Because, as I argue, foster families also subsidize public child welfare programs, a study of foster care highlights the ways women's unpaid and low-paid care work have been vital, yet often barely visible, parts of welfare provision.

The foster care system, although never intended as such, has become a critical part of the modern American welfare state, its twists and turns intricately tied to the fortunes and ideologies of other better-known programs such as Aid to Dependent Children (ADC) and Old Age and Survivor's Insurance. Foster care is substantially different from these welfare programs, however, in its reliance on private citizens to provide services. Foster care is also linked to programs like day care, which failed to become part of federal welfare provision, and to homemaker (or "mothers' aid") services, which were never fully implemented.

Child welfare reformers conceived of a public-private partnership for the care of dependent children. The federal government (or the states) would provide security to families so they could keep their children with them, as well as support for a state and local child welfare infrastructure that would offer specialized services (including foster family care) to those children who remained in need of them. As historians such as Gary Gerstle and Brian Balogh have argued, state-building in the United States has been facilitated through partnerships with both private corporations and private charities, which have helped finesse constitutional limitations on federal power and preserve Americans' sense of individual freedom.[21] Public foster care, too, emerged often in partnership with private child-placing agencies. The private-public partnership extends in an additional direction in the case of foster care, though, into American homes. Private families would be the main provider of public foster care, with professionally trained social workers mediating and supervising relationships between children and their caregivers. Fundamental to this conception, although not explicitly stated, was that child welfare would be partially public (paid for with public funds) and partially private (paid for by the families actually providing the care).

If foster care was unlike other forms of welfare provision, it also differed in significant ways from adoption, especially in the period this book examines. At the turn of the twentieth century, the informality of "adoption" and the broad meanings of "foster care" meant that the two terms were often used synonymously. By the mid-twentieth century, however, adoption and foster care had come to represent two quite different paths. Adoption created permanent, loving families, while foster care was a "system."[22] Adoption would come to be celebrated as the "best solution" for all members of the adoption triad,[23] whereas foster children, their biological parents, and their foster parents were viewed with suspicion by much of the public and even by the agencies that served them. Placement workers understood the pool of potential adoptive parents to be different from and superior to the pool of foster parents. The great demand for adoptable children meant adoption workers could be highly choosy about which parents they accepted, whereas the low esteem in which the public held foster children contributed to a constant shortage of foster parents. Adoption created permanent homes for children, while the explicitly temporary nature of foster care often left children in limbo.

By the turn of the twenty-first century, adoption and foster care have again become closely entwined. New policies and laws promoting adoption of foster children by their foster parents have replaced older practices that explicitly forbade foster parents from providing permanent, adoptive homes to their foster children. These are recent changes, however. At midcentury, foster care and adoption were as radically separated as they have ever been. This separation again highlights the often hidden role that private families have played in implementing publicly funded child welfare services and helps illuminate the unique relationship of foster care to the welfare state. Was foster care a way to create new families, or a way to accommodate an inadequate social safety net? Were foster parents analogous to adoptive parents, in that they provided substitute families for children unable to live with their biological parents? Or were they more accurately seen as laborers whose "job" was to provide love and care to foster children for remuneration? If workers, were they best viewed as low-paid, unskilled female care workers (foster *fathers* received very little attention, especially early on) or as quasi-professionals? Were foster parents the colleagues of agency staff? Their employees? Or were they their clients? Was foster parenting a job? A service? A role? As they tried to understand the system they were creating, midcentury professionals, policy makers, and foster parents themselves meandered uncomfortably between these imperfect, often contradictory, analogies. Each had its pitfalls. Each was revealing.

Midcentury reformers wanted to shift foster family care away from being a program intended only for children of the poorest families and reposition it as one of a number of specialized, professional services available to children at all income levels based on their unique, individual needs. As part of that transition, reformers sought to vet and secure better-trained foster parents who would be qualified according to the new "science" of child placement and who would operate as an arm of the agency, in line with its goals for the child. Reformers would come to realize that they could not retain foster parents who met those criteria without compensating for their services, yet they remained deeply uncomfortable with the idea of paying for parenting. By the late sixties and early seventies, the New Deal–era vision had collapsed. Foster care was overwhelmingly serving poor children and becoming increasingly punitive toward biological parents; public programs were not enough to provide the family security envisioned by reformers; and the idea of creating "professional foster parents" was bumping up against the agendas of foster parents, who sought more and more to help delineate the foster parent role for themselves.

Today, poverty and poverty-related neglect play a critical part in determining which children are removed from their families and placed in foster homes. This would have troubled child welfare reformers in the early to mid-twentieth century, believing as they did that they were creating something quite different and much better for children and their families. Foster care was once part of a broader vision of publicly provided family security, in which poverty alone would no longer force the break-up of families. But that vision was likely doomed from the start. Foster care would become a disparaged form of "welfare" that would stigmatize the women who provided it, the children who received it, and their families. This book tells the story of that vision and its demise.

Communities have long wrestled with questions about how best to provide for those who would come to be known as "dependent or neglected children." The meanings of this term is not at all straightforward. Of course, we understand *all* children to properly be dependent, in the economic sense that they *depend on* their parents for support. As Nancy Fraser and Linda Gordon have explained, by the nineteenth century, American understandings of dependency included "good" kinds (the dependency of wives and children on male heads of household) and more dubious kinds (dependency on charity or public support). Indeed, the term "dependent" was initially applied, between the 1890s and the 1920s, specifically to children in order to distinguish their appropriate state of need from the illegitimate status of paupers. Only after World War II would the term come to be widely and negatively applied to adults who received aid.[24] Thus, all children were properly dependent; yet only those who were not able to be solely dependent on their parents were "dependent children" in need of foster care, or, after passage of the Social Security Act in 1935, in need of "Aid to Dependent Children." (The word "dependent" in the name of the ADC program referred to the dependency of children themselves yet would come to stigmatize the mothers who were conduits of assistance to poor children). In the child welfare system, the term "dependent child" referred more specifically to children who, in the absence of parents able to provide proper care, became "dependent" on the wider community for the maintenance normally provided by parents.[25] The parents of a "dependent child" might be dead, in prison, or otherwise absent, or they might simply be too poor to care for their children.

"Neglected" children had parents, but their parents were not caring for them adequately. Often it was the parents who came to this conclusion themselves and, in their desperation, sought help through child placement. In other cases, some authority deemed a child to be neglected and in need of protection. Perhaps the child did not have proper shelter or clothing or food; perhaps she was not attending school or was exposed to immoral activity, such as gambling, drunkenness, or promiscuity. Although a child from a prosperous family could, in theory, be neglected, neglect was also linked to poverty. As historian Tim Hacsi notes, "The line distinguishing dependent children from neglected children was elusive." Once they entered foster care, neglected and dependent children were "in practice" treated the same.[26] Writing in 1947, longtime child welfare advocate Emma Lundberg noted that dependency and neglect had two main causes — those associated with the home and those associated with the conditions of the community. Often what appeared to be home conditions leading to child dependency or neglect in fact, Lundberg emphasized, had "their source in economic insecurity and health hazards properly chargeable to community conditions."[27] As scholar Karen Swift has explained, in writing about child welfare in Canada, "The concept of child neglect arose from conditions of social and economic deprivation." Reformers believed parents, especially mothers, were responsible for their children. Yet their poverty often prevented parents from providing the care that reformers believed was warranted.[28]

Foster care today also serves children who have been physically and sexually abused. The early to mid-twentieth-century preferred term for the children served by foster home care — "dependent and neglected" — did not explicitly list "abused," although victims of physical abuse would have fallen under this rubric. Child welfare agencies and child protective services, though, believed that incidents of physical cruelty against children had declined after the 1920s, despite what historian Linda Gordon argues has been the "tenacity and constancy" of child abuse.[29] The so-called rediscovery of child abuse in the early 1960s and the later advent of mandatory reporting laws would considerably alter understandings of the purpose and scope of foster family care.[30]

Historians of gender, race, and welfare policy have taught us much about the origins of gender and racial inequality in the welfare state.[31] But while they have focused on American assistance to poor women and their children, for the most part these scholars have not included foster care in their scope. Examining the origins of welfare inequality in the 1935 Social Security Act, they have looked primarily at Aid to Dependent Children (later called Aid to Families with Dependent Children, or AFDC), often contrasting its meager and punitive provisions with the more generous entitlements of workplace programs such as Old Age and Survivor's Insurance, and exploring the gender and racial dynamics at play in their development and implementation. More recently, Eileen Boris and Jennifer Klein have looked at the origins of home health work in New Deal work relief programs that put poor, often minority women to work in private homes providing care to children and the elderly. As they observe, this was "public work performed in private homes."[32] So, too, was foster care.

Indeed, foster care, I suggest, has been deeply connected to many New Deal programs. Child welfare reformers in the 1930s saw New Deal programs as a means of preventing out-of-home placements of children because they would provide security to families and prevent family breakdown and collapse. Social programs that had begun in the private sector became public responsibilities, first at the state level and then, by the thirties, at the federal level. This included basic relief, care for the disabled, and social insurance programs. It did not include day care or health care, which would become benefits provided (when provided at all) through private employment encouraged through incentives.[33] New Deal welfare programs would include care for dependent children, but much of that care remained privately subsidized and implemented. Thanks to other New Deal welfare policies, reformers hoped, children would no longer be removed from their homes and placed in foster care for reasons of poverty. Yet by the late 1950s, researchers were discovering that it was still the case that the majority of children coming into care were, in fact, poor. Indeed, I argue, the assumptions and prejudices concerning class, gender, race, family, and welfare that kept many families outside the web of New Deal family security left foster care as the only option for the children of those families.

Policy historians now recognize that gender and racial assumptions shaped the development of the American welfare state, particularly social insurance and Aid to Dependent Children.[34] Foster care developed in tandem with those systems, and thus reformers' normative notions about male breadwinning, female dependency, female caregiving, and the relative worth of children also helped shape the system of foster care. So too was the place and shape of foster care affected by the social programs that the United States did *not* implement, such as federally funded childcare or a guaranteed income. The shifting fortunes of foster care also illuminate how the professionalizing agenda of social workers and their vision of child welfare meshed with a still uneasy relationship between public *funding* of services and private (often sectarian) *implementation* of them, as well as the corrosive erosion of services when they come to be funded as "welfare."[35] As Tim Hacsi suggests, the development of public foster care (along with state mothers' pensions and federal Aid to Dependent Children) can be seen as a kind of public takeover of a role previously served largely by nongovernmental entities — the care of dependent children moved from the largely private realm of orphan asylums to public support of single mothers and publicly funded foster family care.[36] I argue, however, that while *publicly funded*, the modern foster family care that emerged in the mid-twentieth century was also *privately subsidized* by the individual foster families whose true costs of providing foster care were never actually covered by board payments. Foster fathers' income and foster mothers' care work made hidden, yet essential, contributions to this form of welfare provision.

The study of adoption history (part of the emerging interdisciplinary field of adoption studies) is not as well developed as the study of social welfare policy, although it has produced exciting scholarship in recent years.[37] Historians of adoption have focused less attention on foster care than on the more permanent relationships created by formal adoption. Foster care certainly shares features with adoption. Each places children who are unable to live with their biological parents with substitute families, and professionals in each field developed a "science" of child placement that scrutinized parents and children. Adoption and foster care both involve questions about the meaning of family and the relative value of children. Historians of adoption have given important attention to the roles of class, gender, religion, and race in explaining which children become available for adoption and which parents were allowed to adopt. Particularly in the postwar years, it was middle-class families who met the criteria to become adoptive parents, often of the out-of-wedlock children of white middle-class teenagers. Studies of more contemporary adoption practices have criticized the ways in which adoption serves to transfer the children of those who are economically disadvantaged (and often non-white) to middle-class homes, both within North America and internationally.[38]

The class and racial dynamics of foster care have been different from those characterizing adoption's history. Foster parents themselves were not typically affluent or even middle class, and child placement experts historically viewed them as exhibiting a number of flaws. Indeed, the origins of foster care reveal that earlier systems of caring for dependent children, such as indenture or boarding out, could serve as forms of assistance to poor families who took in children. Receiving the labor of children or payment for their care could be integrated into the broader household economy of families living on the margins. Unlike adoptive parents, mid-twentieth-century foster parents received remuneration (albeit minimal) for board costs. This created anxiety among child welfare professionals who, on the one hand, recognized the need to reimburse foster parents (namely women) for their expenses yet, at the same time, were deeply suspicious of the motives of women who accepted payment to care for children. This anxiety I connect to more broad and persistent denigration of all paid care workers, a term that refers to those who perform jobs that "provide a face-to-face service that develops the human capabilities of the recipient."[39] Furthermore, foster children did not possess the same value that children available for adoption (especially white infants) had, due to their age, backgrounds, behavioral problems, and status as "welfare" or "government" children (as they were sometimes known).

Race played an important role in determining the perceived value of foster children and their families. While today African American children are overrepresented in foster care, for much of the period I examine, this was not the case. Few agencies served black families and their children. Like many other forms of social provision, foster care was generally seen as a "service" whose clientele was primarily white and from which African Americans were largely excluded.[40] When reformers began expressing concern about racial discrimination within the system, as some did in the 1950s, they focused on home-finding campaigns to increase the number of families able to take in African American children. Under conventional wisdom and the often unwritten policies of child welfare agencies, children were only placed in homes where the foster parents were of the same race and religion as the child. A lack of licensed foster parents of color was frequently named as a reason why African American and Native American children were not receiving foster care, even when there was a perceived need. Of other underrepresented groups, such as Mexican Americans and Asian Americans, midcentury child welfare experts rarely made any note at all. In the 1950s, some agencies launched campaigns to recruit black foster parents and to find white families willing to take in Native children, but the results were not always as intended.

There are four crucial perspectives in a study of foster care: those of biological parents, foster parents, foster children, and social work professionals. In this book I try to offer analysis from all four. Professionals are the best sourced, through their voluminous professional papers and writings. But letters to the Children's Bureau offer compelling (albeit fragmented) insights into the views of biological parents and foster parents as well. It is hardest to access the views of the children themselves. Children in foster care had very little say concerning their placements, and their perspectives in the record are almost always mediated through adults. Although the protection of their interests and their welfare was presumably at the heart of the entire system, children's voices are unfortunately marginalized in this work (as their voices continue to be, in practice, many would argue).

In terms of the adults in these stories, I take a position that some might suspect is overly rosy or in need of a dose of cynicism. I assume that most child welfare workers and professionals were in the field because they genuinely cared about the welfare of children, even if some of the policies they pursued and practices they endorsed now might appear profoundly misguided; I assume that foster parents frequently cared deeply for their charges, even though other individual foster parents did indeed behave cruelly toward children in their care; and I assume that most birth parents loved their children, even though they did not always have the financial, material, emotional, or community resources to care for them. I have found nothing in my research to undermine these general assumptions. This perspective may not sit well with some, especially readers who have witnessed biological parents, foster parents, or social workers behaving callously, indifferently, or abusively. Individual adults made plenty of mistakes. But the larger problems with the midcentury American foster care system stemmed from the failure of the welfare state to offer true family security, the inherent problems of private/public welfare provision, and the persistent undervaluing of care work (both the care work performed by low-income birth mothers and that performed by foster mothers).

Indeed, if there is a way to make foster family care truly work well, the United States has not yet found it. While observers complain bitterly about the system today, my research suggests that there was never a time when Americans thought foster care was a well-functioning system that genuinely worked to the benefit of children and families. Yet midcentury reformers had a vision of something better, which they strove to implement. One longs to root for them, even when their project seemed flawed, misguided, and ultimately doomed. Although child welfare professionals did not always speak with one voice on all matters, they developed a general consensus around a number of issues. Foster family care, they envisioned, would cease to be a poverty program designed for only the most destitute children. It would lose its link to poverty and become a much rarer practice, one available broadly to all families that required it. It would develop into a small but important, efficiently administered therapeutic service performed by high-quality foster parents who had been vetted and trained by experts. Foster care would serve children and families, not just protect communities from the problems associated with dependent children. Foster family care would reach children from difficult families whose problems were more complex than those of mere poverty, thus requiring the casework and child-placing expertise offered by specialized professional social workers. And foster family care would be specially tailored to an individual child's needs and provided by a loving, trained, quasi-professional foster family.[41] Reformers articulated this vision over and over. But that vision was idealized, contained inherent tensions, and conflicted with many of the social, economic, and political directions toward which their society was moving.

In exploring foster care at midcentury, this book follows a generally chronological structure. Chapter 1 briefly surveys the origins of foster care in earlier methods for supporting dependent children, whose beginnings date back to the colonial period; chapter 2 addresses the significance of the New Deal to the development of publicly funded foster care and its relationship to the nascent welfare state; chapter 3 examines the impact of World War II, which increased the need for foster care, decreased the supply of foster parents, and exacerbated tensions over women's roles as workers, mothers, and caregivers; chapters 4 and 6 address the ambiguity of foster parents' roles, as both *parents* and *workers* in the postwar period, and the struggles of professionals to come to terms with that ambiguity. Chapter 5 examines the notion of the "hard-to-place child" and the emergence of the idea that foster children were inherently damaged; while chapter 7 explores the policy changes of the 1960s that made foster care a more punitive system, now firmly linked to public assistance, in which children of color were overrepresented.

Among the images I copied from the archives during the course of researching this book is a passport-sized photograph of a mother and baby. The mother — I have called her Ruth Parker in these pages — had attached the photograph to one of the many letters she wrote in her broad, scrawling handwriting. Her red hair is curled, and she sports bright red lipstick. She clutches her daughter, who is dressed in a pale blue coat. The colors in the image are striking. I imagine this picture was taken for a special occasion and that it was precious to Ruth, whose child was no longer living with her when she wrote her letters. Indeed, the point of her voluminous correspondence — she wrote repeatedly to agencies in Washington and even to President Truman — was to convey her frustration and despair at having lost custody of her daughter. Her hopes that the federal government would intervene for her were quixotic at best. Yet she parted with this treasured photograph, trusting, presumably, that it might convey to her reader the strength of her bond to her child and compel action on her behalf. I do not know what happened to Ruth or her daughter and am not in a position to judge what *should* have happened, but Ruth's anguish is palpable. I have looked often at her photograph as I have written this book in an effort to keep central the thousands of individual, sorrowful stories that make up the collective history of our foster care "system."

As a system, foster care is quite diffuse. It operates at a macro and a micro level. In the big picture, foster care is a system, a bureaucracy of regulations, rules, procedures, budgets. At the more intimate level, it concerns families and other personal relationships that are made up of unique experiences and often painful stories. Anyone who has intersected with foster care knows that to do so is to expose oneself to heartache, to joy, to anger — in other words, to any number of profound and affecting emotions that have lasting implications. In writing this account of foster care's history, I know that I have generally opted for scholarly detachment. To the extent that I have failed to capture the intense emotional entanglement of foster care in this book, I take comfort in the fact that others have accomplished what I have not — especially through memoir and journalistic accounts.[42] Mine is a different approach, which I nonetheless hope will resonate with readers who care deeply, as they should, about foster care.

CHAPTER 1

INTO THE FAMILY LIFE OF STRANGERS

The Origins of Foster Family Care

In 1928, Angelo Costa, an Italian immigrant living in Minneapolis, found himself in crisis. His wife and newborn baby had recently died. Struggling to hold steady work due to a war injury and with a young son and two daughters to raise, Angelo faced a dilemma — how to both provide for and care for his children. Where and to whom could he turn? Out-of-home care for his children would turn out to be one of his only options. But this was not yet the modern, bureaucratic, publicly licensed system of supervised foster care that would arise within a few decades. Angelo's crisis happened at a time when that system was only just beginning to take shape.

The "story of the development of supervised foster care as it now operates," as one curious child welfare worker would later put it, extended far back into foster care's roots in much older traditions of caring for poor and dependent children.[1] A number of these traditions have been explored at length by other scholars, but briefly reviewing them helps us to appreciate the daunting task that child welfare professionals would face in the mid-twentieth century as they tried to make out-of-home placement conform to their developing understandings of families, of child welfare services, and of the role of the state in providing those services. Such a review also assists us in focusing on the traditional power relations within families, communities, and the nation that helped shape the precursors to modern foster family care. As Tim Hacsi has argued, "Without an understanding of how poor children have been cared for by charity and welfare, no study of politics or economic development can fully explain what the American welfare state does *not* do very well. And of all the welfare state's failures, none is more glaring than its inability to provide for poor children."[2]

The long history of foster care in the United States extends back to various colonial practices of indenture and apprenticeship. Indeed, the National Foster Parent Association has, since 1974, heralded Benjamin Eaton, a seven-year-old boy bound out by his widowed mother in 1636, as the nation's "first foster child."[3] The NFPA didn't seem to know much about Eaton when it claimed him (and got some important facts wrong), but we can find him in the historical record. His father, Francis, a resident of Plymouth colony, died insolvent in 1633, leaving four minor children, including Benjamin. Like Angelo Costa several centuries later, Francis's widow, Christian, faced a crisis of care. She found herself with four youngsters but no financial resources from her husband's estate to help with their care. Three years later, in February 1636, Christian apprenticed Benjamin to Bridgett Fuller for fourteen years.[4]

Even if Eaton was the "first" recorded case of a European child bound out as an indentured servant in the Massachusetts Bay Colony — possible, but not likely — we know that Native American, African, and mixed-race children regularly found themselves in situations not all that different from Benjamin's. And what does it mean to read our modern conception of "foster child" back into the seventeenth century, when ideas of family, the state, and child welfare were profoundly different? Indenture and apprenticeship of children, practices brought to the colonies from England and modeled on aspects of Elizabethan Poor Law, were part of a labor system. Masters signed contracts with a child's guardians, promising training and support in exchange for the services of the child.[5] From their apprentices, households and craftsmen received the advantages of household labor. In this sense, children paid for their own support.

Indenture was a labor system, but it was also an early means by which communities provided for the welfare of dependent children, an obligation derived from the Poor Law tradition of *parens patriae*.[6] Such arrangements were not to be — or, at least not intended to be — one-sided. The head of household was expected to act like a parent by supporting, nurturing, and educating the child in his or her care and provide training in a useful skill. Even in cases where indenture was a private arrangement between two families, the state was at least tangentially involved through the use of contracts, enforceable through the courts, to seal these agreements. Furthermore, communities had to pay to bind out an infant, who, unlike an older child, did not come with an ability to work. As with more modern foster care practices, poverty was a significant reason why a child like Benjamin Eaton would be placed with another family.

Community morals and standards of behavior also played a role. In colonial Virginia, churchwardens could bind out children whose parents they considered to be "idle."[7] By 1660, the selectmen of Massachusetts were authorized to remove badly behaved children from their homes and apprentice them to masters who would do a better job of forcing them to "submit unto government."[8]

The practice of indenture may seem remote from that of modern foster care. Whatever the problems with the system today, foster care is at least intended to promote children's interests, not exploit their labor. But the idea that children were to be valued purely for the emotional attachment adults felt for them is a fairly recent one. Viviana Zelizer maintains that such sentimental understandings of children first became engrained for middle-class urban families only in the mid-nineteenth century.[9] By that point, indenture had been gradually giving way to wage labor. And, as antislavery sentiment grew, so too came the suspicion that indenture, under which many children of all races continued to be bound, looked itself to be too much like enslavement.[10] Yet by the early nineteenth century, urbanization and the concentrations of poverty associated with it would mean a growing need for out-of-home care for children. Public almshouses, insane asylums, and even adult prisons came to house many poor children who had nowhere else to go.

Orphanages were meant to be a more humane and specialized alternative to almshouses or adult prisons (though only for some children). The "vast majority" were local undertakings, managed and funded privately. This meant directors could be selective in choosing the children they would serve. Religious selection was common, as many of the orphanages were constructed to serve specific faith communities. Almost half of children in orphanages at the end of the nineteenth century were living in Catholic institutions.[11] Orphanages tended to be restricted to white children, although a few black orphan asylums were created, sometimes by African Americans themselves but more often with white sponsorship.[12] According to Tim Hacsi, by 1880 there were over six hundred orphanages in the United States serving more than fifty thousand children.[13]

Despite their name, orphanages did not strictly house full orphans and, in fact, often served as a safety net for poor parents. Able-bodied children whose families were unable to raise them due to poverty, illness, or death might be turned over — often reluctantly or unwillingly — to orphanages.[14] The parents of children with disabilities, meanwhile, were encouraged to place their children in institutions such as schools for the blind, homes for crippled children, or asylums for the feeble-minded.[15] Parents were expected to pay an orphanage something toward the care of their children, although not all did. Placements were often temporary, with children returning to their families when they became old enough to go to school, when a widow remarried, or when an unemployed father found work.[16]

The relationship between public and private support for orphanages was complex and would help shape the development of foster care. Once state legislators began banning the placement of children in almshouses starting in the mid-1870s, the states had to care for dependent children in other ways, leading them, in some cases, to establish public orphanages at the state or county level.[17] As Andrew Billingsley and Jeanne Giovannoni have argued, the shift from private to public child welfare services meant more services available to black children as African Americans "inevitably fare better where the givers of services are publicly accountable."[18] But that shift from public to private was uneven. States with a powerful network of preexisting private orphanages, like New York, chose not to establish public institutions but instead to provide subsidies to those private orphanages housing children committed by courts or public relief agencies.[19] Because private institutions were free to turn away children who were poorly behaved or who exhibited particular defects of body or character, it was the children perceived as challenging, different, or less desirable (a group which typically included black children) who ended up in state institutions.[20] In the South, even many public institutions served white children only.[21] Many child welfare reformers would later see public subsidy of private institutions as inherently problematic, but the practice developed for quite pragmatic reasons. In states where private orphanages were in place long before public ones, states simply "drifted" into the practice of subsidizing existing private institutions because it was less expensive, because it was easier, and because "public" welfare carried more stigma for recipients than did private charity.[22]

Not all mid-nineteenth-century child welfare reformers saw orphanages as appropriate alternatives for children in need of homes. Theology student Charles Loring Brace was, like other reformers, profoundly distressed by the conditions of the street children he observed when he first came to New York City in 1848. Especially troubling to Brace were the large numbers of homeless children he encountered who were begging, selling flowers, or working as prostitutes. In 1849, reformers estimated that as many as forty thousand of

New York City's children, many of whom were immigrants or children of immigrants, lived on the streets.[23] Yet Brace was not persuaded that orphanages were an improvement over adult institutions, because they were, after all, still institutions. What destitute children needed, Brace believed, were the wholesome effects of family life. In 1853 he created the Children's Aid Society and soon instituted his famous "placing out" program, better known today as the "orphan trains." The homes that took in these children were also sometimes called "free homes" because no money was given in exchange for care. Although Brace did not invent the system, his would become the name most associated with it. Orphan trains sent impoverished, able-bodied children from the rough and dirty streets of the cities to live, often permanently, with rural families in nearby states and eventually in farther away parts of the Midwest, the South, and the West. In what one historian has described as Brace's recreation of the "old concept of indenture" in a "new form," children were still expected to work for their new family within the context of household labor, yet they were not bound out by contract.[24] Through the ennobling effects of outdoor rural living, character-building labor, and wholesome family life, children's lives would be transformed.[25] Society's cast-off waifs would become productive citizens.

Like orphanages, these placing-out programs did not exclusively serve orphans. Certainly some youngsters were placed out by the Children's Aid Society because their parents had died or had abandoned them. In other cases, parents voluntarily pursued placement with the Children's Aid Society to address immediate economic crises in the family.[26] But Brace also sought out children whose families appeared to be too impoverished or culturally problematic. And his agency at times applied intense pressure to parents to give up their children. For Brace, the biological families of poor children were a large part of the problem; the solution to child dependency and neglect was to remove children from the influences of those urban, immigrant, impoverished (and often Catholic) families and place them in homes he felt would provide a more stable and wholesome atmosphere — rural, native-born, and Protestant. Brace and his colleagues saw placing out as a solution to the problems of urban poverty and, later, of escalating immigration.[27]

Although the Children's Aid Society was a private organization dependent on donations, its child placement program was also subsidized by New York City and New York State and therefore can be seen as form of proto-public child welfare services.[28] Public subsidy did not yet bring public accountability, however.

Neither did the Children's Aid Society offer its own oversight. Brace's program initially did not screen receiving parents, nor did it provide any systematic follow-up with children once they were placed.[29] As a consequence, while some receiving families were loving and treated their new children as their own, others were merely seeking something akin to a servant or a free farmhand. This was particularly the case with older boys, who were also in greatest demand.[30] Although Brace's "orphan train" system is well known, rural placements also occurred much closer to home, as midwestern states sought solutions for their own dependent children through farm placements. According to historian Megan Birk, between 1850 and 1900 farm placement was so widespread in the Midwest that between 20 and 30 percent of farm homes included children who were not biologically related to the adults.[31]

The orphan trains are often cited as the origins of the modern foster care system and Brace as foster care's "father."[32] Certainly the placing-out model played an important role in the development of twentieth-century child welfare practices, particularly in its premise that dependent children were better off in nonkin families than in institutions. Brace's system would be picked up by other child-saving organizations in New York and elsewhere.[33] But the placing-out system looked more like informal adoption arrangements, on the one hand, and indenture, on the other, than what would come to be known in the twentieth century as "foster family care." Most children who rode the orphan trains were not formally adopted, as adoption was still a rare practice in the late nineteenth-century United States. But Brace thought or hoped that these placements would lead to permanent homes for children. The families who opened their doors to needy children were supposed to raise them as their own, provide them with decent food and clothing, and allow them to go to school.[34] Motivations were meant to be charitable, although all parties assumed that children would contribute their labor to the household economy. Child labor had to retain a certain legitimacy for these free home placements to be effective. Children were expected — as was normal in nineteenth-century rural families — to be "useful," by working. It was considered a "fair bargain" that families would receive help with a variety of tasks in exchange for board, clothing, and a little education.[35] Indeed, Megan Birk insists that there were so few differences between indenture and rural free placement that the terms were often used synonymously. Rural placements were often "indentures without the paperwork."[36]

Both orphanages and the orphan trains were important precursors to foster family care and have received considerable treatment by historians.[37] Yet the lesser-studied practice of "boarding out" had, in many ways, more in common with modern fostering.[38] Boarding arrangements were typically informal ones between families, without the involvement of any agency. Under these arrangements, parents facing hardships — such as the death of or abandonment by a spouse, unemployment, or prolonged illness — might temporarily pay another woman to board their children while they waited for circumstances to improve. Like orphanages, boarding homes were part of a cobbled-together system of family support that families suffering from crushing poverty turned to when they were in need.

Boarding was not just a survival strategy for hard-hit families who could not care for their children, however. These arrangements were part of the survival strategies of boarding mothers as well. Indeed, informal boarding arrangements might best be characterized as a "circulation of children" between one group of poor and often single-parent families who could not care for their children and another group of poor families who desperately needed the added income that boarding mothers received.[39] Child boarding was part of the long tradition of women's home work, in which working-class women also took in adult boarders, laundry, or factory piecework to help support their families. Such work allowed women to continue performing household responsibilities for their families, including child-rearing, while earning necessary income through their domestic skills. And boarding children could be more appealing than other options, as it was less grueling and provided more autonomy than did industrial home work, which typically meant backbreaking labor, long hours, and exploitive piecework wages.[40]

Although boarding arrangements traditionally were informal ones between families, agencies would experiment with their own boarding programs beginning in the 1860s, when the Massachusetts State Board of Charities started paying women to board children in its care. Other agencies would adopt similar practices. In the 1890s, for example, the New York Foundling Asylum was placing its charges with "nurse mothers" who were paid to breastfeed and otherwise care for the infants. Indeed, in some places agency boarding programs were initially tied to the need to find homes for the youngest children, who could not justify their care through their labor. By the late nineteenth century, as middle-class children's advocates became increasingly uncomfortable with ascribing economic value to children, it came to appear unseemly to place youngsters with families who expected their labor in exchange.[41] Many midwestern states began experimenting with paid fostering due to concerns about abuse, neglect, overwork, and lack of oversight in free placements. According to Birk, the isolation of children in rural placements, together with the lack of supervision and record keeping, made placed-out children "exceptionally vulnerable." The hope was that by paying board to house children in towns and cities (rather than on isolated farms), agencies could keep better track of them and engage in better record keeping. In non-farm homes, children were also more likely to have access to schooling.[42]

Thus states "drifted" not only into subsidizing private orphanages but also into subsidizing care provided by boarding mothers in private homes — another less overt form of public-private partnership in child welfare provision. By paying board even for the care of children who were old enough to work, an agency ostensibly secured assurance that children would not be exploited for their labor. But board payments, too, conflicted with the idea that a child should be valued purely for his inherent worth and not as a source of income, a conflict not easily resolved.

Brace, for his part, opposed the use of boarding homes, fearing they would lead to exploitation. His fear reflected concerns that have continued to inform suspicions of foster parents. What, after all, was the difference between boarding out and the horrors of commercial "baby farming," a practice with a terrible reputation in which women were paid to take in infants (usually of illegitimate birth) who often perished in their care?[43] Brace argued that boarding transformed the act of taking in a child from one inspired by "a deep and fervent [Christian] spirit of humanity" into one "purely of business."[44] For Brace, economic and charitable motivations were not compatible. Even for child placers who supported boarding care, it was imperative that boarding not be profitable. Thus, agencies and orphanages, when they launched boarding programs, preferred to keep board payments lower than the actual costs of caring for a child, the balance being made up by the philanthropy of boarding families themselves. That gap, that balance, has persisted into the present. Acknowledging it is to acknowledge the hidden role of women's unpaid care work in sustaining American public welfare provision.

As the photojournalist pioneer and reformer Jacob Riis wrote in his classic exposé of life among the urban poor, mothering for pay had significant economic value for struggling immigrant families. "The money thus earned," he wrote, "pays the rent of hundreds of poor families. It is no trifle." Yet for Riis, in contrast to Brace, the economic aspects of boarding did not preclude emotional connections between boarding mothers and their charges. Riis reported that he had seen boarding mothers reduced to tears when, at age four or five, the children they cared for were sent west to permanent homes.[45] Riis's focus on boarding *mothers* was intentional, for boarding children was a decidedly female occupation. Although husbands were also present in many boarding homes, their role was not considered particularly necessary. Women had primary responsibility for children — both their own and those for whom they were paid to care; men's contributions to family life were understood to come primarily from breadwinning. Homes headed by widows (where there was no man present) were perfectly acceptable for boarding children.

Gradually, agencies developed more formal practices of boarding. American child welfare professionals came to see boarding homes as a more palatable option, when compared with free homes. The rise of the juvenile court system in the first decades of the twentieth century also contributed to the growth of publicly funded boarding programs, as it increased the number of youth becoming wards of the state.[46] Yet boarding homes were only slowly accepted by American child welfare professionals, who, along with the public more broadly, remained uneasy with the idea of paying for care. A further problem was financial. Identifying what would turn out to be an ongoing problem, one frequent writer on child welfare noted in 1926 that to secure a child a place in a "reasonably normal home environment," an agency required "an outlay of funds which the general public is quite unprepared to meet."[47]

The 1923 census showed that 64 percent of dependent and neglected children under care were living in asylums. Meanwhile, 23 percent were in free homes and only 10 percent in boarding homes.[48] Five states in 1923 indicated that they did not have a single child placed in boarding care, and sixteen additional states reported placing less than 1 percent of dependent children in such homes.[49] Meanwhile, independent placements continued to be negotiated between families. A struggling Missouri parent placed a typical ad in a local paper in 1924: "WANTED — Good homes for four children, three girls, ages 10, 7 and 5, the boy, 8 years. They may be taken separately or as desired."[50] Any boarding placement resulting from ads like this one would not be reflected in the statistics above.

Well into the twentieth century, a number of prospective foster mothers would continue to understand fostering in terms of the boarding arrangements of the past — in other words, as an opportunity to earn extra income by performing the kinds of "women's work" for which they felt best qualified. But in understanding fostering in this way, such women would be increasingly at odds with a developing child welfare system. Child welfare professionals, in the early decades of the twentieth century, began to transform child placing into a state-monitored, scientifically based professional service, driven by new concepts of child development and by more recent "sentimental" understandings of children's value. That transformation would leave child welfare workers, paradoxically, in search of trained and qualified boarding mothers while at the same time deeply ambivalent about paying for the care of children.

The development of adoption in the United States was also clearly connected to a growing need to address the problem of child dependency. Although initially a rarely used means of clarifying inheritance in families of considerable wealth, adoption came to be promoted by some philanthropists hoping to help homeless children.[51] Indeed, the backgrounds of children available for adoption raised concerns for Americans profoundly anxious about "bad blood." A skeptical William Whitmore wrote in 1876 that the "fact that the subjects of adoption are so largely taken from the waifs of society, foundlings, or children whose parents are depraved and worthless; considering also the growing belief that many traits of mind are hereditary and almost irradicable; it may be questioned whether [adoption] is for the public benefit."[52] Such fears of the "bad blood" of society's waifs were also entwined with late-nineteenth-century anxieties about immigration.

In an attempt to counter these kinds of fears, efforts like the *Delineator* magazine's "Child-Rescue Campaign" encouraged readers to pity, rather than fear, such children, stressing that adoption could be a rewarding act of child rescue. From late 1907 to early 1911, the magazine published a monthly series featuring photographs and heart-wrenching stories of individual children, usually of immigrant background, living in institutions. The series encouraged its affluent female readers to consider adopting such a child as an act of charity and of female civic duty.[53] As Julie Berebitsky argues, these profiles effectively used the popular literary convention of "the rescue" to present "pathetic tales of children who languished in institutions, abandoned by unfeeling parents or orphaned through tragic accidents." Women who took the next step and inquired about adopting a child could feel that they were saving a child from a "wretched fate."[54]

By the 1920s, however, adoption began to lose its association with child welfare and child rescue, and experts would begin separating those seeking adoption and foster care services "into distinct populations along social, economic, and ethnic lines."[55] The rhetoric of child saving in discussions of adoption was replaced by that of "sentimental adoption." Rather than focus on the benefits of taking in a child in exchange for board payments or labor or on the duty to rescue a child as a magnanimous act of charity, modern adoption stressed the joy that children would bring to childless couples.[56] Adoption was still commonly included among the various practices considered to be forms of "foster care" into the 1920s. But the new emphasis on companionate marriage, family planning, and scientific motherhood (each of which stressed the merits of choosing the kind of family one hoped to have) helped drive the separation of adoption from the wider category of foster care (which still included orphanages, work homes, and boarding homes). The idea of "kinship by design," which stressed the possibilities for adoption to create families not based on biological ties, served to make adoption less frightening to a skeptical public.[57] This new notion that true kinship could be created through adoption also served to further separate adoption (which created "real" families) from what would eventually become known as "foster family care" (which did not). As adoption became a practice distinct from foster care, the latter emerged as an institution in and of itself, one that was not sentimentalized as adoption was, one that did not emphasize the "realness" of the "families" it created, and one that retained and became marinated in the stigma of "welfare." Adoption became a means of addressing a private need, such as a couple's coping with childlessness.[58] Yet the public responsibility to address the welfare of dependent children remained.

Child welfare became ever more a public concern over the course of the nineteenth century. Beginning in the 1870s, some cities enacted legislation intended to protect children from "cruelty," and private charitable societies arose to enforce such laws. Most Societies for the Prevention of Cruelty to Children remained allied with law enforcement rather than with social services agencies.[59] As Linda Gordon argues, these SPCCs tended to target the drinking habits of immigrant men and thus envisioned "cruelty to children" as something that "'they'—the immigrant poor—did, never 'us'—the respectable classes." In the Progressive Era, the emphasis on immigrant male alcoholic cruelty gave way to a focus on the broader category of child neglect, which reformers linked to poverty and in which they understood women to play a larger role. Attention to child neglect became part of the child welfare branch of the new social work profession. Not until the late 1950s and early 1960s did social welfare agencies really turn their attention to protective services.⁶⁰

The emergence of a new generation of college-educated women seeking fields where they could claim expertise, together with contemporary attention to the unique needs of children in a democracy, contributed to a fresh concern about child welfare in the early twentieth century.⁶¹ Contemporary scholarship on child welfare would lead a wave of reformers to criticize traditional orphanages for their regimentation, for the separation and stigmatization of their young residents, and for the general grimness of the life they offered. Progressive Era reformers sought to bring such institutions up to date and to get them to better reflect modern child-rearing practices.⁶² Increasingly, reformers would come to believe, like Brace, that for most dependent children, placement in an individual family setting would be more conducive to their development. However, by the late nineteenth and early twentieth centuries, child welfare advocates began to depart from Brace's low regard for the immigrant families of poor children. According to Cybelle Fox, social workers became the defenders of European immigrants "against a hostile public," although their advocacy did not extend to black families, whom they tended to ignore, or to families of Mexican origin, toward whom they would grow progressively more hostile.⁶³ For impoverished immigrant children, social reformers would come to see family preservation, rather than family disruption, as the best solution. Reformers were horrified by the numbers of children being shunted to orphanages, free homes, and boarding care, not only for the impact on individual children but for the impact on the very future of the nation.

Alarmed by the state of childhood in an increasingly urbanized and industrialized country, reformers convinced President Theodore Roosevelt to convene the White House Conference on the Care of Dependent Children in 1909. This conference proved to be a pivotal moment in Progressive Era history, women's history, and the history of child welfare. The two hundred or so attendees focused on the needs of orphans and other impoverished children and, in a departure from established practice, emphasized the positive role that government could play in protecting dependent children. Indeed, the conference would lead to the creation of the U.S. Children's Bureau three years later. In keeping with their profession's skepticism about child removal and institutionalization, conference attendees emphasized — for white and European immigrant families — "prevention, government regulation, and aid to families so that children might stay within their own homes."⁶⁴ The conference paid almost no attention at all, however, to the unique needs of African American, Mexican, or Native children.

In stressing the importance of mother care, the conference strengthened the growing case for mothers' pensions as a solution to the problem of child dependency. Under such policies, states would provide a stipend to single mothers so that they could care for their children at home. Mothers' pensions were supposed to prevent single mothers — especially widows, but also unmarried mothers — from having to place children in orphanages or boarding homes or from leaving them unattended while going to work for wages. Max Mitchell, of the Federated Jewish Charities of Boston, captured the argument for mothers' pensions: "Instead of breaking up a home and paying for the board of her children in a private family, while the mother is taught a trade under the impression that she will develop an earning capacity, let the amount involved be paid to the mother in the exercise of her own trade, which she already knows — a mother's trade — the bringing up of her children, the highest and noblest calling."⁶⁵ Like board payments, mothers' pensions, which most states would enact by the late 1920s, were kept deliberately low. Many needy families fell outside their reach, and in a number of states with especially high African American and Mexican populations, little use was made of mothers' pensions at all, essentially preventing such families from receiving public support. Indeed, mothers' pensions were lowest in the South and Southwest, created, as Fox argues they were, with European immigrant populations of northern and eastern cities in mind.⁶⁶ Mothers' pensions clearly had their limitations. Yet in favoring family preservation, supporters of mothers' pensions were insisting that immigrant parents (even unmarried mothers) were not necessarily to blame for their poverty and thus could be considered decent and worthy. This policy preference also rested on the idea that a child's biological ties to those parents were usually profound.

Attendees at the 1909 conference unanimously adopted a platform, which famously argued that children should remain with their families of birth whenever possible and called for an end to the haphazard placement of children in various out-of-home situations that families had used as safety nets through hard times in the past. Poverty should not break up families, they believed. The 1909 conference concluded that home life was essential to children and that they should never be deprived of it except for "urgent and compelling reasons."⁶⁷ Among these "urgent and compelling reasons" were when "immoral" parents exposed children to depravity, a loophole open to interpretation and ripe for mischief. Yet child welfare reformers at the conference declared that "poverty should not be considered indicative of immorality" and stated that children should be separated from "worthy" parents or placed in institutions only as a last resort.[68] As Linda Gordon has astutely argued, however, even when reformers insisted that children should not be removed for reasons of "poverty alone," they could not "keep this promise because poverty is never alone."[69] Even in their defense of poor families, reformers maintained distinctions among the poor, suggesting that the noble or "moral" poor were different from the "immoral" poor in terms of their right to keep their families together. There would always be families that were not worthy of preserving.

For those children who did require placement, an emerging generation of trained social workers was ready to step in and help. During the Progressive Era, the latest social science approaches to child development and social work gave rise to a new class of professional child welfare experts and social workers whose approach to child placement favored casework methods, careful record keeping, and the prudent matching of children with foster parents to achieve the most suitable placements for all parties.[70] Although a number of its prominent leaders would be men, this was a field dominated by women. As such it suffered from low prestige but offered fulfilling, professional work opportunities to a generation of women whose options were otherwise limited. As Robyn Muncy notes, professional women at the turn of the century were "constrained by a culture that increasingly granted respect, financial resources, and effectiveness to those who could convince their public that they possessed esoteric knowledge on which the public's welfare depended."[71] Child welfare reformers would go on to create the field of foster home placement, applying relevant theories developed and taught at prominent professional schools, including the influential New York and Pennsylvania Schools of Social Work. They would create this field not out of nothing, though, but rather drew from the myriad existing means for assisting dependent children that poor families were already using.

By the 1920s, foster care services remained local and often nongovernmental. But these services were now part of a field with growing national presence. Child welfare was a subfield of social work more broadly, which was just reaching professional status, a process that was uniquely challenging in a field dominated by women.[72] To achieve professional status it needed to do what other emerging professions did — separate "old-fashioned" dabblers from modern, trained professionals. This meant developing specialized training, professional organizations, insider vocabulary, professional standards, and scientific methodology. In the 1920s child welfare work was acquiring these trappings. But continued skepticism about whether or not social work itself was a "real" autonomous profession would haunt the field and nourish a "long-lasting professional self-consciousness and self-doubt."[73]

The scientific method for social workers — what warranted specialized training, specialized journals, and research — was what practitioners called "casework." Casework was a process, first formally articulated by Pennsylvania's Mary Richmond in 1917, that included lengthy, detailed interviews with clients and their families. Those interviews would lead to a diagnosis of the problem, ranging from the practical (lack of a job) to the psychological (maladjustment), and a corresponding treatment.[74] This methodology tended to view problems (and solutions) first in individual and family terms rather than as a call to address broader structural problems such as poverty. The casework method was inevitably subjective, but it longed to be rigorously scientific and neutral. Casework would be essential to the "science" of child placement, which nascent professionals concerned with foster care were just beginning to develop in the twenties.

By that time, two national institutions were emerging that would shape the field, the U.S. Children's Bureau and the Child Welfare League of America. While the Child Welfare League was "national," though, and the Children's Bureau "federal," both had, at least early on, an orientation to the Northeast and Midwest and a policy focus on European immigrant populations. Congress established the Children's Bureau, located within the Department of Labor, in 1912, after several years of prodding from prominent settlement house workers Lillian Wald and Florence Kelley.[75] This move was significant in that it acknowledged federal responsibility for children. The idea of such a bureau had been promoted through the 1909 White House conference, which concluded that the needs of children not only should be a federal responsibility (novel in itself) but also should be "considered as a whole by one governmental agency."[76] This "whole child" approach would be central to the Children's Bureau's philosophy and to its arguments for its authority. The bureau would go on to play an important role in defining childhood and the needs of children and in shaping the parameters of public policy directed at children. Its original mandate was to investigate and report on "all matters pertaining to the welfare of children and child life among all classes of our people."[77] Initially it did so primarily in the areas of mothers' pensions, infant mortality, and child labor but would later also be the voice in the federal government insisting on the need to improve foster care.

The Children's Bureau became the focal point of the network of organizations and agencies that Robyn Muncy has called a "female dominion" of policy making, which reached its peak of influence in the 1920s and early 1930s.[78] It would also serve as a seat of female power in the federal government. This meant that the bureau was in a position to put services to dependent children, including foster care, on the national agenda in the 1930s, when the New Deal administration began building its welfare state. The Children's Bureau suffered, however, from persistent stereotypes that its work was not of serious importance and that social workers were overly sentimental and not really professional. Although it would lose some of its status by midcentury, it remained the most important voice for children in Washington.

Unlike the Children's Bureau, which was a center of female government influence, the New York–based Child Welfare League of America, founded in 1920, was nongovernmental and, while it employed a largely female staff, was led by a series of male executive directors, beginning with C. C. Carstens. The fifty-five-year-old Carstens, who had immigrated to Iowa from Germany as a child, had substantial experience in child welfare. In Philadelphia in the early twentieth century, he worked under casework pioneer Mary Richmond and then served for thirteen years as director of the Massachusetts Society for the Prevention of Cruelty to Children, a private charity. In that position he had championed a greater role for the state in protecting children and was known as an advocate for standardized laws and practices in the field. He was an early advocate of paid foster family care.[79]

The Child Welfare League and the Children's Bureau played critical roles in professionalizing the field of child placement. By offering the broader child welfare field the legitimacy of having its own federal agency, the Children's Bureau was particularly important not only in establishing child welfare as a profession but also in establishing it as one in which women with leadership, policy making, and communication skills could find an outlet for their talents. Indeed, through the hiring strategies of its first leader, Julia Lathrop, the bureau would go on to be dominated by women. Former settlement house worker Grace Abbott would serve as bureau chief throughout much of the twenties and thirties. Abbott, her staff, and her successors would help define areas of concern, promote research, and advocate policies. Abbott, who had studied political science and law and had lived for many years at Chicago's Hull House, had a particular passion for ending child labor and promoting maternal and infant health, but the bureau would reach into other areas as well. Through effective use of media, the organization also helped establish itself as a national, governmental authority on child welfare through coverage in women's magazines and other outlets.[80] That presence made it a resource for ordinary women, who wrote hundreds of thousands of letters to the bureau. These letters would include voluminous correspondence from birth mothers and foster mothers, which the bureau dutifully answered, sometimes in great detail, outlining current thinking on the subject of foster placement.

The Child Welfare League's audience, by contrast, was primarily the scores of agencies engaged in child placing that had to meet minimum standards to come under the league's umbrella. Thus one of the league's most significant influences on modern foster care would be its work in assembling, codifying, and disseminating the specialized knowledge of child placement. It worked from its beginning to establish and disseminate professional standards for a number of services for children, including foster care. Foster care in the 1920s, as should by now be clear, was quite a diffuse system, relying as it did on thousands of individual and fairly autonomous foster families and scores of agencies, many of which were not at all up to date in their understandings of the theory and practice of child placement. The services for dependent children were so diverse and frequently slapdash in their methods and varied so much from state to state, from north to south, and from rural to urban areas that it was hardly feasible to forge them into one unified system. Initially sixty-eight member organizations came under the league's aegis, growing to ninety-eight two years later.[81] Most were private agencies, given that few states at the time had "effective" state departments of public welfare, although this would shift as the public child welfare infrastructure expanded in the 1930s and 1940s. Among the first public agencies to join the league were the state agencies of Ohio and Minnesota, along with local public agencies in Westchester County, New York, and Cincinnati.[82]

Many in the field, including C. C. Carstens, had been calling for the development of standards for a number of years by the time of the Child Welfare League's founding. The league would go on to craft standards of best practices for a number of services, including foster care, and to communicate those standards across the country. The standards were meant to help improve services and were targeted at child welfare service providers, at state licensing agencies, and at schools of social work.[83] In the 1920s, the Child Welfare League was still at the beginning of this endeavor, publishing its first round of *Standards* in the 1930s, including volumes on foster family care (first released in 1933) and protective services (1937). Practiced according to such standards, foster care could become a *service*, a modern professional one intended to promote children's well-being.

Public foster care services were modernizing, but they remained imprinted with the legacies of the past, including a history that differentiated among children, even among those already seen as society's castoffs. In 1937, Carstens described the nineteenth-century history of his field as one in which "in succession, groups of dependent, neglected, and delinquent children were extracted [from almshouses] to be given better care in separate institutions or foster families."[84] While this depiction may be accurate as a general overview for white Americans and European immigrants, it makes some significant omissions. Notably, the history of the care of dependent black, indigenous, and disabled children does not fit the pattern Carstens described. In the early nineteenth century, black children in almshouses were less likely than white children to be moved into orphanages because so few orphanages would take them. Those orphanages that did accept black children tended to develop as segregated institutions. Similarly, the orphan train system did not place dependent African American children (or other children of color) in private homes, partly because there were so few black farm families to take them.[85] In midwestern rural placement programs, most placed-out children were white. For the small numbers of placed-out black children, it made a great difference whether they were placed with a black family or a white one. If placed in a black home, a child had at least a chance of being treated as family, whereas in a white home, he was "clearly there to work."[86] Under juvenile court systems developed in the early twentieth century, delinquent African American children were far more likely to be sent to adult prisons than were white children.[87]

Billingsley and Giovannoni have noted, with irony, that the "major child welfare institution for Black children" before the Civil War was slavery, as it was the institution under which the largest number of African American children lived.[88] Under plantation slavery, biological parents did not have rights to their children. Children were considered property of their "master," and families could be separated at his whim. Even if enslaved parents were living on the same estate as their children, those children were often cared for by others. A slave woman's productive labor was seen as more valuable than the labor of child-rearing. Thus it was often older, weak, or ill women (who could not perform harder labor) who were given the tasks of "mothering." As a consequence, new patterns of child-rearing emerged in enslaved communities, with a variety of adults and older children raising youngsters. Historians have shown that networks among enslaved women were crucial to facilitating adequate childcare. This reality, coupled with the more expansive notions of kinship that West Africans brought with them to America, led to a more extensive notion of kin, as well as a tradition of "othermothering" and mutual obligation. Many scholars argue that these traditions carried on long after slavery, leading to the widespread practices of informal adoption and foster care.[89] These traditions have thus affected the relationship between the child welfare system and black families. We see the effects of this history not only in the deep distrust many black families have toward the predominantly white child welfare system that holds the power to break up black families but also in the difficulty that white child welfare workers have sometimes had in seeing the contours and strengths of black families that operated within boundaries less familiar to Euro-Americans.[90]

Late nineteenth-century child welfare practices also reflected the organized system of racial segregation that developed in the wake of emancipation and that left most southern black families facing dislocation and poverty. Indenture, often to former slave owners, became a chief means of caring for poor southern black children.[91] There were a small number of southern orphanages that served black children.[92] But as Tuskegee Institute founder Booker T. Washington noted in 1909, relatively few black children lived in orphanages, and the southern states (where the majority of African Americans lived at the time) spent very little on the care of "dependent negro children." For Washington, these observations spoke to the strength of black families and communities. He noted with pride that the "number of dependents among my own race in America is relatively small as compared with the number of dependents among the white population." Washington boasted that in Alabama, a state with an African American population of 900,000, only 301 black children resided in children's institutions. He argued that "this condition exists because ... the negro, in some way, has inherited and has had trained into him the idea that he must take care of his own dependents." Indeed, he insisted, black communities saw it as a "disgrace" for any child to be taken out of the community and placed elsewhere. Black children in need were cared for by black churches, by family members, or by community members. Of orphanages founded and run by African Americans themselves, Washington was suspicious.[93]

To his white audience, Washington presented a picture of strong southern black families and communities with no need for services because of their traditions of self-reliance. Certainly it is true that black voluntary associations and self-help efforts made up the "dominant mode of care for dependent black children immediately after emancipation and beyond."[94] As LeRoy Rowe shows in his study of Missouri's State Industrial Home for Negro Girls, however, when public children's institutions were actually available to black families, they did make use of them to address their own family circumstances.[95] And as Kriste Lindenmeyer notes, Washington avoided the conclusion that "discrimination and racism rather than a lack of need" might account for the small number of black children in orphanages.[96] In fact, segregation laws and the indifference of white legislators and child welfare agencies meant that dependent black children, especially in the South, were likely to end up in jail or reform school even when not charged with a crime because of the lack of more appropriate services. Well into the twentieth century there were reports of black children being housed in jails because there was nowhere else for them to go.[97] Yet Washington's insistence that black communities and families took care of their own would provide the field with justification for its tendency to overlook the needs of dependent black children. In this period, Cybelle Fox argues, social workers in general — not just child welfare specialists — tended either to ignore African Americans altogether or to perceive them as far less dependent on relief than were European immigrants.[98]

Meanwhile, policies toward indigenous children and their families were dramatically different. For American Indian children, the very purpose of institutions ("boarding schools" set up by the Bureau of Indian Affairs) was to separate children from their families as part of government efforts to assimilate native peoples into Euro-American ways, allegedly for their benefit. These boarding schools, set up in the late nineteenth and early twentieth centuries, separated indigenous children from their families and communities both physically and culturally (as children were typically forbidden to speak their native languages). Removal was coercive and traumatic and "threatened the very existence of

Indigenous communities." Not until the 1950s would institutional placement fall out of favor for Native children.[99]

Children with mental or physical disabilities also followed a different trajectory than that described by Carstens. Beginning in the early nineteenth century, reformers such as Laurent Clerc, Thomas Hopkins Gallaudet, and Samuel Gridley Howe worked to build schools where young people who were deaf, blind, deaf-blind, or "idiots" could be educated "to their fullest extent." Initially these were private ventures, but by 1849 the Massachusetts legislature established a state School for Idiotic Children and Youth, starting a trend toward state support. While such institutions provided education and training for many, the quality of these institutions varied, and even in the best of circumstances youngsters were separated from their families and communities.[100] There was little sense that such children might also benefit from the merits of family life.

Thus, while Carstens's generalization about the movement of dependent children from prisons and almshouses into foster homes is accurate to a point, it contains some fundamental oversights. His omissions speak to how Americans in the twentieth century would understand the role of foster care in preserving families (some families more than others), valuing children (some children more than others), and investing in services (for some children but not all). Even for able-bodied children of European descent, comprehensive child welfare services did not yet exist by the early twentieth century. Foster family care would become something distinct from adoption in its association with welfare and child dependency, yet modern foster care would also emerge as a practice quite different from other methods Americans had used to care for dependent children. Unlike indenture, binding out, work homes, or almshouses, foster family care was intended to nurture and protect children; unlike orphanages, foster family care rested on the assumption that children were best cared for in a family setting; unlike state mothers' pensions (and later federal Aid to Dependent Children) and homemaker services, foster care served children outside of their biological families. And finally, unlike the boarding home arrangements of the nineteenth and early twentieth centuries, modern foster family care occurred under agency supervision, would increasingly use public monies, and would be monitored under developing professional standards.

By the 1930s, when the heart of this book really begins, out-of-home placements for children were taking a number of forms. Some of these forms, such as free homes and work homes, were on their way out, while others, such as orphanages and boarding care, were modernizing to meet new understandings of family and child development. By this decade, child welfare advocates were turning more often to boarding homes to meet the needs of dependent children. Between 1923 and 1930, the proportion of children in both institutional care and free homes went down, whereas the use of boarding homes went up, especially in states that provided direct public care of dependent children.[101] In 1933, 27 percent of dependent children in out-of-home care were in boarding homes, up from 10 percent in 1923.[102] Although raising their own concerns, boarding homes seemed the best solution for children needing out-of-home placement. Paying board to foster parents offered some assurance that children would be cared for in a family that did not value them merely for their labor. And, unlike adoption, boarding homes did not require that parents permanently sever their ties to their children.

To itemize the various options available for dependent children, though, is to miss the complex tapestry of aid that families wove as they tried to make do. To better suggest the state of services for dependent children on the eve of the Depression, as well as the ways that family and community resources, private philanthropy, and public services were cobbled together to meet a family's needs, I return to the story of the Costas of Minneapolis, as told through the records of the city's Children's Protective Society.[103]

In 1928 the Costas were struggling. Angelo Costa was a good-looking forty-year-old man who spoke English with the strong accent of an Italian immigrant. He had served the United States in World War I, where he had suffered a spinal injury. He now worked periodically as a laborer, but back problems from the war injury limited the steadiness of his employment. From time to time, he had to enter the veterans hospital for treatment. Although he received some compensation from the Veterans Bureau, his family could not support itself while he was in the hospital and not working. In those periods, Angelo turned to local relief agencies to help sustain his family. Despite this economic instability, the Costas owned their own home. Angelo and his wife, Ana, had three children in fairly rapid succession: Giacomo, almost six years old; Maria, age three; and Filomena, age one and a half. Ana was expecting a fourth child in the spring.

On March 11, Ana died in childbirth, leaving behind a baby boy who died two weeks later. Ana was only twenty-six years old. As a low-income immigrant woman, Ana probably did not have a hospital delivery, and childbirth remained quite dangerous, especially due to the risk of deadly infection. Angelo, disabled and between jobs, was left to care for his three surviving children. Although his son would be starting school in the fall, his young daughters still required constant care, which he felt unable to provide.

Minneapolis had a Catholic Charities Board and a Children's Protective Society. But those were not the first places Angelo turned to for help. He had no other biological kin in the United States, yet he did live in a neighborhood with many other Italians, including two families, the Solaris and the Gallatis, who were godparents to his daughters. It was to these families that Angelo would turn for help in caring for his young girls.

In one version of events, Angelo dropped Maria and Filomena off with their godmothers and demanded that the women care for them. In another account, the women rushed to Angelo's side upon the death of his wife insisting that they were duty-bound, as Italian godmothers, to care indefinitely for the girls. In either case, the godmothers — or at least their adult sons — soon became annoyed with Angelo, wanting him to relinquish his daughters permanently, reclaim them, or begin paying five dollars a week board.

While the Solari and Gallati sons may have been frustrated, Angelo was apparently satisfied with the initial arrangement. He believed his daughters to be in the good hands of fellow countrywomen eager to help. But complaints that Angelo was neglecting his children brought him to the attention of the Children's Protective Society. To the agents there, he indicated that he needed additional treatment at the veterans hospital but could not seek it, for that would leave no one to care for his son, Giacomo.

In 1928 there was little to offer a man like Angelo Costa. The Children's Protective Society agent suggested that he might marry again or obtain a housekeeper to help with cleaning, meals, and childcare. Otherwise, Angelo would need to have Giacomo boarded. This he was reluctant to do, though, and he thus put off plans to go to the hospital. By July, he had determined that he could no longer care for Giacomo and had approached the Catholic Charities Board about boarding arrangements. Catholic Charities, however, did nothing because the public Children's Protective Society was already involved with the family.

The case is full of confusion and contradictions. The agents of the Children's Protective Society had difficulty speaking with the godmothers, as neither was fluent in English. Both Mrs. Solari and Mrs. Gallati used their adult sons as mediaries — sometimes as translators, sometimes as their representatives. Thus it is hard to know exactly how these immigrant women understood their duties and obligations. In any case, both sons seemed incensed that Angelo had not paid board to their mothers as they believed he had promised. They returned often to the argument that as Angelo was receiving a stipend from the government for his military service, some of that money should go to the women who were raising his daughters. Meanwhile, Angelo's community gave conflicting reports about his household. To one neighbor, Mrs. Fabio, Giacomo was obviously neglected and the home unsuitable. She reported that Angelo had a woman friend, Mrs. Williams, who often spent the night, that he often held late-night parties, and that he drank a lot and was possibly a bootlegger. To others, Mrs. Fabio was simply a neighborhood scold whose information was unreliable. Angelo was a good father, his son was well cared for, and Mrs. Williams was simply a housekeeper in his employ. Giacomo's teachers in his first year of school reported no concerns.

Meanwhile, Mrs. Solari and Mrs. Gallati, as presented by their sons, were growing only more aggravated. After twenty months, Mrs. Solari had received only ten dollars in total from Angelo for Maria's care, despite promises to pay five dollars per week. Furthermore, Mrs. Solari (through her son) reported that Angelo showed little interest in his daughters and that Giacomo was neglected and was smoking cigarettes. The sons were considering filing nonsupport complaints against Angelo.

In November 1929, a neglect complaint was filed on behalf of all three children, but a month later the complaint was dropped. A year later, all three children were back living in Angelo's home with Mrs. Williams as "housekeeper." In March 1935, six years after Ana Costa died (and after a gap in the record), the complaint of neglect finally went to juvenile court. The children were placed in the temporary custody of the Children's Protective Society. In May the children were committed to the general guardianship of the Catholic Charities Board. Giacomo was placed in a Children's Protective Society boarding home. There is no further record of what became of the children.

The case of the Costa family illustrates something of the state of child welfare services at the onset of the Depression. For one, the abrupt end of the record suggests the problem scholars would later identify as "foster care drift," in which children could linger indefinitely in foster placements. And in the existing record itself, we see the immigrant widower Angelo shifting among friends, quasi-kin, the federal government, local public services, and local charities in an effort to care for his children after his wife died. In turn, neighbors, local child protective services, and Catholic charities felt a duty to weigh in on the care his children were receiving. Did Angelo's difficulties in caring for his children stem from poverty, his disability, his lack of a wife, or his own allegedly immoral behavior? Who was in charge of making that determination, and what were the consequences? Who should pay to care for Angelo's children? None of these questions had particularly clear answers.

One could hardly claim that a foster care "system" was in place at the time Ana Costa died, although what would come to be known as foster family care was emerging. Families continued to make do, with the help of relatives, boarding homes, orphanages, and limited local relief resources. The boarding-out practices that would become foster family care existed as a loose network of public and private boarding home placements arranged by agencies and a more informal system of independent arrangements between families without participation of an agency. Even when agencies were involved, their staff more than likely had received little to no training in child placement methods, which experts were only beginning to develop. Agency placements were inevitably uneven in their availability and of uneven quality.[104] Primarily run by white social workers, foster family care was seriously limited in its ability to adequately serve nonwhite families. Services were scant in rural areas and were rarely available to families of disabled children. They were also a mix of public and private and of voluntary and coercive efforts.

In these ways, foster care was not unlike other forms of social provision in the United States. As Walter Trattner notes, the United States (in contrast to most European countries) has never had one overarching "legal code affecting social welfare matters." Instead, social welfare policy has arisen through many different state and local laws, sometimes in response to court rulings. And usually public responsibilities have been met through some kind of uneasy partnership between public resources and private philanthropy.[105] That "private philanthropy" included not only the well-organized charities but also the services of individuals like Mrs. Gallati and Mrs. Solari who — with little or no compensation — cared for the children who were considered dependent.

By the early decades of the twentieth century, though, foster care was beginning to develop into the modern, public system that would dominate by mid-century. That "system" of foster care had grown largely through private institutions and practices. Yet it would become an essential arm of the welfare state.

CHAPTER 2

THE NEW DEAL, FAMILY SECURITY, AND THE EMERGENCE OF A PUBLIC CHILD WELFARE SYSTEM

"There are at the moment," noted the Committee on Economic Security in its proposal for what would become the Social Security Act of 1935, "over 7,400,000 children under 16 years of age on the relief rolls. The lives of some of these children, who have never known a time when their father had a steady job," who have experienced "nothing but the threat of being scattered, are lost beyond full restoration to their physical and social fulfillment." Hundreds of thousands of these children were disabled, delinquent, illegitimate, or dependent and neglected, but most lived in homes where nothing was "wrong with the environment but their parents' lack of money."[1] For no reason other than poverty, too many of these children were doomed to be separated from their families and consigned to foster care, institutions, or other out-of-home placements. Such scenarios made a mockery of the child welfare field's principles, established during the Progressive Era, which rejected splitting up families simply because of poverty.

The Great Depression would strain skeletal foster care services to the breaking point. But it also led to the development of a nascent welfare state that many in the profession sincerely believed would diminish the need for out-of-home placement altogether. On the one hand, the country's economic troubles meant crisis for thousands of children and families and stretched what limited child welfare services existed. More children needed care, yet the households of boarding mothers were themselves often in economic distress, and agencies lacked money to pay staff salaries or board. Thus at precisely the moment when child welfare advocates were trying to replace what they saw as out-of-date methods of caring for dependent children with a rationalized, bureaucratic system governed by standards, licensing, and best practices, their ability to do so was severely compromised. On the other hand, the development of a federal welfare state in response to the economic crisis presented opportunities to begin to truly create a comprehensive public child welfare system, one that included foster family care.

If the onset of the Depression marked a setback for the delivery of child welfare services, the promise of a more rational system of federal welfare provision raised many hopes. By the end of the 1930s, the network of child welfare professionals located in private agencies, public departments, the Child Welfare League, and the Children's Bureau had grown optimistic that federal New Deal programs — such as Aid to Dependent Children and federal survivor's and unemployment insurance — would bring an end to the family insecurity that separated children from their families and that compelled some women to see boarding other families' children as their only way out of desperate circumstances. Such programs, these reformers expected, would eliminate (or at least diminish) the role poverty played in separating children from their families and complete work toward the Progressive Era goal of sharply reducing the number of children placed in out-of-home care altogether. Meanwhile, as foster care developed into a more specialized service, child placers would be able to select a better quality of foster homes. Yet, New Deal programs were limited and likely to reach some kinds of families more than others, leaving a gap between the optimistic expectations of reformers and the realities of the uneven effects of economic hardship.

The Great Depression was hard on families. Parents of young children struggled especially when an already fragile family faced a major crisis. The model family supported by a male breadwinner and a female caregiver was vulnerable if either of those pillars was weakened or lost. Indeed, the economic crisis brought a corresponding "crisis of care" that could be staggering.[2] In Canton, Ohio, where unemployment approached 50 percent in the winter of 1933–34, Robert Davidson abandoned his wife and four young children. His wife, Helen, tried to apply for a state mothers' pension in order to sustain her family but was told she was ineligible, presumably because her husband was still legally responsible. She therefore had to find employment as a housekeeper in order to support her young family. Her job made it a challenge for Helen to supervise her children, and she voluntarily placed them in foster care.[3]

Loss of a male breadwinner, as in Helen Davidson's case, made it difficult to care for and economically support children at the same time. Loss of a caregiver could also lead to crisis. This was the case for the Simpson family of Washington, D.C. Charles Simpson's annual income of $1,100 was meager (about $19,800 in 2016 dollars), but he was able to support his wife and their four-year-old child, and the family was at least making ends meet. Then in 1934, his wife "suddenly became insane" and was hospitalized. With his wife absent, Simpson was forced to stay home from work indefinitely in order to care for his child.[4]

An even more desperate situation was that of the Brinkley family of Pennsylvania. In 1937, Evelyn Brinkley died of gangrene, leaving a husband, Jim, and eleven children. Jim Brinkley was managing somehow, but in January the following year he was stricken with tuberculosis and needed to enter a hospital. Fortunately, doctors were optimistic that he could be cured in three years' time. Yet Brinkley's oldest son, Emery, who was only twenty, was simply unable to care for his ten younger siblings by himself while waiting for his father to recover.[5]

When parents tried to better their circumstances for their children, those same children could, ironically, be obstacles to doing so. In the summer of 1934, Gladys Speck, an unmarried mother from Texas, dreamed of becoming a nurse. She planned to relocate to New York in the fall in order to attend a three-year nursing program at Bellevue Hospital. Yet she had three young children to support.[6]

Unemployment and underemployment. Desertion and illness. Unwed motherhood. In each of these cases, families struggled to support children financially while also caring for and supervising them. While many distressed families in similar circumstances were able to turn to relatives, religious institutions, or private charities, such resources were themselves severely compromised during the Depression. Helen Davidson, Charles Simpson, Emery Brinkley, Gladys Speck, and thousands of others turned instead to local child welfare agencies and to the U.S. Children's Bureau for help. These families sought placement because they saw no other option. Indeed, as late as the 1950s, the majority of children in foster care were there because their parents had requested placement.[7]

In none of these examples did local agencies or courts have much to offer. State mothers' pensions were one option, and at the end of 1934 approximately

230,000 children were benefiting from these payments.[8] In the cases described here, however, parents were unlikely to have been eligible. Some states were still sending children to almshouses, a practiced that had been "condemned" and largely phased out back in the early nineteenth century.[9] The 1930 Children's Charter, drafted by the White House Conference on Child Health and Protection, advocated home care over orphanages for dependent children.[10] But orphanages remained an option — especially for white children. Between 1923 and 1930, the proportion of children cared for in institutions had declined from 64 to 59 percent.[11] Yet, the early years of the Depression saw a record number of children — over 140,000 — housed in the nation's orphanages, most of which were under private auspices.[12] Still, the growing consensus that most children were best cared for in a family setting had begun to diminish the role of institutions. Work homes for dependent children were now considered exploitive. And increasing urbanization had sharply reduced the supply of so-called free homes, in which children were incorporated into rural household economies without payment from any agency.[13] Public assistance, homemaker services, or day care, which might have helped families stay together, were inadequate or absent altogether. This meant that most often the only service available to families who wanted to avoid orphanages was out-of-home placement of the children.

At the end of 1933, the third year of the Depression, 102,577 dependent and neglected children in the United States were in official foster family homes (an unknown number of children were in independent, unlicensed homes). Of those, 66,350 were in boarding homes, 31,538 in free homes, and another 4,689 in work or wage homes. Half of the states had more than tripled their use of boarding homes over the previous ten years, although many child welfare professionals accepted this change only reluctantly.[14] Because orphanages and adoption were largely closed to them, black children were more likely to be in boarding homes. This had some advantages, according to scholars Andrew Billingsley and Jeanne Giovannoni. The shift to boarding homes meant more direct involvement of African American communities in child welfare services. Most orphanages that took in black children were white-run. In the developing foster boarding home system, however, even though agency staff members were white, racial matching policies ensured that black adults at least had key roles to play in providing care.[15]

Both public and private welfare agencies offered boarding homes as an option for families needing temporary homes for their children. Increasingly, agencies came to be staffed by professional social workers who made use of newer techniques of casework, bureaucratic record keeping, and boarding home licensure. In the independent boarding-out systems of the past, arrangements had been made privately between households without licensing, record keeping, or casework. But mid-twentieth-century child welfare professionals considered independent boarding to be risky for all parties.[16] They worried that without agency involvement, children would end up in homes without benefit of the "science" of selecting the proper home for the individual child. "Social disaster often follows," wrote one expert, "when a child is separated from his home without accurate knowledge of his needs."[17] Furthermore, in independent boarding situations, parents frequently failed to pay board, sometimes even abandoning their children.[18]

While some parents coped with economic stresses by seeking boarding arrangements for their children, other families *took in* dependent children for many of the same reasons. In 1936, Marjorie Frisbie of Maine hoped to board several young children and promised she could provide good care. She and her husband had five children of their own. Earle Frisbie was working to the point of exhaustion but was not earning enough to feed his family, to "say nothing about clothes and the bills that are piling up." Mrs. Frisbie hoped that conditions would improve soon but meanwhile felt she "*must* do something" and so wrote to the Children's Bureau with hopes of receiving child placements.[19]

Like Marjorie Frisbie, Berta Washington, an African American widow, thought she needed to do "something to help" herself. She had boarded a seven-year-old girl during the summer of 1933 and by the fall was interested in receiving additional children. She wrote to the new secretary of labor, Frances Perkins, asking for help "in getting two or three girls ranging in age from five to twelve years of age." She also inquired about the "price I would get for their board."[20] Mrs. Henry Nickerson wrote the Children's Bureau wanting to know "how and where I can get one of these well fair [sic] children to keep at $4.00 a week and how I might get one by the last of March or first of April."[21] One Ohio woman, whose husband was disabled by arthritis and living in a sanitarium, tried to cover all bases in seeking additional income. She wrote the Department of Agriculture asking for advice on raising young poultry, on the one hand, while at the same time inquiring as to how she could secure boarding placements of young girls and be paid for "the keeping and caring of them."[22] Frances Gaines of Wisconsin did not hide her desperation. "In all this world," she pleaded, "isn't there some children I can have to take care of for money[?]"[23]

These letters provoke discomfort in those of us who have thoroughly absorbed the modern view of children — that children's value lies in the joy they bring and in their essential worth as human beings rather than in any income they might bring their caregivers. Children, unlike poultry, should not be a source of profit. And, indeed, the practice of paying board to foster families was by no means settled policy. Critics insisted that for most boarding parents, "it is only the money[,] a pure and simple business condition."[24] For many poor and working-class families in the 1930s, the transition from "economic" to "sentimental" understandings of children's value, which Viviana Zelizer describes, was not yet complete.[25] Children, especially in rural areas, were expected to contribute to the household economy. And for widowed women, or for married women whose husbands were unemployed, disabled, or barely earning, boarding children was one of the few ways they could imagine earning money for the household.[26] "I don't want relief," wrote Pauline Wagner of Indiana. "But I do want this sort of work as it is the only kind I know."[27]

Martha Dempster of Delaware expressed a similar view. Dempster had been boarding children successfully for a Jewish agency (probably the Hebrew Charity Association) for several years. In 1933, however, the agency decide it would no longer place Jewish children in non-Jewish homes, like the Dempsters'. After the agency dropped her as a foster mother, Dempster tried to find other placements but was unsuccessful, despite good references from the Jewish agency. Given the thousands of children in need at the time, she wanted to know "why cannot I have several children here who need care and good food to bring them to a normal condition?" She needed more children in her home "that I may have at least a livelihood assured, at the same time that I am doing the work I love, a necessary work, a work that I can do, that I have proved I can do successfully."[28] To women like Martha Dempster, for whom child-rearing was the only work she knew, a "job" boarding children of misfortune made sense.

If such attention to board payments and earning a livelihood on the part of foster mothers is troubling, it is also worth pointing out that children's own parents were not always purely sentimental in their attachments. In Washington State, Walter Townes's neighbors reported that he had whipped his adolescent daughter. In response, authorities then sent her to the Yakima detention center, with plans to move her to a children's home in Seattle. Now, four months later, Walter and his wife wanted their daughter back. "My wife is a cripple and sick most of the time," Walter wrote to Eleanor Roosevelt; "she has nerve trouble and has histeric [sic] spells so she can't be left alone. I can't afford to hire anyone to stay with her or do the house-work as I'm a old man." He continued: "Our girl is all we have and we miss her so, she is fifteen and was always good to help with the work and cooking until they took her away."[29] Mr. and Mrs. Townes may have loved their daughter, but they also valued her for the labor and care she could contribute. Sentimental and instrumental impulses could both be present in the feelings of parents toward their children and of foster parents to their foster children.

Prospective boarding mothers who wrote to various federal officials in Washington (and whose letters were forwarded on to the Children's Bureau) were typically misinformed about procedures for becoming a foster parent or about the kinds of board payments available. The federal Children's Bureau was not in the business of matching dependent children with boarding mothers. Indeed, it had no authority to do so. Women with an interest in boarding were supposed to seek state licensure and register with a local agency. Meanwhile, independent boarders, who did not work through agencies, found children through word of mouth or by placing classified ads in their local newspapers, the legalities of which varied from state to state.[30] Formal foster placements were set up by local agencies (both public and private). They were not, as some letter writers seemed to believe, arranged by Eleanor Roosevelt, the Department of Labor, the Department of Agriculture, or even the Children's Bureau.

In fact, foster placement was not a federal responsibility, and federal dollars did not pay for care. Furthermore, board rates were typically so low as to be unlikely to provide relief from serious economic troubles. "Many foster families," the Children's Bureau's Agnes Hanna acknowledged politely but firmly to one letter writer, "spend much more for care of the children than the amount paid by the agency."[31] Hanna was the bureau's social services director in the 1930s and handled much of this kind of correspondence, often sending detailed, individualized replies, at times even writing local agencies to follow up on the letters she received. The care and engagement shown in these responses (and those of subsequent bureau employees such as Mildred Arnold) is noteworthy, given that the bureau actually had no jurisdiction over local child placement decisions.

The women who wrote the Children's Bureau of their desire to board children may have been ill informed. But their hopes of finding work for which they were well qualified were certainly understandable, reflecting not only the kinds of work experience and skills they already had but also undoubtedly some understanding of the traditional roles child boarding had played in household economies. It is not surprising that many women would settle on the expertise they possessed as mothers of their own children as their best hope for employment. Not only was "mothering" the work they knew, but there were considerable practical reasons for pursuing it as well. Women seeking to board children — with their own youngsters at home or aging spouses to care for and few other job skills — did not have a lot of other options.

While many potential boarding mothers were open about their need for supplemental income, there were plenty who also emphasized themes of altruism, rescue, and sentiment. Lois Bolinger had been the foster mother to a young girl who came to her at the age of six. The girl, now fourteen, had been recently removed from Bolinger's home in order to live with the girl's adult sister. Bolinger was devastated. The girl, Bolinger held, is "very much attached to us and we are to her, we have no children of our own."[32] The Oakleys of Iowa had boarded neglected children for seven years and were "heartbroken" when, in 1939, the state inspected all boarding homes to issue licenses and found the Oakley home to be too small. "We feel like we would be doing something worth while if we could do this," Mrs. Oakley lamented. "We all love children and would give our full time to their care. There is nothing more grand than the appreciation that little tots give you for good food care and attention and a mother's love."[33]

Despite real affection for their charges, plenty of boarding families who had been approved during better economic times found that board payments took on new significance during the Depression. Katherine Turner, wife of an Ohio insurance salesman, had been receiving five dollars a week, paid once a month in advance. In June 1933, that rate was cut to twenty dollars a month. At the beginning of 1935, the rate was cut again to sixteen dollars a month, and payments were "from one to three months in arrears." Turner noted proudly that in her community, "none of the 83 foster mothers affected has turned out her charges." But, she stated, "it is very hard." Turner seemed uncomfortable discussing her work as a foster mother in economic terms, but she was blunt about her concerns. "When I started in the work it was with the humanitarian side of it alone in view," she explained. But her husband then fell seriously ill and was unable to work for eighteen months. This downturn in family circumstances meant that the boarding care she provided took on new importance, bringing "the finances end of it into the picture so strongly."[34] For these boarding families, the line between instrumental and sentimental considerations was blurred. Boarding mothers like Turner needed income but wanted to be paid for work they loved and felt they were good at.

Indeed, while poverty clearly affected the demand for boarding homes, it affected the supply as well. Poverty not only made it difficult for some parents to care for their own children; it also had an impact on the ability of even long-term foster families to provide the care they had been able to in the past. The St. Louis Children's Aid Society had a stable network of rural homes within a hundred-mile radius of the city in which it had been placing a number of its adolescent boys. These homes relied on their own kitchen gardens to provide the fruits and vegetables consumed in a year. In the mid-thirties, though, drought destroyed orchards and vegetable gardens as well as the "money crops" that provided cash to rural families. Many of these families likely faced foreclosure or eviction if they fell behind on payments. Administrators saw the effects that drought had on those foster families. Without cash reserves with which to purchase the green vegetables and fruits they could no longer grow, these families were hard-pressed to provide their foster children with the balanced diet they had offered in the past and that the aid society believed was needed. The families received board payments to cover some of the costs associated with caring for children. Yet, George Swartzott of the aid society noted (not unsympathetically) that his agency was "inclined to feel that the cash these foster parents derive from the board we pay on these children will go toward paying taxes, interest, etc. rather than toward the purchase of vegetables and fruits." What could be done, Swartzott wondered, to assist these foster parents through the coming winter "so that an adequate and well balanced diet can be supplied the children in their care?"[35]

Agencies preferred to work with foster families who were themselves economically stable and for whom the "finances end of it" was not so salient. The state of Louisiana was typical in its official policy that agencies not use foster homes in which the "economic standards of the family are so insecure and the margin of the income is so narrow that the child will not receive any more sense of financial security than he has experienced in his own home."[36] In other words, foster families should have some source of income other than board payments. Not only was the boarding family's income relevant, but so was the sense of the wider neighborhood. Foster homes should not be approved in neighborhoods in which there were "many rooming houses" or that were "composed largely of a transient population."[37]

As the field professionalized, new (or even existing) standards would rule out traditional boarding families who could not meet changing expectations, as many of the stories in this chapter suggest. The onset of the Depression coincided with a period in which a number of agencies were beginning to impose more consistent standards of care, and, in 1933, the Child Welfare League of America published its first *Standards* for foster placement.[38] Dorothy Hutchinson, a recognized expert on home finding who taught at the New York School of Social Work, described the older attitudes about vetting foster parenting as one of cultivated naïveté. In the past, she explained, when children were placed in free homes without board, it was assumed that anyone who took in a child "*must* be benevolent." If social workers looked too closely at the people taking in children, there was always the danger that they might find out something they did not like and therefore would not be able to place the children. Furthermore, it "wasn't good manners."[39] By the early twentieth century, however, child welfare advocates had become concerned that free homes were ones in which adults merely wanted household help. And the advent of casework, with its emphasis on meeting the needs of an individual, meant that not just any home would do for any child.

With professionalization, other considerations also entered into the new practice of formally licensing boarding homes. The size of the existing family and its home needed to be taken into account. Agencies typically engaged in religious and racial matching in determining placements, either according to law, agency policy, or unspoken custom. And children were not to be desired for their labor or for the board payments they would bring. In trying to impose these standards in the 1930s, child welfare workers frequently found themselves butting up against the financial realities of struggling boarding families and against long traditions of boarding care.

Otto Hocker, for one, was outraged by the imposition of new bureaucracy and standards. Hocker was an unemployed man living on Long Island whose wife had been boarding children for some time. The New York State Department of Social Welfare had recently established a number of regulations concerning boarding homes for children that were, in Hocker's opinion, designed to "pick on poor Boarding mothers." Regulations that Hocker did not fully understand had led social services to take away his wife's boarding license and remove from their home a nine-year-old and an eleven-year-old who had been with him and his wife since birth. The problem seems to have stemmed from the fact that the two unrelated children were sharing a room, a practice discouraged under emerging standards. Hocker and his family missed the children horribly and had heard reports that they were doing poorly. Although the agency believed it was acting in accordance with practices that would better serve children, Hocker felt himself to be subject to an irrational dictatorship that had rendered him powerless. "We do not need to direct our Eyes to Europe's Dictators," he declared. "I think we have enough of them here."[40] Child welfare professionals were now advocating licensing, standards, individualized casework, and diligent record keeping. It may have seemed to Hocker that these developments were creating a bureaucracy as powerful as Hitler's. Yet, in reality, the child welfare infrastructure remained skeletal in the early 1930s.

Meanwhile, the gradual shift from free placements to boarding homes required, of course, funds to pay board. This was no small matter. Funding was a constant concern and would alter the balance between public and private child welfare services. Most agencies providing boarding care services had traditionally been private, often developing as expansions of the services offered by sectarian orphanages. Public child welfare services rose gradually alongside the private agencies that had existed for decades. While the relationship between the two was rarely untroubled, in many states a constructive division of labor and balance were on the way to being achieved. The Depression would change that. By 1932, private charity was at its highest level ever and public welfare spending (almost all of it at the local level) had doubled from the previous decade. But this was not enough to meet the enormous needs of the thirty million families suffering the effects of unemployment.[41] As with other charitable organizations, private donations to children's agencies dried up, staff had to be laid off, and services were cut. Private agencies were forced to address their clients' needs for basic material relief (food, clothing, and shelter) rather than attend to the "constructive and rehabilitative work for which they were originally designed."[42]

As more taxpayer money became available for social services by the late thirties, public agencies would begin expanding rapidly. In some cases, public agencies took over services formerly provided by private ones. But this was not a simple process. Private agencies typically had decades of experience in the child welfare field, not to mention considerable financial investments in infrastructure, including the real estate, buildings, and grounds that housed orphanages themselves. Public agencies were often newcomers to child welfare. They lacked expertise and suffered from extremely high caseloads. Whereas private agencies could turn away children they believed they were ill equipped to handle, public agencies could not. In some cases, public agencies hired trained personnel who had previously worked for private agencies. Additionally, private agencies at times requested and received public funds to bridge the gap created by a drop in charitable donations and to enable them to continue providing services. Turf wars and friction ensued.[43] Indeed, states made "substantial subsidies" to private agencies, as did town and county "poor funds."[44] In other words, it was not simply a matter of public child welfare services replacing private, sectarian ones. The modern field of child welfare services in the United States would develop as an at times bewildering mix of public and private.

The "private," nongovernmental aspects of foster care were not limited to private children's agencies, though, but also included the boarding homes themselves into which children were placed. Paying board to foster mothers had been established practice in some agencies for decades, and many orphanages had boarding programs for their youngest charges. Yet, a number of child welfare professionals found the shift to boarding homes deeply troubling for both philosophical and practical reasons. On the one hand, they were frankly suspicious of women who received money to care for children (an issue that will be addressed more fully in chapter 6). At the same time, agencies simply did not have the funds to pay adequate board, relying on a child's own parents to partially meet the costs of boarding (which many could not), private donations, or local or occasionally state appropriations. The difference was made up by foster families themselves. In 1936, only twenty-nine states were funding foster home care. A few of these states used government monies to subsidize private agencies that placed children in foster homes. The Children's Bureau took a dim view of this practice, reflecting the widespread belief among social workers that "public funds should be used only under public administration."[45]

The lack of stable public funding for child welfare services was not a new concern in the 1930s, but the problem became particularly acute during the Depression. In December 1934, eight million children under age sixteen were living in families receiving emergency relief.[46] Relief undoubtedly kept many families together. But relief was inadequate, and other families collapsed under financial strain, turning to child welfare agencies for help or coming under the scrutiny of courts that then removed children they considered to be neglected. The prevalence of both scenarios meant the need for homes in which to place dependent children greatly surpassed the availability of free homes. And the funds to pay for boarding homes were scarce, leading to decisions that professionals felt were not always in the best interest of children.

We see the dimensions of the problem through the case of a Connecticut man who — perhaps because his wife had died, or perhaps because she had left him; the record does not say — placed his two children in a boarding home in October 1935. He made regular payments (of around $4.50 per week) for the children's board until, as with so many wage-earning men, his employment became irregular. With the father no longer able to pay board consistently, no public funds earmarked for such cases, and no private funds to bridge the gap, the children had to be placed in an institution, not because such a shift was considered best for them but simply because of the "financial aspect."[47] The child welfare agency had money allotted for institutionalization of children but not for boarding homes.

Not only were the needs great and the resources scarce, but also inadequate child welfare staffing could result in poor options for children and their families. In Connecticut, many districts lacked even a single staff member assigned to the "rehabilitation" of families whose children had been removed, rendering the return of children to their relatives "practically impossible."[48] J. Prentice Murphy explained in 1930 that often out-of-home placement was not needed, even though a parent might request it. Murphy, one of the early leaders of what had by 1933 become the Pennsylvania School of Social Work, had strong ties to both the Children's Bureau and the Child Welfare League and was a frequent writer on matters concerning child welfare.[49] A truly "modern children's agency," Murphy argued, would study each request for placement, examining factors such as the home, kinship ties, and social and economic factors. When this process was done well, Murphy noted, 75 to 85 percent of applications were refused, "the children proving to need instead the services of family relief, health, neighborhood, educational, and other types of agencies rather than the services of foster care organizations."[50] But the nation's support for families simply was not that robust.

The critical need for foster care funding in the early years of the Depression led some child welfare advocates to look to federal options. Indeed, that vision of a federal role in foster care evolved alongside and in conversation with broader discussions of federal responses to the Depression and of the creation of a welfare state. Even before Roosevelt took office, there were voices asking whether funds allocated to nascent federal relief programs could be made available to state and local providers of child welfare services. Local agencies, despairing at their inability to provide foster home care for all needy children, pleaded with the Children's Bureau and other federal agencies to see if there were "any possibility whatsoever of federal aid."[51] This was the case with the Louisiana Children's Home Society. With its assets frozen, the private agency had to close its doors in March 1933. "Men get releif from th employment releif," the society's supervisor, Judith Douglas, wrote to the Children's Bureau. "Why cannot the helpless and dying children get Releif from the R.F.C. [Reconstruction Finance Corporation]?"[52]

The Reconstruction Finance Corporation (RFC) was President Hoover's late-term effort to bring about economic recovery. Although initially intended to stabilize banks and industry through government loans, the RFC eventually turned to issues of relief as well. In the last year of Hoover's presidency, Congress appropriated $300 million for unemployment relief to be administered by the RFC. States faced pressure to define "unemployment relief" broadly so as to enable RFC funds to go toward other kinds of assistance.[53] President Roosevelt had just taken office when the frustrated Douglas wrote to suggest the possibility of a change in policy. Douglas saw an opening. But Roosevelt's federal relief administrator, Harry Hopkins, would rule in June that federal relief funds could not be used for foster care, continuing the policies of the Hoover administration.[54]

There were other possibilities. Those who believed the country needed a more comprehensive and viable federal relief program, including social workers and members of Congress, drafted what became the Federal Emergency Relief Act which was approved in just two months after President Roosevelt took office. The act provided an initial appropriation of $250 million for grants to the states to provide unemployment relief.[55] Some in the child welfare field hoped these funds might be used for the care of dependent and neglected children. Indeed, Hopkins reportedly joked that his friends had warned him that children's advocates would try to unload "all their burdens on his shoulders." Senators Robert LaFollette and Robert Wagner argued, however, that the first priority had to be family security. In other words, if unemployed breadwinners received relief, their children could be cared for and protected in their own homes.[56]

"Relief" was not precisely defined, however. Secretary of Labor Frances Perkins and Children's Bureau chief Grace Abbott successfully pushed for language in the law allowing for a more capacious understanding of "relief" that could include provisions for the health and welfare of dependent and neglected children. But it was up to Federal Emergency Relief Administration head Hopkins — not Perkins or Abbott — to interpret the act's language. The administration was overwhelmed with handling direct relief and was not at all prepared for the more specialized and complicated tasks of addressing the needs of dependent and neglected children. Hopkins, who had spent much of his own social work career working in private agencies, had come to see weaknesses in voluntary agencies and to believe in the need for strong public institutions. Private institutions at this point still played a large role in foster family placements; to allow federal money for board payments would inevitably mean federal subsidy of private agencies. Hopkins ruled in June 1933 that FERA funds could not be given to private agencies and that the funds could not be used for boarding children, either in orphanages or family homes. Although some in the child welfare field were "shock[ed]" by this ruling, it reflected the position shared by many leading child welfare experts that the "first line of defense for children is in their own homes" and fit with the principle of not separating children from their families for reasons of poverty.[57] Indeed, by the mid-1930s, federal relief funds were supporting in some capacity the families of more than seven million children under the age of sixteen.[58]

Child welfare advocates saw additional opportunities for federal support of child welfare when President Roosevelt went on to pursue more sweeping measures to help families. In 1934, he established the Committee on Economic Security to draft plans for what would eventually become the Social Security Act. A year later, B. H. Robinson of Utah's Juvenile Court Commission urged the committee's assistant director to steer the proposed legislation in such a way as to make federal funds available to pay the board costs for foster children. In Utah, Robinson explained, after several years of "crippled public revenues," juvenile courts had become reluctant to assume custody of children living in deplorable conditions because counties and states had "no financial ability to provide for boarding home charges." With the county unable to pay for foster care, an estimated 150 children were remaining under "home conditions which offer no advantages."[59] Needed, Robinson believed, was legislative authorization to use federal money to pay for foster care.

Robinson's plea went unheeded. Although the Social Security Act included what its architects referred to as "the most far reaching child welfare program ever considered in this country," the legislation allocated very little federal money for foster home care and none at all for board payments.[60] Instead, New Dealers, including those with ties to the child welfare field, planned to develop programs that would systematically provide security to families, thus, they hoped, rendering foster care mostly unnecessary. To Grace Abbott, who herself had been a member of the president's advisory council drafting the bill, "provision for the unemployed is a child-welfare program and if we get the aged taken care of, it means that there is more money available in the families for the care of children."[61] Security for families, including aid to the aged that would free young parents from the need to support elderly relatives, would mean security for children and an end to out-of-home placements altogether.

This vision of family security was a deeply gendered one. As Margot Canaday notes, men's "neediness alarmed policymakers in a way that women's did not."[62] Thus the solution to poverty in both women and children was to boost the breadwinning abilities of men so that they could protect and provide for their families. The architects of the Social Security Act aimed to reduce government "dependency" among the eighteen million Americans receiving emergency relief and the ten million more having no employment other than relief work. About 40 percent of those on relief were children. For children, "dependence [was] normal" but best provided through the security of their own families.[63] Strengthening the earning power of fathers and providing aid to mothers when fathers died or deserted would enable children to be raised by their families of birth. This vision had been pursued by Progressive Era reformers, who had supported legislation at the state level to create state mothers' pensions, unemployment insurance, and minimum wage laws. Under the New Deal, similar measures were enacted at the federal level. The Social Security Act of 1935 contained provisions to shore up male breadwinning, including federal unemployment insurance and old age insurance. These measures were complemented by the National Labor Relations Act of the same year, which established the right for workers to join a union and bargain collectively over terms of employment, and the Fair Labor Standards Act of 1938, which instituted a federal minimum wage.

Abbott; her successor at the Children's Bureau, Katharine Lenroot; and another bureau colleague, Dr. Martha Eliot, who would later serve as bureau chief herself, were all represented on the team drafting the legislation. Thus the Social Security Act bore the bureau's imprint. The strategy of advancing child welfare by promoting overall family security was in keeping with the Children's Bureau's philosophy of treating the "whole child" and of viewing children's interests as entwined with those of their parents. They left their mark in other parts of the act as well. In addition to family security measures such as unemployment insurance, the 1935 Social Security Act also included several other provisions of great interest to child welfare advocates.

Title IV, Aid to Dependent Children, targeted the needs of children being raised by single mothers. To bypass the deficiencies of state mothers' pensions, which were ever financially strapped and uneven in coverage, Title IV provided federal grants on a matching basis to states that established ADC programs meeting federal guidelines. The hope was to make ADC more widely available than mothers' pensions had been. Substitutes for male breadwinning would be available not only through ADC but also through the more generous Old Age and Survivor's Insurance (Title II of the Social Security Act as amended in 1939), which provided support for the minor children of a worker (in covered occupations) if he died, as well as for his widow.

Family security measures, together with ADC, were intended to be the most significant for improving the lives of children. But the Social Security Act contained additional measures to address children's health, the needs of disabled children, and other "child welfare services" (Title V, part 3, which included foster care). Child welfare measures (including ADC) were crafted largely by Abbott and Katharine Lenroot. Lenroot, like Abbott, had deep roots in the women's reform network and was a protégé of her friend Emma Lundberg, fellow Wisconsin native and head of the bureau's Social Services Division.[64]

Under Lenroot's leadership, the bureau remained committed to its "whole child" approach, advocating that all government programs addressing children's needs, including ADC, be housed under one roof. Under the whole child approach, foster care would be only one resource available to offer to families. To the bureau, child welfare services and ADC should not be classified as poverty programs because they required rigorous casework carefully tailored for individual children and their families. In Lenroot's view, foster care was "distinct from public assistance, and should not be provided as part of a public assistance program, but in relation to a comprehensive and flexible child-welfare program." Foster placement was, for Lenroot, a very "delicate" process and could be done effectively only by workers with the proper training. Attempts to integrate child welfare services and public assistance programs "presented many problems because of differences in concept, function, and method."[65] The Children's Bureau was given jurisdiction over most children's programs, including maternal and infant health, services to crippled children, and child welfare services. Child welfare grants to the states were to be administered by the Bureau's Child Welfare Division, headed by Mary Irene Atkinson. However, the administrative responsibility for ADC went to the Federal Employment Relief Administration and eventually to the new Social Security Administration. Losing out on jurisdiction over ADC marked a defeat for the Children's Bureau's status as a seat of female influence in Washington and a defeat for proponents of holistic child services.[66] ADC would go on to be administered locally not by caseworkers with training in child welfare but by public assistance departments. The Children's Bureau lost control over ADC, but the program remained a key area of interest as it federalized the mothers' pension idea that the bureau had been so important in promoting decades earlier. And ADC's fortunes would remain deeply connected to those of foster care.

This New Deal's vision of family security, rooted in Progressive Era thought, rested on firmly held notions of male breadwinning and female dependence and caregiving. Yet this long-held family wage ideal, which was reinscribed in the Social Security Act, remained unobtainable for many families.[67] Within the programs of the New Deal, some families were better protected than others. For example, under the Social Security Amendments of 1939, the widow of a man covered by Old Age and Survivor's Insurance received more generous benefits than other single mothers who were eligible only for ADC.[68]

The kind of government benefits a child received depended on the kind of family she lived in. Canaday observes that with the end of the Federal Transient Program in 1935, which had briefly provided for single men who were homeless, "less and less assistance would be delivered outside the family economy."[69] But some children stood outside of this vision of family security altogether. The Social Security Board concluded in 1939 that only "a fraction" of needy children were being reached by new federal programs, although it was impossible to determine precisely how many.[70] ADC, although a federal program, allowed states to pass individual eligibility criteria that would continue to prevent many poor children from receiving assistance because local administrators considered their mothers to be unworthy. In the 1940s and 1950s, several southern and western states would pass laws restricting ADC eligibility to homes considered "suitable."[71] Especially in the South, such rules were used to keep African

American female-headed families out of the ADC program. Those married couples in which the father worked in occupations not covered by social insurance, minimum wage laws, or the National Labor Relations Act lacked protection for their breadwinning ability, a problem that also disproportionately affected rural black and Mexican American families. Due to occupational restrictions and state oversight, the Social Security Act was "like a sieve with holes just big enough for the majority of blacks and Mexicans to fall through."[72] But it was not only children of color who found themselves outside the circle of the welfare state. A widower with young children could not collect survivor's benefits, even if his wife had worked in an occupation covered by survivor's insurance.[73] And he was unlikely to receive ADC. Men could not be both worthy and dependent.

New Deal reforms intended to promote family security supported a racialized ideal of male breadwinning and female dependency. Such provisions assumed that dependency and caregiving were normal and desirable for white women but never for men and only rarely for women of color. The point was not to enable women's economic self-sufficiency or to allow men's caregiving but to make it possible for women deemed deserving to care adequately for their children and for men in covered occupations to financially support their wives, children, and survivors. The boundaries of family security, then, did not encircle all families or all children. Yet reformers were optimistic that most would be reached through New Deal programs, ending pitiful scenarios in which children were separated from their families simply because their parents were too poor to provide for them adequately.[74]

By the mid-1930s, the passage of a number of New Deal measures convinced child welfare reformers that conditions for America's most vulnerable children would improve. With economic need "correctly lodged in government responsibility," child welfare casework would be freed up to fulfill its original purpose as a treatment for individual personality maladjustment.[75] Child welfare advocates and policy makers were distinguishing children whose families were poor but upstanding from those who were permanently dependent, orphaned, or chronically ill treated. With the advent of New Deal programs, only the latter children would now need foster care. Certainly, foster care would require better funding and wider availability than in the past; yet children should be removed only after all the new possibilities for "maintaining the child in his own home under proper conditions" had been explored.[76]

Under the Social Security Act, states would have only indirectly received federal money to cover the costs of children's placement in foster family care. Although earlier in the decade, many had sought federal money for foster care under federal relief funds, the Social Security Act did not supply any funds specifically for board payments. But Title V, part 3, did provide grants to the states in order to promote additional "child-welfare services" for dependent and neglected children, especially in rural areas.[77] As the Children's Bureau envisioned, such services would be available for children in cases of "extreme neglect..., feeblemindedness in parents and children, cruel and abusive parents, illegitimate children without competent guardians, children who are delinquent..., or who suffer from mental disturbances." These situations required "skilled investigation of the individual needs of the child" in order to determine and provide the appropriate services that were available.[78] The bureau's initial budget for such grants was $1.5 million. In 1946, under a government reorganization that transferred child labor responsibilities away from it, the bureau's budget for child welfare grants did increase to $3.5 million.[79]

Unable to use Title V funds for board payments, the various states made use of the funds in other ways. Some focused on improving recreational opportunities for children, some attempted interventions to prevent juvenile delinquency, and others used funds to train new workers. Often the use a state made of Title V funds was related to how well public child welfare services already were established in that state.[80] What these services entailed was not spelled out in the 1935 Social Security Act, but they could include homemaker, casework, child protective, adoptive, and disabled children services and other programs for children in their own homes — along with foster home care. Early visions of "child welfare services" omitted day care, still considered suspect among child welfare experts.

References to other "child welfare services" are somewhat confounding. In terms of formal policy, the phrase appears in the 1935 Social Security Act but was not defined at that time. Social workers and other experts used the term constantly, implying that there was more to "child welfare services" than just foster care. But they rarely did much at all to explain what those "other services" were, nor when, where, to whom, and to what extent they were actually being offered. The term at times seemed to include homemaker services (in which agencies provided a housekeeper to a family whose mother was absent or incapacitated to care for children, prepare meals, and do housework); so-called services to unmarried parents (which involved enabling or even encouraging young unmarried women to relinquish their children for adoption); services for disabled or convalescent children; and protective services (for children whose parents had been charged with abuse and neglect).

Key to experts' understandings of most child welfare services (with the exception of protective services) was that they were *voluntary*. That volunteerism, they believed, enabled the most constructive working relationship between agency staff and birth parents and was best for all parties involved. Parents in distress would seek help from public agencies. After thorough intake by a trained caseworker, staff and parents would determine what the family needed and choose from a range of child welfare services available. At times a parent might request foster placement, but it might be possible to receive other services, such as a housekeeper, that would enable the child to remain in the home. The phrase "other child welfare services" implied a whole menu of unspecified services. Yet the only service the term clearly and consistently referred to was foster care itself. Over the next decades, these additional services remained largely ill defined, precisely because, in reality, the main child welfare service most agencies were able to offer to families was foster care.

Although foster care was certainly understood to be part of child welfare services, Mary Irene Atkinson, head of the Children's Bureau's Child Welfare Division, spoke for many of her colleagues in 1939 when she optimistically anticipated that foster home placement would develop as only "one tool among many" intended to help solve a child's problems.[81] By the late 1930s, ADC was already supporting "far more children than institutions and foster [family] care combined ever had."[82] Funding remained an obstacle to achieving a broader vision of child welfare services. The initial appropriation for Title V child welfare services in the Social Security Act was only $1.5 million—compared with nearly $25 million for ADC and, for unemployment insurance, $4 million the first year and $49 million thereafter—and was to be used to provide modest grants to the states, averaging $11,000 to $73,000.[83] Significantly, Title V funds could not be used to pay for foster care itself. The prohibition on using federal funds for board payments stemmed partly from the private status of so many agencies providing foster placement. The private/public mixture of the foster care "system" meant that reformers and policy makers alike were reluctant to use federal money to pay for care. Instead, the main purpose of the child welfare provisions of the Social Security Act was to help coordinate the work of local governments, promote standards based on professional understandings of best practices among them, and help local units hire and train social workers who would be qualified to investigate cases of neglect and dependence — in other words, to expand services to areas where they did not already exist and to move toward a time when all those placing children would have the kind of specialized training in child placement promoted by professional social workers themselves, thus further moving away from earlier informal models.[84]

At the time of Title V's passage, most states had "few precedents" for child welfare services that were both *public* and staffed by trained professionals. Private agencies and orphanages had developed in large urban centers with concentrated populations of needy children, leaving sparsely populated rural areas relatively untouched by the field. One area administrator, for example, noted in 1935 that services in rural Ohio were in a "practical state of collapse."[85] In 1935, child welfare services remained concentrated in large urban centers. Only a quarter of the states had a system of county public child welfare services.[86] Eleven states at the time had no statewide public child welfare agency at all. With the introduction of federal money for child welfare services, however, every state by the end of 1939 did, although services did not necessarily extend to all counties. By 1946, only one-sixth of the nation's counties had at least one full-time child welfare worker.[87] In 1938, twenty-three states required boarding homes to be licensed; an additional nine states required a license to board children under age two or three but not for older children.[88]

As state agencies expanded with the help of federal Title V funds, they often did so in uneasy relationship with more established private agencies that were deeply invested (both materially and philosophically) in maintaining focus on their own missions, often to particular geographic or sectarian communities. By 1944, the division between public and private child welfare agencies had been upended. It was by that point "increasingly recognized," according to Alice Nutt of New York City's Committee on Child Welfare in a letter to the Children's Bureau, that "primary responsibility for care of all children in need of such care rests with the public agency; and the responsibility for supplementing the public agency through specialized services rests with the private agency."[89]

Foster care belonged to the child welfare network's broad vision of publicly provided family security. But foster care was to be a last resort. Child welfare reformers believed that the 1935 Social Security Act would be a godsend for children in general, keeping families together and enabling more children to be raised in their own homes by their own parents. Children would be protected through programs designed to provide family security. Ideally, the welfare state would support the male breadwinner; when no male breadwinner was present, it would grudgingly support single mothers who met certain standards of need and propriety. Only when there was no mother or a mother deemed inadequate or unworthy would state, local, or private funds support a substitute mother in the form of foster family care.

In 1938, near the end of her life, Grace Abbott felt she had reason to be optimistic about the direction of child welfare in the United States. Having devoted much of her career as a reformer to improving the lives of children, to strengthening the security of the families in which they lived, and to advocating for a greater role for government in providing that security, Abbott trusted that much had been accomplished. Child welfare was in the early stages of becoming a bureaucratized system, overseen by state authorities and increasingly by staff with professional training. And out-of-home care for children, she believed, was becoming a thing of the past. Mothers' pensions, since 1911, together with workman's compensation, unemployment insurance, better wages, and more general public relief, meant that children were "now rarely removed from parental care on the ground of poverty alone."[90] Under the New Deal, those state-level programs had been federalized, meaning more families would fall under their scope. Foster care, it seemed, was on its way to becoming unnecessary.

Foster care as a public welfare provision for children would be supported only indirectly by the federal government. It was instead sustained by a combination of modest board payments from a public or private agency, the foster father's income, and the foster mother's unpaid care work. But what was intended now to be therapeutic would remain a poverty program, and the implications of its reliance on private families would remain largely unexamined.

CHAPTER 3

HELPING AMERICA'S ORPHANS OF WAR

In September 1939, British parents worried about what might happen to their children if Germany were to begin bombing British cities or if a land invasion were to occur. These fears only intensified after the fall of France, Holland, and Belgium less than a year later. In June 1940, Parliament created a Children's Overseas Reception Board to send children abroad for the duration of the war. This organization built on earlier programs to evacuate working-class children out of densely populated areas and send them to the countryside and, ostensibly, out of harm's way.[1]

Americans responded with a wave of concern and generosity. In June 1940, publisher and philanthropist Marshall Field III founded the U.S. Committee for the Care of European Children (USCOM) to coordinate activities of professional, religious, and other private agencies hoping to assist "refugee children." Although a private group, USCOM worked in cooperation with the U.S. government (including the Department of State and the Children's Bureau). First Lady Eleanor Roosevelt was named honorary chairman, while Field served as active chairman. In the summer of 1940, when USCOM issued a call for temporary homes for British children, its New York offices were apparently "besieged" by interested families. USCOM reportedly received 22,000 inquiries by late July. A Gallup poll suggested that millions of American families were willing to take in a child for the duration of the war.[2] The Child Welfare League of America and USCOM braced for an onslaught of children in need of homes.

For American child welfare professionals, this undertaking meant enormous investment, planning, and oversight, an indication of how much had changed since the orphan trains of the nineteenth century. In harmony with the trend toward professionalization of the child welfare field, one of USCOM's primary concerns was to ensure that children be placed in a "supervised" manner and not in a "hit or miss fashion with families who might not understand them."[3] In order to travel to the United States, all children had to have "affidavits of support" secured for them and presented to the State Department.[4] Although most British child evacuees (more than 6,500) went to Canada, somewhere between 800 and 1,600 were placed in the homes of American strangers; others went to relatives or family friends.[5] Because most children bound for North America were evacuated first to Canada, the process had to be coordinated with British and Canadian as well as American officials. Once children arrived in the United States, they needed to be received by social workers. Stranger placements had to be in homes approved by a child-placing agency. Thus social workers would use their expertise to conduct detailed child histories in order to properly match each child with a carefully vetted host family. While in transit to their foster homes, children would also need to be vigilantly supervised. Once placed, homes would have to be monitored. Fund-raising, too, would be important to the project's success. Coordination of these efforts through USCOM was a public-private effort, with the Children's Bureau selecting and advising the agencies with responsibility for overseeing the foreign placements. Three Children's Bureau staff members were temporarily assigned to work with USCOM, including Delinquency Division director Elsa Castendyck. Castendyck, who had visited Europe in 1939 as part of a League of Nations effort to investigate the refugee situation, strongly supported an American role in addressing the child refugee crisis and was thus an obvious choice to work with USCOM on this project.[6]

Public child welfare agencies had recently been expanding at the state and county level, thanks to the inflow of money from Title V of the Social Security Act. The field was in the early stages of establishing guidelines for best practices. The Child Welfare League had released its first *Standards* for foster home care in 1933, which it would update in 1941, and was beginning its national studies of board rates, the first of which would be conducted in late 1941.[7] The relationship of public to private agencies remained complex.

In other words, to receive mass numbers of refugee children would require a more efficient and more fully realized child welfare "system" than actually existed in the United States at the time. The *New York Herald Tribune* editorialized that the prospect of receiving British children served to shine needed light on "our defects" and to propel, in a way not possible before, the ongoing efforts of the

Child Welfare League to bring American child placement up to the standards it advocated.[8] (And, indeed, by early 1944, league membership would grow to over 400 agencies, 180 of which now met the league's accreditation standards).[9] Organizers initially expected so many children that they anticipated having to set up regional offices and other bureaucratic mechanisms to coordinate the effort.[10] The British evacuation would be, one observer wrote, a "test under glass of most of the theories and practices" developed by child welfare experts during the previous twenty-five years.[11] For a field still just beginning to develop the bureaucratic apparatus, tools, and networks of professionalization, the prospect of receiving many thousands of children from overseas was both daunting and inspiring.

American discussions of aid to refugee children typically referred generically to "European children," and USCOM intended to serve children "of all nationalities." In the end, though, it was primarily British children who found safe haven in the United States.[12] USCOM anticipated bringing others and certainly received requests to do so. Some refugee children did come to the United States from France, Spain, and Romania.[13] Yet, the possibilities of accepting other children were limited by immigration quotas, as well as by naval blockades that prevented transport of children other than British. In Britain, the idea of sending children overseas was never universally embraced. Prime Minister Winston Churchill opposed the evacuations because he believed it made Britain appear to be retreating in fear. The program was also risky. One ship, the SS *City of Benares,* was torpedoed in September 1940, leaving nearly two hundred passengers and crew dead, including around seventy-seven refugee children. (None of these children, who were bound for Canada, had been sponsored by USCOM.)[14] In October 1940, only a few months after the endeavor was begun, Britain stopped its official evacuations of children, although it continued to grant exit visas to parents who wanted to make their own independent arrangements.[15]

Thus in the end, the numbers of children entering the United States never came close to what had been first anticipated. Yet the wartime demand for American foster homes was real, even if the children in need of homes were not the British children USCOM prepared for. Rather, it was American children themselves who would need temporary homes during the war. That hundreds of thousands of America's dependent children needed foster homes was not new. The war itself, though, would provide a compelling language for framing that need. Savvy child welfare reformers, long concerned with the plight of dependent children in the United States, hoped to capitalize on the unprecedented attention to child welfare infrastructure and the public sentiment toward child saving, both of which were kindled by the prospect of receiving thousands upon thousands of British children. World War II would be a catalyst in the development of modern foster care.[16]

Deeply held gendered ideas about caregiving and breadwinning faced consistent challenges from the realities of wartime family life. The child welfare field approached the needs of children in wartime within a continued preference for mother care and opposition to day care. For a number of reasons — including the government's deliberate recruitment of mothers of young children into the workforce — the war would recast the need for foster care. In an attempt to meet those needs, child welfare professionals would turn to the rhetoric of war service, celebrating foster mothers' caregiving as part of the war effort. As was also the case for other women working in war industries, however, their champions celebrated foster mothers' motivations in traditionally feminine terms while often downplaying the very real economic considerations also at play.

Economic depression had contributed to the need for foster homes in the 1930s. New Deal family security programs were intended to ameliorate the damaging effects of male unemployment on family life. The coming war in Europe, though, essentially eliminated the unemployment crisis, creating opportunities but also serious challenges for American parents. The Depression era unemployment rate, which peaked at nearly 25 percent in 1933, had dropped to under 5 percent by 1942 and to a little over just 1 percent in 1944.[17] Millions of Americans moved as they entered the armed forces or pursued new employment opportunities. But for those who were parents, taking advantage of those opportunities came with their own complications, including housing and day care shortages.

Certainly, for some families, the economic opportunities afforded by war mobilization offered hope of being reunited with children whom they had reluctantly boarded out during the Depression. Robert Norman had worked on a WPA job during the late 1930s but "scarcely made a living wage." It was a struggle for the Normans to provide for their seven children. The county children's worker encouraged the couple to place two of the youngsters in a private boarding home "in order to lighten the mother's load." By August 1942, the family's economic circumstances had, happily, improved. Mr. Norman had found well-paying work as a carpenter on a defense project, and the family had been able to move into a better home. Now he and his wife hoped for the return of their children.[18]

But for other parents of young children, taking advantage of new opportunities could also create additional challenges. Unemployment may have evaporated, but problems of family insecurity did not end. Mobilization, mass migrations, and the resulting housing shortages created their own family disruptions, leading some children to be exposed to "abnormal family and community life in war-congested areas."[19] Consider the family of Sergeant Bob Gutowski, who was stationed at Fort Meade in Baltimore. For a time, Sergeant Gutowski was able to live near his base with his wife and his young son and daughter. Then he was transferred to a base in the West. This transfer would only be temporary, he believed, so he sent his family to stay with his wife's mother, who lived about 150 miles from Baltimore, in rural Virginia. Unfortunately, this proved to be an unhappy arrangement for Mrs. Gutowski, who had a contentious relationship with her mother. She returned to Baltimore, where she found work at Eastern Aircraft, a division of Chevrolet that had recently begun manufacturing key parts of the navy's torpedo bombers. Mrs. Gutowski rented a room from a woman named Mrs. Norris, who was also housing three of her own adult children, a daughter-in-law, a son-in-law, and a grandchild, in addition to three other adult boarders. While Mrs. Gutowski was at work, Mrs. Norris looked after the Gutowski children.[20]

Mrs. Gutowski's mother objected to her grandchildren living in a household with such a large number of adult boarders and to their being cared for by a woman who had so many other responsibilities. Yet this type of arrangement was how families coped with the wartime housing crisis, high rates of mobility, and the high cost of living. They doubled up, moved in with relatives, or took in boarders. Women like Mrs. Gutowski, whose husbands were away and who had found good work, needed to find someone to care for their children. When appropriate arrangements could not be made, such children became, in the eyes of many child welfare professionals, not just cases of neglect but casualties of war.

The prospect of war work promised more than simply economic benefits for Betty Mosby, who lived with her husband, James, in a small town in upstate

New York; it enabled her to consider leaving her husband, who was physically abusive and earned little income. Betty was able to secure a job in a defense plant in nearby Syracuse and badly wanted to move out. But in order to make the move, she needed someone to care for her young sons.[21] Like Mosby, Gloria Jones addressed the challenges of single parenting by seeking boarding care. Jones, an unmarried mother, obtained work with the New York Shipbuilding Corporation in Camden, New Jersey. To make it possible for her to go to work, she boarded her three-month-old daughter over two hundred miles away on a farm in Troy, New York. When the boarding mother announced she could no longer keep the child, Jones was in terrible straits. "I have no other form of income except working," she wrote to the Children's Bureau, "so I would be unable to keep the baby with me." She was now seeking a "reliable place" to board her daughter, hopefully close by in New Jersey or Pennsylvania.[22]

Sometimes, of course, parents faced with wartime stresses simply abandoned their children, or at least that was how it could appear. Evelyn Murphy was an independent boarding mother in New York City who, in 1943, was caring for the child of a Harlem couple named Wilber. While Horace Wilber was stationed with the army in Texas, his wife, Louise, made arrangements to board their child with Murphy. In June 1943, Murphy complained that she had received no board payments since January and that the mother appeared to no longer want her baby.[23]

Single parenthood was a significant factor in foster placement during the war, whether due to unmarried pregnancy as in Jones's case, or to separation as in Mosby's, or to a father's absence due to military service as in Wilber's. Unmarried pregnancy increased and millions of fathers of young children went into service. Almost one in five families were female-headed during the war, and these single mothers had few options.[24] If they fell behind in board payments as Louise Wilber did, they risked being seen as having abandoned their child.

In the story of the Dearborns of Birmingham, Alabama, we see the disruptions of war interacting with other causes of family insecurity and conflict. The Dearborns had a five-year-old, and in the summer of 1941 Arlene Dearborn gave birth to another child. Not long after the baby was born, Mr. Dearborn joined the army, partly, it seems, as a means of separating from his wife. After entering military service, he continued to contribute ten dollars per month to Arlene, which helped support the children.[25]

Not all servicemen were able to do this. Fathers in the armed forces were given some assistance for their children, but payments were not always timely or sufficient. Soldiers could not apply for their dependent allotments until they had been in service for one month, after which there was another month's delay in processing through the Office of Dependency Benefits. Sometimes fathers failed to apply for these benefits in a timely fashion, which only added to the problem.[26] For men who were paying to board their children before entering the military (perhaps due to divorce, separation, or a wife's death), military service could lead to interruption in board payments. Because of the long lapse between their entrance into the armed forces and the granting of the war allotment, these fathers were not always able to make their regular board payments. One agency in Canton, Ohio, found itself over $2,000 in the red for the boarding of the children of seven such men.[27]

In the Dearborn case, however, Mr. Dearborn seems to have successfully applied for his allotment, which was going to his children as intended. Yet, the family faced additional problems. Mrs. Dearborn became afflicted with tuberculosis, which alarmed her estranged husband. He filed a complaint with the juvenile court to have the children removed because of his wife's health. The children were subsequently placed in a boarding home, and their mother was allowed visits.[28]

The circumstances Mrs. Dearborn reported after visiting her children in their foster home suggest some of the complications of foster placement during the war. She was dismayed to find that the boarding mother was seventy years old and that her husband was over eighty. The couple, childless themselves, were boarding eight children under the age of twelve.[29] This was not acceptable, according to standards of the child welfare profession. The 1941 edition of the League's *Standards* for foster care maintained that foster parents should be a "suitable age to meet the needs of children," that there be "adequate space for separate sleeping rooms for children," and that "not more than two unrelated children should be placed in each house, and preferably children from only one family." Most states refused to grant licenses to homes boarding more than three children.[30] But the acute shortage of foster homes during the war led agencies to be more flexible (or less discerning). Mrs. Dearborn, however, was not of a mind to be sympathetic and, concerned about the welfare of her children, removed them from the boarding home to place them with her sister. The court then threatened her with arrest.[31]

The repercussions of the wartime shortage of foster parents that led Alabama to contract with an older couple in the Dearborn case were felt across the country and intensified over the course of the war. In March 1945, Gertrude Prack of the Missouri Social Security Commission wrote of the "serious plight" that St. Louis County was facing in this regard. She estimated that 250 to 300 homes were needed immediately, noting, "We have only been able to accept real emergency cases for months. There simply is no place in our present state where we can place a child."[32] Earlier that same year, child welfare workers in Massachusetts were reporting that "there are not sufficient boarding homes available; that many of those which they are using are not acceptable; that large numbers of children are in one home; and that they do not have sufficient staff to adequately supervise those which are in use." When boarding homes could not be found, dependent children had to be placed overnight in jails or committed to state reform schools.[33]

By D-day, the shortage of foster families had become so severe that agencies across the county found it necessary to be even more flexible in their standards for foster homes. Many agencies, according to Elsa Castendyck, were putting less emphasis on the "physical aspects and more on the emotional security [the home] has to offer the child." Dorothy Hutchinson, an influential social work professor at the New York School of Social Work, proposed some ideas for care that the Child Welfare League was working hard to define as substandard — that single women be considered as possible foster mothers and that two children be allowed to share a room.[34] In Worcester, Massachusetts, the dire shortage of homes led the local American Legion to take on child placement work, despite having no one trained in that area, because the organization felt that local child welfare services were not doing the job.[35] The Travelers Aid Society in Washington, D.C., continued placing youngsters with one boarding mother, despite reports that the woman had ten to fifteen babies in her home and the Travelers Aid Society's own complaints that she was neglecting the babies in her care.[36]

The chronic shortage of foster families was compounded by the wartime housing crisis. Many of the same challenges that contributed to the explosion in the number of those needing care led also to a shortage of foster homes — the spare bedroom that might have housed a foster child in the past was now home to an aunt who had relocated because of job opportunities or to an adult boarder who paid more in rent than did a child welfare agency, whose board rates could not keep up with wartime rises in the cost of living.[37] Rates for boarding foster children in 1941 ranged from a low of $9 per month to a high of $26 (a range of $148 to $427 in 2016 dollars). Higher rates were found in eastern cities. The Child Welfare League's 1942 board rate study noted that the problem was particularly acute in towns where defense industries were centered: "These towns and cities have literally doubled and trebled their population overnight. A serious housing shortage has been created which affects the foster home program in several ways. As rents rise, some families must move into smaller quarters, which reduces a potential source of foster homes.... The housing situation in defense areas is an overwhelming problem that cannot be minimized." One agency noted that families could now rent rooms in their homes to defense workers "for as much as $20.00 to $24.00 per room per week," significantly more than what agencies paid to board children.[38]

Foster parents who were renters could find themselves at the mercy of landlords who did not always like the idea of their tenants housing foster children. This was the situation described by Peggy Crawford of Woburn, Massachusetts. Crawford lived with her husband and two school-age daughters in a rented seven-room home. For a time, to the consternation of her landlady, Crawford boarded "two state children that were as much to me as my own." The Crawfords, who had lost several other children, presumably through miscarriage or early death, hoped to board additional children. Their landlady, however, according to Crawford, was determined to "find a way to make us vacate if we have anymore in the home."[39]

In Key West, Florida, local child welfare workers and the Federal Housing Authority developed an innovative use of funds to meet the need for foster homes. In 1944 there were no homes in Key West for children needing emergency care, no county children's institution, and no development of licensed foster homes. When a need arose, an agency would go door-to-door in neighborhoods asking who might be able to take a child. This was a makeshift plan that often separated siblings. Key West was "jammed with people" including locals, navy personnel, civil servants, and tourists. With every available apartment and home "filled to capacity" and almost every employable person already working outside the home, a local child welfare worker approached the Federal Housing Authority with a plan to work together. The federal agency allocated a three-bedroom furnished housing unit to be used for temporary, emergency foster family placements. This move was justified "on the basis that the provision of foster shelter care for children is essential to the war effort." As would also be the case with federally funded day care, supporters successfully invoked national security as a rationale for drawing the federal government into new areas of public funding. Child welfare funds paid the rent for the foster family plus an additional five dollars per week per child when children were in the home. By 1945, Key West had three foster homes in federal housing units, which were able to accommodate eight children total.[40]

The Board of Public Welfare in Washington, D.C., was less hopeful about its subsidized boarding home program. It had funds in 1945 to subsidize eight foster homes but had secured only two. The superintendent of home finding, Helen Cooper, was reportedly willing to take "almost anyone who would consider" operating such a home. The two subsidized homes she had arranged were "Negro homes," and Cooper believed it impossible to find any white ones. The thirty-five-dollar-per-month subsidy (on top of twenty-five to thirty dollars per month in board) was simply too low.[41]

The mobility of the American population during the war and the related housing shortages clearly contributed to the wartime foster care crunch. Another factor was what modern readers might recognize as a "day care crisis" but that child welfare professionals were inclined to understand as a crisis caused by mothers "rushing into war industries."[42] As philanthropist Marshall Field put it, "There is every indication that the problems of children are increasing in direct proportion to the increased demand for manpower."[43] One Wichita social worker described as typical a family that had tried to keep its children at home but struggled to do so because of "lack of adequate supervision.... The parents working on a ten hour shift are unable to get sufficient rest and give children any supervision."[44]

The real issue for experts, of course, was not working *parents* but working *mothers*. Indeed, in 1941, 1.5 million women were working in war industries, and by the end of the war 5.5 million mothers of children under fourteen were doing so.[45] Female workforce participation was actively encouraged by government, industry, and the popular press as a patriotic act, necessary for the war effort. Yet Americans still tended to view working mothers as anomalies, and the nation was utterly lacking in the infrastructure necessary to enable mothers of young children to engage in wage work. Accounts from the early months of the war described "children being left alone or locked in cars in parking lots while their mothers worked."[46] Some child welfare agencies reported that women were placing their children in foster family care simply because of that lack of day care.[47]

Such stories led to calls for subsidized child care for working mothers, what until recently had been disparaged as "charity for the poor."[48] Under the Lanham Act, Congress authorized the use of federal money, beginning in August 1943, for day care in so-called war impact areas — areas of the country central to war production. The cost to mothers was capped at fifty cents per day, later raised to seventy-five cents, with the federal government providing 50 percent matching (around seven to eleven dollars per day in 2016 terms). Over the course of the Lanham Act's existence (until 1946), 3,102 federally funded child-care centers provided day care to around 600,000 children. At its peak in 1944, approximately 130,000 children were being served. Every state but New Mexico received Lanham funds, although the bulk went to California, where the majority of the war industries were located. Indeed, nearly 25 percent of all children enrolled in Lanham Act day care programs were from California. But even at the height of the program, only about 13 percent of children needing day care received federal help.[49] And for those living in parts of the country not designated "war impact areas," federally supported day care was not an option at all.

Child welfare experts had long been dubious about group care for children, especially young children. During the war, they expressed grave concern about the poor quality of staff in many childcare institutions and independent boarding homes, as well as about the lack of oversight and personalized care.[50] Even the National Association of Day Nurseries was grudging and suspicious in its thinking about the use of such resources. Indeed, one 1939 article on day nurseries suggested that the "real needs" of parents were not always the ones they claimed when seeking day care. A woman might say she wanted to work and needed child care to do so. "But we find she has had a quarrel with her husband and left him in a fit of anger," the article continued. "If nursery care were provided in such a case, it might widen and make permanent a break."[51] The Child Welfare League, which would absorb the Association of Day Nurseries during the war, reflected its own long-standing opposition when its leader, Howard Hopkirk — who became head of the league in 1940 after the death of C. C. Carstens — predicted that there would be "tragic consequences if the demand for woman power leads to widespread care of infants in groups in nurseries."[52]

The league may not have enthusiastically embraced wartime day care, but it did set out to assess its effects. In a study of communities affected by the war emergency, the league described an institution caring for eighty children, ages five and under. The staff was "small and admittedly incompetent." Conditions were appalling and included "the presence of vermin, filth, and odors." The majority of the babies suffered from "prolonged diarrhea." There was no program of child development, and the children had few toys. Most of the children were not toilet trained and were described as "noticeably retarded" in their development. Even among the older children, many sat on the floor "rocking and mumbling."[53] Such conditions were disturbing. But working mothers had few options.

One factory-run center described by the league as "unusually good" operated two nurseries on a twenty-four-hour schedule, caring for a total of around 740 children. The twenty-four-hour schedule enabled parents working swing shifts to secure care for their children. Children, even the youngest, were in groups of twenty-five to thirty with an average of three teachers per group. They received meals, depending on which hours they were in care. While the league found this particular center to be better than most, it still concluded that in "no institution or day nursery" visited during the course of its 1944 study were young children (under age two) receiving "satisfactory care."[54]

The day care crisis contributed to the wartime foster care crisis as families resorted to using foster care to make up for inadequate day care. Child welfare professionals at times endorsed this option, under certain conditions, as an alternative to day care in institutional settings. As day care skeptics and champions of their own specialized knowledge, the Children's Bureau and the Child Welfare League preferred what they called "foster day care" to group care, as child welfare professionals had a hand in placements in the former. "Foster day care" was an arrangement similar to what today would be called "licensed in-home day care," only more regulated. A woman, often a mother herself, would be paid to accept a small number of children into her home during the day while parents were at work. The "foster mother" would be licensed by the state. But oversight did not end with licensure. Trained caseworkers would be the ones to refer children to the boarding mother, and casework services would be available to both mothers and children.[55] Consensus expert opinion held that children ideally belonged with their mothers. If that were not possible, an alternative homelike setting to which children had been carefully matched was a preferable alternative to both unlicensed boarding homes and group care. The heads of both the Child Welfare League and the Children's Bureau supported foster day care; however, the Children's Bureau's medical adviser (and future chief) Dr. Martha Eliot worried that such care in a home could cause confusion for children, possibly leading to psychological problems.[56]

The development of licensed foster day care was inhibited by a ruling of the Federal Works Administration, which oversaw the Lanham funds, that those funds could be used only for institutional care and not to pay foster day care providers.[57] The Child Welfare League's Howard Hopkirk testified before Congress on the need to include foster day care in updated legislation for 1944 but to no avail.[58] One implication of the ban on using federal funds for foster day care was that the fees for foster family day care tended to be more than twice as high — $1.35 a day for foster day care versus $0.50 for group care.[59]

While the Child Welfare League preferred licensed boarding homes, it noted with alarm the "unprecedented number of children" placed during the war in institutions, nurseries, and unlicensed foster homes. Many of those, the league reported, were commercial establishments. The league worried especially about this type of care. Even in states where licensing laws existed to protect children, commercial and independent unlicensed homes were inserting advertisements in the classified sections of local newspapers, which appeared to be encouraging the use of these resources.[60]

Some newspapers were by now refusing to carry these kinds of ads.[61] Yet plenty continued to run postings such as one from the *New Orleans Times Picayune* seeking "ROOM and board for my 2 preschool age daughters. Suburban home preferred" or one from the *San Francisco Chronicle* offering to "give complete care to under school age child in my home."[62] In 1945, Indiana, like many other states, passed a law requiring that boarding homes be licensed. To encourage compliance, the state's Children's Division produced pamphlets encouraging relevant parties to see the law not as a restriction but as a form of protection. "Boarding Parents! Protect Yourselves with a License!" read one. "Mothers! Protect Your Children if They Must Live Away from Home," read another.[63] In most states, even independent boarding homes had to be licensed by the state. But child welfare professionals remained skeptical of independent placements, convinced that specialized matching and casework services were required to truly meet the needs of families.

Helping America's Orphans of War | 79

"Board Wanted." Newspapers continued to run want ads in the 1940s for both boarding homes and children to board, although some states were beginning to ban such notices. (*Baltimore Morning Sun*, October 7, 1945.)

In this same period, adoption professionals were campaigning against independent adoptions and in favor of agency-supervised ones. Adoption experts presented independent adoptions as risky for all parties, for such placements did not benefit from the "science" employed by professional adoption workers to match a child with the appropriate family and to ensure that children were not exploited through baby-selling. By advocating agency adoptions, adoption caseworkers also helped assert themselves as professionals whose skills were essential in ensuring a successful adoption. Meanwhile, many birth mothers and potential adopters continued to prefer to avoid the red tape of agency adoptions in favor of independent or "gray market" adoptions.[64] Similar themes were at play in professionals' campaigns against independent boarding homes and families' continued use of them.

A tragic fire at a Maine boarding home offered a cautionary tale of the potential perils of independent boarding. The private boarding home in Auburn for the babies of working mothers had lost its state license because it was found to be boarding more than the allowed maximum number of children. The home, run by Mrs. Eva LaCoste and employing three other adult women, was legally allowed to house sixteen babies but was boarding as many as twenty-one at the time the fire broke out in January 1945. Sixteen children and one adult woman, employed as a nurse in the home, perished in the fire, which occurred at night when the occupants were asleep.[65] "Mothers who turn their children over to unlicensed agents and to people who flout or ignore laws intended to protect their children," Katharine Lenroot commented, "are, like the bereaved mothers in Maine, running tremendous risks."[66]

To the Child Welfare League's Howard Hopkirk, the tragedy was an argument for finding the funds to support additional foster homes across the country. Hopkirk had studied at Union Theological Seminary and the New York School of Social Work and had previously served as a consultant on institutional care for the league in the 1920s and 1930s.[67] In a Child Welfare League pamphlet issued in response to the fire, he asked, "Has your community tolerated the inadequate rates of board which still make the boarding of children in foster homes impractical under the high cost of living and other economic pressures of wartime? Has foster mothering been considered the essential activity which it is?" Hopkirk further connected the tragedy to wartime. Several of the babies who died in the fire were the children of servicemen, whose wives had to board their infants while they worked. As Hopkirk noted, "Wives of service men increasingly are compelled to rely upon the cheapest available nursery care while they are at work."[68]

Undoubtedly, the war exacerbated the foster care crisis in the United States. The war also, though, provided a compelling language for the advocates of foster children to make their case that the American public needed to pay more attention, as Hopkirk's plea to consider wartime foster parenting an "essential service" suggests. Apparently learning from the outpouring of interest in providing homes for British children in 1940, child welfare professionals built on the rescue rhetoric of the British case to present America's foster children as the country's own "war orphans"— victims of the war itself who deserved an outpouring of patriotically inspired support. To meet demand for foster homes for American children, child-placing agencies embarked on publicity campaigns that presented foster mothers as patriotic "war workers" and foster children as victims of the war in ways that strategically evoked the plight of British children whose homes and communities were under attack. This analogy was far from perfect, to say the least. But it suggests much about the problems and opportunities presented by the war to child welfare workers concerned about placing dependent children in foster homes.

The generous and positive responses of the American public to the British evacuation program seemed to create an opportunity to channel those impulses toward American children who also needed out-of-home placement. Heartened by the outpouring of support for young victims of the European war, the Child Welfare League tried to tap into that sentiment and urged the public to extend the "generous impulse aroused by the plight of the British children" to the 250,000 American children in need of foster care.[69] Staff at the Child Welfare League and the Children's Bureau worked to link the nation's own needy children to the tragedy of war. One child welfare worker referred to American children needing foster care as "Lend-Lease babies," in reference to the controversial American policy of "lending" arms to the Allies (before the United States entered the war) as a means of getting around American neutrality laws. The term "lend-lease" suggested the temporary nature of foster care but also evoked the war effort, implying that American foster children were themselves casualties of war. As Children's Bureau chief Katharine Lenroot put it, "Family life is being bombed every day in the United States."[70]

During the war, some pamphlets aimed at recruiting foster parents began describing supposedly typical foster children as youngsters who were "temporarily orphans of the war" because their fathers were fighting overseas.[71] This was strategic. In reality, American foster children on the whole did not require placement because they were literally "war orphans." (Neither, incidentally, did most British child evacuees). In 1946 Lenroot estimated there were only about sixty thousand children orphaned due to their fathers' deaths in military service.[72] As Emma Puschner of the American Legion's Child Welfare Division put it, finding an American child who was a full orphan due to war was "like looking for a needle in a haystack."[73] Rather, American children needed homes due to more long-standing reasons — unwed pregnancy, illness, homelessness, poverty, or loss of a breadwinner. Many of those problems were most certainly exacerbated by the war. American deployment led to an increase in unwed motherhood, a highly mobile population, additional stresses on families, a shortage of housing, children being supported on inadequate servicemen's pay, and an explosion in the number of mothers of young children in the workforce. The Social Security Board did eventually interpret a father's absence due to military service to be a qualification for Aid to Dependent Children, and some states did allow soldiers' wives to receive it. Yet by 1943, only 700,000 families were collecting ADC, whereas experts estimated that as many as 1.1 to 1.3 million might have been eligible.[74] All of these war-related factors contributed to children being placed in foster homes.

Hopkirk echoed this theme of children as casualties of war in titling a brief 1942 article "War Hits Our Children." But while Hopkirk noted, nine months into the war, that there were indeed American children who were fatherless as a result of the conflict, he emphasized that the real issues for most children in foster care were family disruptions due to mothers being drawn into industrial war work and "unwholesome moral hazards" of wartime resulting in "twice as many children of unmarried mothers under care" in some cities.[75] In 1943, approximately seventy thousand children were born to unmarried mothers annually.[76] These certainly were conditions that could be linked to the war. But they were apparently not the kinds of problems guaranteed to provoke the sympathy and generosity offered to British children, who were viewed as literally fleeing the bombing of their homes. Hence most publicity materials on foster care in wartime were noticeably more vague about the precise links between dependent children and war.

If American foster children were casualties of war, than the foster mothers who cared for them were patriots engaged in the essential war service of preserving the nation's human capital. In promoting foster mothering as a war service, child welfare professionals tried to counter the prevailing view that industrial work was the highest form of female patriotism. "Taking children into your home is as truly war work as the construction of ships in the Navy yard," argued Anna King of Fordham University's School of Social Work. "Every time a child is kept happy and well, you are producing something greater than a ship."[77] Children's services agencies, in appealing for foster mothers, tried their best to counter the propaganda that women could best show their love of country by taking factory jobs. They produced pamphlets describing foster care as "a war job for you in your own home."[78] Another declared, "We cannot all fight for freedom in the active theatres of war... but we who remain at home can line up against the evils which undermine the physical, mental and spiritual development of our children's lives, armed with the realization that there is no greater antidote for such evils than the daily living and growing in a wholesome family home."[79]

The Child Welfare League wrote disapprovingly of the employment of mothers of young children, especially of the fact that government and industry

("A War Job for You in Your Own Home!" ("Share Your Home with a Child," ca. 1943, 7-3-3-2 Foster Home Care — Placing Out May 5, 1943, box 168, CB Central File 1941–1944.)

seemed to be "actively recruit[ing]" mothers for war work, noting that in Britain, women with young children had initially been exempt from national service.[80] The Child Welfare League implied that in urging women to take on war jobs out of patriotism, the U.S. government and American industries were inadvertently helping to create America's own "orphans of war." Children's Bureau chief Katharine Lenroot observed that while women now had "increasing responsibility for the war effort, it must not be overlooked that their primary duty is to their homes."[81] A conference on day care held in the summer of 1941 concluded that "although women are needed as an essential part of the defense program and it is a public responsibility to provide appropriate care of children while mothers are at work, it should be emphasized that mothers who remain at home to provide care for children are performing an essential patriotic service in the defense program."[82] So too, it would seem, did foster mothers. As Lenroot described, the work of foster parents needed to be considered to play a "vital part" in the struggle to "carry on a free society in the postwar world."[83]

84 | Helping America's Orphans of War

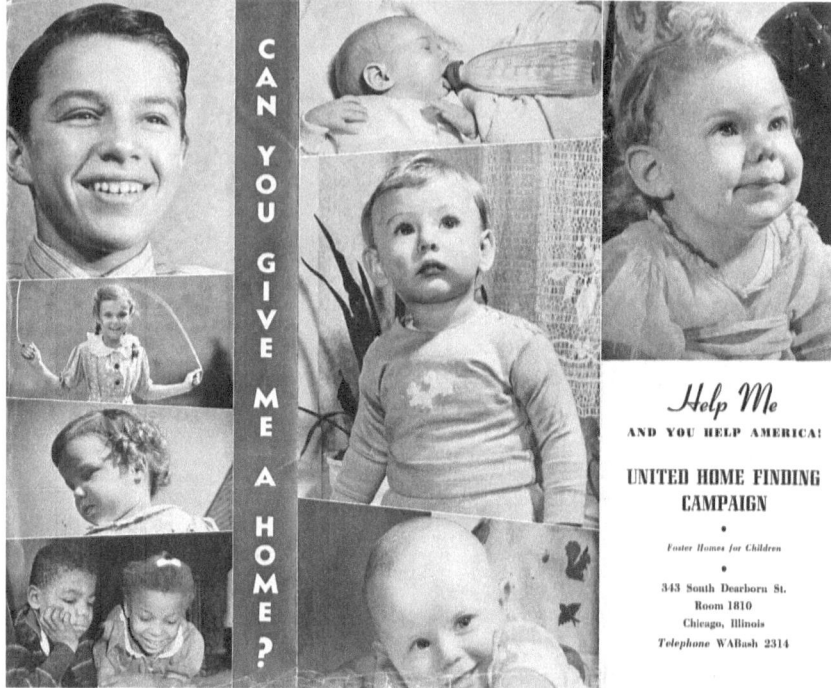

"*Help Me* and You Help America." (United Home Finding Campaign [Chicago], "*Help Me* and You Help America!," ca. 1943, 7-3-3-2-Foster Home Care — Placing Out May 5, 1943, box 168, CB Central File 1941–1944.)

Serving as foster parents, the message ran, was a way that women could "make a great patriotic contribution to the war effort" and do their part to "help secure the future of America for which we are now fighting."[84] One Connecticut pamphlet reasoned that "to care for a homeless child is to help strengthen our home defenses" and asked, "Won't you choose this as your war job?"[85] A pamphlet from Boston described foster care as "a patriotic service in war and peace."[86] Others featured photos of infants and toddlers with the words "Help me and you help America."[87]

The children pictured in recruitment materials were mostly white, but several pamphlets also displayed images of African American children, including one young boy featured in a Connecticut Child Welfare Association pamphlet who appeared to make the plea, "I'll pay my way in joy and cash and you'll be doing your part in the War effort."[88] Most recruitment materials downplayed

Joy and cash. Most recruitment materials downplayed board payments as an incentive for fostering. This image, targeted at African American parents, was an exception. (Foster Homes for Children Campaign [Connecticut], "*Won't You* Give Me a Home?," ca. 1943, 7-3-3-2 Foster Home Care — Placing Out May 5, 1943, box 168, CB Central File 1941–1944).

the importance of board payments; thus it is noteworthy that this particular pamphlet, clearly targeted at black mothers, highlighted financial incentives among the reasons to take in a foster child. While experts preferred to work with foster parents unaffected by financial considerations, the challenges of finding homes for black children would at times lead them to modify those expectations when working with black families, as will be discussed further in chapter 5.

As was the case with most references to foster children as war casualties, such pamphlets did little to expand on the alleged connections between foster care and wartime other than to suggest that "war conditions have increased the need."[89] One of the few that did go into more detail (a pamphlet produced by the Children's Department of the Boston Council of Social Agencies and the Massachusetts Child Council) asserted that there was a shortage of foster homes "directly attributable" to the war. It went on to elaborate on various reasons: "the moving of families from old home areas to war industry centers; to crowded living quarters; to men entering the armed forces; to housewives replacing men in industry."[90]

As was the case with the need for foster placements, the chronic shortage of foster parents, although not *created* by the war, was exacerbated by it. The war played a role in creating the need for foster homes by leading families to relocate for military service and jobs and by providing women who might have served as foster parents in the past a chance to pursue better economic opportunities. As the Child Welfare League noted, board rates for children (placed both in full-time foster care and foster day care) were unrealistically low, especially given wartime inflation and the high cost of living. "Compensation for the foster mother's services must be added, " the league argued, "if women are to be attracted to this from other occupations."[91]

Some women did indeed see foster parenting as akin to a "war job," whether because they read recruitment brochures or articles in newspapers and magazines that featured these themes or because they made such connections on their own. Before the United States had entered the war but while mobilization was already underway, Mrs. Bradbury Townes, a thirty-three-year-old woman who lived on a farm in Ohio, sought information about jobs that might be opening up for women "due to the present emergency." She preferred a job in her home and proposed caring for several preschool-age children. "They could be underprivileged little ones," she offered, "but they must be white, and not crippled or too much dependent."[92] Peggy Crawford described herself as wanting to "do something for the country that would prove worthwhile without leaving my children-husband and home."[93] Rose Vogt of Kentucky was another who embraced the idea of foster mothering as women's patriotic war service. She had seen in the news that there were "50,000 homeless children in the U.S.A. made so by the war." The Vogts had four children of their own. Mr. Vogt, an electric welder, did not earn a lot of money, and the family did not own their own home. Rose wanted to help with the war effort (and perhaps earn extra income), but the small town they lived in had no defense plants. "I would like to help out if I could, and I thought you might help me to get one of those homeless children to care for."[94]

During the Depression, some potential boarding mothers had explained their desire to board in economic terms — that is, in terms of their need to earn money doing work they loved. During the war, similar economic arguments were given a new frame — the desire to serve one's country. Nora Hoyt, a single woman who was a licensed nurse from Massachusetts, wanted to work "for a cause" by boarding ten babies in her home. "I want to do my share in war effort," Hoyt noted in a telegram to the president.[95] And Mrs. Mabel Gibson, a widowed teacher with two school-age sons, wanted to board two more school-age boys. "We are dependent upon my salary," she noted, so she would need to be paid. She had in mind the "fathers in the service or about to be called who are much concerned about the welfare of their motherless children."[96] As single women, of course, neither Hoyt nor Gibson would have met the boarding qualifications of the more exacting agencies.

Local publicity campaigns presenting foster parenting as war service did have important effects. A Chicago home-finding effort (part of the United Home Finding Campaign, which brought different agencies together in launching drives for foster homes) conducted from April 19 to June 1, 1943, resulted in about 2,900 applications. Many of those applications were not found to warrant further pursuit, but the director of the project insisted that the number of applications told only part of the story. It seemed to him that "great good has been accomplished by this cooperative campaign in bringing to the attention of the community, in a dramatic manner, the work of these agencies and the total nature of the dependent child problem, while at the same time paying a very important and deserved tribute to foster parents."[97] The Child Welfare League's Henrietta Gordon saw another advantage in the home-finding campaigns, which were conducted in several other cities as well: foster parents who were previously "embarrassed to tell their friends of this service they were rendering" were now "boasting" about it. Increasing the "sense of dignity and importance" of the foster parent job would, she hoped, bring more applicants than before.[98]

In suggesting that families might previously have been "embarrassed" to admit that they were serving as foster parents, Gordon showed she understood the limitations of Americans' sympathies for dependent children. Reframing American foster children as war casualties and those who cared for them as rendering patriotic service to their nation was a means of addressing those limitations. Children needing homes because of poverty or homelessness or because their mothers were unwed or employed apparently did not promise to generate the same kinds of responses as did British children perceived more genuinely to be victims of the war.

Here class seems to have played a significant role. "In our opinion," wrote Elsa Castendyck in 1943, "there are relatively few people in the higher income brackets who are willing to accept the responsibilities involved in the care of homeless children simply as a patriotic duty." Part of the reluctance, she suspected, came from prejudice against children of recent immigrant backgrounds. Although Castendyck acknowledged that the Children's Bureau did not have "statistical data" by which to prove her point, others in the field shared her impressions.[99] Cheney Jones, of the New England Home for Little Wanderers, noted to Katharine Lenroot a year later that, having had "considerable experience with British evacuee children," he could not help "continuing to think that by some means or other we could succeed in interesting a class of families in becoming foster families of American children who heretofore have not been used."[100]

That the evacuation of British children to American homes was likely to place affluent children into affluent homes was an idea reflected in *Now That April's There*, a juvenile novel by Daisy Neumann, published in 1945. In Neumann's novel, part of which first appeared as a short story in the *New Yorker* in 1944, Wincy and Angus Turner return home to Oxford after several years in America. The children of an Oxford University classics professor, Wincy and Angus were sent overseas by their parents for their safety and were placed with a Harvard University chemistry professor and his wife. In their foster home, Wincy has the opportunity to learn to play the violin, and Angus becomes adept at building and repairing household items. Upon their return to England, the Turner children's parents worry that Wincy did not study Latin in her American school and that she has picked up an interest in Freudian psychology.[101] While the Americanization of their children was surely troubling to some British parents, such concerns were of a different degree from those of someone like the tubercular Mrs. Dearborn, who feared the overburdened elderly couple with whom her children were placed could not give even basic, adequate care.

In the case of British children, American families in large numbers willingly opened their homes to these children of strangers who were imperiled by war. Yet if the British children's seemingly more authentic status as victims in need of rescue would seem to explain the greater response, we must also look at another group of young war victims who did not fare so well in public opinion. A year and a half before the evacuation of British children, after Kristallnacht, the Wagner-Rogers bill had proposed admitting twenty thousand Jewish children from the Reich into the United States above and beyond the numbers allowed under immigration law. The bill was widely opposed and never became law. Jewish children failed to generate the outpouring of support that might have helped the bill. There are a number of reasons why Wagner-Rogers failed, including anti-Semitism, economic anxiety, and a widespread reluctance to tamper at all with immigration law. A compelling child rescue narrative in and of itself was not enough. Many Americans found Jewish children to be threatening in ways that British children were not. While child rescue narratives offer the potential to frame policy proposals in ways that generate sympathy and support, there are no guarantees. Children are not blank slates, and rescue narratives are not constructed in social and political vacuums.

In recognizing that the war offered an opportunity to generate sympathy for dependent children that might otherwise be lacking, child welfare professionals were tacitly acknowledging the low regard in which many held such children. It was easier, apparently, to generate sympathy for British children who were described as having "survived bombs and torpedoes."[102] Creating similar concern for American "welfare children" was more challenging. The image of children fleeing the Blitz was a powerful one, and it resonated with American families. In the end, around 4,200 British children came to the United States, although only 1,600 at most seem to have been evacuated by the British government through the Children's Overseas Reception Board.[103] The remaining children were sent by private arrangement (like the fictional Turner siblings), indicating that their families were of some means. In other words, the foreign children to whom Americans opened their hearts and homes were not orphans; many were not even poor; and one could even argue that they faced as much danger in being transported overseas than they had faced in Britain itself. Yet the "rescue" narratives that tend to permeate child-saving enterprises hit home.

Americans understood that war brings suffering to children, and child welfare professionals leveraged this as best they could. During the Second World War, in order to meet the demands for care of dependent children, child welfare professionals in the United States used the context of the war to reshape the public's image of foster children as victims of the war and to insist that foster parenting was a patriotic activity helping the war effort. Essentially they argued that helping poor children would help America as a whole. But that argument has not often been a winning one, which partly — although only partly — explains the ongoing difficulty in finding foster homes for children. Child welfare professionals understood that American children — even white children — were already coded as problematic, as would become even clearer in the decades to come.

CHAPTER 4

PROVIDING LOVE AND CARE

Foster Parents as Parents

In the spring of 1945, *Woman's Day* ran a profile of a New York foster mother named May Gill. Reporter Dorothy Blake visited Gill's home and watched her juggle the tasks of making lunches for a preschooler and four school-age children, who all came home at different times. Two were the biological children of Gill and her husband; three were foster children, two of whom had been with the family for three years. Blake noted that the tenor of the home—"warmth of kindness and laughter and love overflowing"—was not the "grim atmosphere" she had feared when she began the assignment. When she asked Gill about the love she had for both the biological and foster children in her home, the woman was thoughtful. "It's nothing you can measure like a cup of flour—your heart just has to be big enough to not sense the difference and to fit them all in and then do your best for each. It's not something you can take up and leave off from one day to the next either—and it's not something that can be paid for in dollars. I'm Aunt May to some and Mother to the others but so long as they all love me—well you see how it is." As foster parents, the Gills received twenty-five to thirty dollars a month per child, which, as Blake pointed out, barely covered the costs of the children's care. The real payment, Blake and May Gill seemed to agree, came from the foster mother knowing that she was helping a child in need.[1]

In drawing a distinction between those who called her "Mother" and those who called her "Aunt May" while insisting that she loved them all, Gill was perfectly aligned with contemporary professional literature on ideal foster parenting. In the years following World War II, the United States relied on private families (like Aunt May's) to fulfill the public's responsibility to care for children who, for whatever reasons, had not found security in their own families despite the programs of the New Deal welfare state. Women providing foster care served as "mothers" who were to supply the intangible qualities of love and nurture to children who were not their biological offspring. In this way, foster care was similar to adoption (a practice that was on the rise in this period).[2] Yet as home workers, foster mothers provided social services for remuneration and signed contracts outlining the parameters of their relationship with their foster children, which made foster care something quite different. These women who were "mothering for the State" (to quote sociologist Teresa Swartz) were at the center of foster care's ambiguity within the American system of welfare provision.[3]

In the postwar period, experts saw foster parents as critical yet precarious components of the child welfare system and, consequently, directed new attention to them. That attention took the form of refined, revised, and expanded volumes of *Standards* from the Child Welfare League, which was increasingly working in tandem with the Children's Bureau and with professors and graduate students at prominent institutions like the New York School of Social Work. The Child Welfare League, in dialogue with its contacts at agencies across the country, reworked and reissued the existing *Standards* and released additional volumes on adoption (1958), homemaker services (1959), and day care services (1960). The Child Welfare League and the Children's Bureau helped sponsor, publicize, and distribute professional literature on home finding, child placement, and foster parent recruitment.

Although children had been placed out and boarded out for decades, not a lot of thought had been given to the receiving homes in the past. In the 1940s there were not even good estimates of the number of foster homes serving children. As late as 1955, the Children's Bureau could only reply "Not available" to a request for the numbers of children in foster care in each state.[4] By the mid-1950s and 1960s, however, child welfare professionals and advocates were producing a flurry of reports and studies on foster parenting as they attempted to determine who foster parents were, how they could best be recruited and retained, and how they could be brought into line with agency understandings of best practices.

Child welfare professionals had a number of reasons to be thinking more analytically about foster parents at midcentury. The chronic shortage of foster parents had only intensified during the war, stimulating a desire to understand this group better. But there was also a developing awareness that the very purpose of foster care had changed considerably from nineteenth-century practices in ways that rendered the foster parent role more fraught. Rather than an open-ended means of providing a physical home for dependent children, foster care was now viewed as a temporary, rehabilitative practice. The goal of most placements was supposed to be — at least in theory — the return of a child to his biological family. And foster children were increasingly seen as damaged in some way. The number of orphans had declined, and furthermore, Aid to Dependent Children and New Deal social insurance programs now provided benefits to many families who previously might have been unable to care for their children. These changes meant, at least according to child welfare professionals, that children were now coming into care not due to the death or poverty of their parents but because there were problems in their families — mental illness, social disorganization, alcoholism, or out-of-wedlock births — as will be discussed in chapter 5.

At the time when therapeutic culture was at its "most dominant" in the United States, then, foster care was taking on tasks that were more explicitly geared toward treatment and rehabilitation.[5] Thus experts on placement became increasingly aware that not just any willing family made a good foster placement. Foster parents remained mysterious, however, and experts often adopted a perplexed, distanced stance when writing about them. As one Philadelphia recruitment campaign from the late 1940s put it, "It is both natural and unnatural to be a foster mother."[6] The goal of foster care was to replicate a "normal" family life for foster children as an alternative to institutional care. But because foster care was supposed to be temporary, it was important that foster homes not perform the task of creating a substitute family life *too* well. Prospective adoptive families were scrutinized for their ability to love an unrelated child as their own. Yet for foster parents to show "extreme love" or "possessiveness" (as was expected of other kinds of parents) was to violate the standards of good foster parenting.[7] Child welfare experts and professionals in the 1950s and 1960s would discover that recruiting, selecting, and retaining couples to play such a role was a great challenge.

Foster families were not seen as "real" families or even as potential adoptive families; yet they were to provide family life to foster children, as part of a community's and the nation's system of social services. Adoption, by midcentury, was now seen as the "best solution" to the crisis of unwed pregnancy among white middle-class girls and the problems of infertility among middle-class couples.[8] Certainly adoption was understood to also benefit children, but the institution was no longer burdened by earlier expectations that it also address social problems of child neglect and dependency. Foster care, however, still held these associations, although now with a new emphasis on rehabilitation.

The advantages foster family care allegedly held over orphanages was the opportunity for the child to live in a homelike, family setting. Placing children deprived of the care of their own parents in a carefully vetted foster family would allegedly offer the healing effects of proper family life to dependent children whose own families were unwilling or deemed unable to properly care for them. Foster placement was also one means of addressing societal problems of juvenile delinquency, unwed pregnancy, and poverty — problems that generated considerable anxiety in the postwar period.[9] (At least one birth mother whose children were in care saw the problem of juvenile delinquency quite differently. "Would you try to make a law, that would void all court orders taking children from their mothers?" Mildred Woods wrote in a letter to President Truman. "I think if more high pressure people would stop taking children from their mothers it would stop over half of juvenile delinquence." Woods was surely not alone in her views, even if they did not reach a wide audience.)[10]

Foster parents were to provide the family life that would serve therapeutic functions for needy children until the agency determined that it was best for a child to be returned to his home or placed with another family. Foster parents were explicitly *temporary* caregivers, although in reality that "temporary" period could go on for years, even for most of a childhood. This temporary nature of foster care was a key part of what made the foster parent role so ambiguous, and it made it difficult for professionals to believe they could trust those who performed that role. As Berkeley social work professor Martin Wolins put it in 1963, "Clarity is lacking. The foster parent is sometimes seen as a client, sometimes as an agency staff member. He is seen as a natural parent, a relative, a stepparent, a 'professional' parent, or he defies classification."[11] As "clients," foster parents were recipients of casework, yet as Children's Bureau research director Elsa Castendyck noted, it was a different kind of casework because the applicant made a request for "the actual person of a child rather than for money or services."[12] Katharine Lenroot noted that in most cases the relationship between a child and her foster parents "cannot be a true parent-child relationship" because the child's biological parents were still in the picture. The foster relationship had to be "more of an aunt-uncle-grandmother, grandfather relationship which involves ability to hold both the child, and if possible, the parents, in mature affection and concern, without jealousy." Lenroot acknowledged that this was "very difficult" but believed it should "be really the aim."[13]

Good foster parents, according to one pamphlet written in consultation with the Children's Bureau, were those who could "give the youngster emotional security, yet relinquish him readily when the agency request[ed] it as best for the child."[14] Professionals recognized that this was hard to do. Wolins wrote of the confusing expectations of foster parents, resulting from agencies failing to make the "rules of the game clear to the other players."[15] David Fanshel even described foster parents as "social deviants" in that they were "willing to undertake a role that the rest of society strongly avoids."[16] Wolins and Fanshel both earned doctorates from the Columbia School of Social Work (formerly the New York School of Social Work), and each would take stints as the Child Welfare League's research director. Wolins, who immigrated to the United States from Poland in 1938, would go on to a distinguished career at UC-Berkeley, while Fanshel returned to Columbia as a professor.[17] Both continued to write extensively on child welfare issues, including foster care.

For those familiar with the current foster care system, two aspects of the midcentury system are particularly noteworthy for their stark contrast to current practice. First, until the last decades of the twentieth century, court-ordered termination of parental rights (known as TPR) was quite rare.[18] Children placed in foster care as infants had typically already been surrendered by their birth mothers and were awaiting transfer to an adoptive home. Indeed, infant adoption depended on a system of temporary foster placement in preparation for permanent placement, although this practice was beginning to fall out of favor by the mid-1950s.[19] In most other situations, however, parents retained parental rights, and children in foster care would either be returned to biological families or remain in foster care or residential care until they turned eighteen.

A second difference was that in the cases of those children who did become available for adoption, the foster parents usually were *not* considered for those adoptive placements. This is at odds with current practice. "Fost-adopt" programs, in which a child's foster parents are the first in line for consideration as adoptive parents should reunification efforts fail, are now viewed as an excellent option for achieving permanence and stability for many foster children.[20] The midcentury prohibition on foster parents adopting their foster children was explained and justified in a couple of ways: agencies did not want to lose good foster parents to adoption, on the one hand. Yet, on the other hand, it was also true that professionals generally believed foster parents to be drawn from a different and inferior pool than were those pursuing adoption. The draft of a 1947 Vermont foster home manual was especially blunt on this subject. The manual addressed the possibility that foster parents might decide they wanted to make a permanent home for a child in their care. The manual acknowledged that such desires created difficulties for the child welfare department. Having already approved a home for foster care, it could be problematic for an agency to later deem the home unfit for adoption. But it is "seldom that a good boarding home becomes even a satisfactory adoptive home."[21]

Such were the rules that went along with the contemporary standards for best practice. Yet, to the consternation of agencies, plenty of foster parents resisted the system and expressed interest in adopting the children for whom they were providing "temporary" homes. In June 1950, a sixteen-day-old girl named Sally was placed with the Cook family of eastern New York by the local child welfare office. The Cooks, who were also the biological parents of a young son, cared for the girl for more than a year until the agency removed her for placement in an adoptive home. After Sally went to her new home, the Cooks were no longer allowed to see her. Mrs. Cook described her family as "broken hearted." She and her husband "were so attached to her and loved her so much and Sally loved all of us to [sic]." More than one hundred friends and neighbors signed a petition on behalf of the Cooks' desire to adopt Sally themselves, but it "seems we are just bouldered against a stone wall." Mrs. Cook found a job in an attempt to forget about the little girl, but two months later she still cried herself to sleep for want of her foster daughter. In a heart-wrenching letter to President Truman, in which she enclosed a photo of baby Sally, Mrs. Cook begged him to intervene to have the girl returned to them and to change the agency's policy so "that they cannot break the hearts of so many foster parents." She also hinted at the tensions that could arise between foster parents and publicly employed child welfare workers. "We vote and pay taxes so these people can live," she complained, "then they call us the small people and think we have no right to things we love."[22]

Mr. and Mrs. Tom Yates of Massachusetts, who became the foster parents of an infant girl in 1947, told a similar story. By the time the girl was a year old, the Yateses had grown to "love her very fondly," and they asked to adopt her. The "State people" said it was not possible because the child's religious background was different from that of the Yateses. Then in July 1950, when the girl was three and a half, two police officers with a court order took the child away. The Yateses applied for adoption, but the judge turned down their request.[23]

Such stories were not uncommon in the postwar years, leading individual states to try to clarify their foster care programs so as to avoid such conflicts. States encouraged workers to be extremely clear with foster parents that their placements were not permanent and even began requiring parents to sign written agreements to that effect (see appendix). Such contracts did not prevent cases arising in which foster parents sought to adopt a specific foster child, although it provided some cover for agencies when such cases went to court. As one Children's Bureau representative put it, it was also helpful "psychologically" when parents signed such an agreement as it emphasized that the child was in the care of the foster family *temporarily* and was not available for adoption.[24]

Nonetheless, foster parents continued to challenge the rules. In 1959, the Tennessee Welfare Department reportedly had "several rather troublesome cases" that went to court involving foster parents who wanted to adopt children placed only temporarily with them.[25] And the Children's Bureau received a number of letters containing similar accounts. Foster parents appealed to the president or to other federal agencies when they felt they had exhausted all hope locally. These letters typically describe a litany of past pleas and petitions to local agencies, to their governors, and to the courts. This problem was compounded by the practice of pre-adoptive placement of infants in temporary foster homes. The Cook and Yates stories both involved foster placement of infants.

The case of Laura Neuberger, which did not involve a pre-adoptive placement, was also somewhat different in the minor notoriety it received, eventually working its way up to the New York Court of Appeals. Laura was born in June 1953 to a seventeen-year-old who lived with her widowed mother and brother. At some point, Laura's mother turned her over to the Department of Welfare, which transferred her to the Jewish Child Care Association. When Laura was thirteen months old, the Jewish Child Care Association placed her with a foster family in Levittown, Mr. and Mrs. Seymour Sanders. Laura's biological mother had only limited contact with her, and after several months, the Sanderses began expressing a desire to adopt Laura. This was in violation of the role they had agreed to perform as foster parents. In 1957, the agency, apparently concerned about the intentions of Mr. and Mrs. Sanders, insisted that they sign a statement agreeing, as a condition of the girl remaining in their home in a fostering relationship, that they would not try to adopt Laura. At one point, when reminded of the plan to eventually return Laura to her mother, Mrs. Sanders became very upset. "I was heartbroken," she recalled, "very worried about Laurie, about how she would react. In fact, that was my prime worry, how she would feel being taken away from her mother and father." By "her mother and father," Mrs. Sanders meant herself and her husband.[26]

After learning that the Sanderses had hired an adoption attorney, the Jewish Child Care Association became concerned that the couple was too emotionally attached and demanded Laura's return for placement in a different foster home. In court, the agency conceded that the Sanderses were providing good care and a good home for Laura but argued that Laura would be better served in a "neutral environment" where she would call her foster parents "aunt" and "uncle" rather than "mother" and "father." At trial, a psychologist testified on behalf of the Sanderses, arguing that removal from the only home Laura had known, just as she was about to begin school, would not be in the child's interests. The court, however, ruled in favor of the agency, a decision that was upheld by the New York Court of Appeals in a 4–3 decision. Indeed, the court of appeals noted with alarm that although the Sanderses had shown Laura "great love," the situation in the home had now "reached such a peak of emotion and possessiveness" that Laura's prospects for eventual reunification with her mother were at risk.[27] This was a case of foster parenting gone awry. The problem, for the agency, was that the Sanderses loved Laura too much.

The lesson agencies seemed to learn from such cases was that they needed to be exceedingly vigilant in screening foster parents, especially foster mothers. The presumed naturalness of women's maternal instincts in combination with the temporary nature of foster parenting made the motivations of foster mothers seem especially elusive. Welfare agencies had to be wary of accepting as foster mothers women who might develop "unbridled attachments" to foster children in their care, as Mrs. Sanders had done in the case of Laura Neuberger.[28] Yet (and therein lay one of the most profound tensions at the heart of foster care) "unbridled attachments" were precisely what was expected of biological or adoptive parents. One contemporary scholar summed up the conundrum as follows: caseworkers, it seemed, came to expect "an almost professional objectivity in foster parents when spontaneity and emotional involvement [were at] the very root of what they [had] to offer."[29]

In a culture that emphasized the primacy of the mother-child relationship over other kinds of caregiving, and to child welfare professionals who insisted that adoptive parents could form close bonds with children who were not their genetic offspring, foster parenting appeared to be an unnatural form of parenting. Certainly, societies have generated other forms of parenting and understandings of kinship, as anthropologists know.[30] There were even other models within the United States at midcentury, if one had looked at indigenous families, African American families, and families from some immigrant communities.[31] Yet in terms of the midcentury professional and popular discourses about family that provided the context for child welfare workers' approach to foster care, foster parenting indeed appeared not to be "natural."

Through this "unnatural" parenting, foster care was somehow to provide "normal family life" for children in care. But what exactly was a "normal" family? Well-publicized scandals like one involving the Whyte home in Canada helped emphasize the importance of "normality." Bert and Bertha Whyte were found to be caring for more than one hundred homeless dependent children in their Bowmanville, Ontario, home when the children were removed in 1959. These children had been independently placed by their parents, without involvement of or supervision by an agency. While favorable publicity referred to Bertha Whyte as a "foster mother with a heart of gold," a Canadian welfare official insisted that the Whytes' household "cannot be called a 'foster home'" because, by housing so many children, it lacked one of the "essential characteristics" of foster care, which was a "normal family life."[32]

Potential foster families generally had to meet basic standards of income and housing. Homes, for example, needed to be sanitary and large enough for children to have their own rooms. Some states explicitly defined such standards in ways that varied according to race. In Louisiana in the late 1930s, standards for foster homes stated that for white children "the community should provide good standards in accordance with those accepted by the members of that race," whereas for "colored children" it need only "make available the same quality of standards as accepted by the Negro race."[33]

The quest for suitable families to provide foster homes went much further than standards of housing, however. As was the case with adoption, postwar foster care experts understood, in historian Ellen Herman's words, that "assessing normality and abnormality was indispensible in family formation."[34] In 1945, Henrietta Gordon, who was in the early years of her nearly twenty-year stint as director of publications for the Child Welfare League, acknowledged that it was "strange" that "at this late date in the history of foster placement . . .

we are only beginning to be aware of what is required of a foster mother and therefore beginning to develop a case work process in foster home finding."[35] Expert literature on foster parents was typically impressionistic or anecdotal (not to mention condescending). Consider, for example, Jean Charnley's casual yet confident assertion, in her classic *Art of Child Placement*, that "many foster parents are lonely people" living "socially uncomplicated lives."[36] Charnley was an engaging writer who was a practicing social worker from Minneapolis and also a trained journalist. Her influential book was not alone in its attitude toward foster parents. Indeed, one child welfare professional complained that there were only two or three manuals for foster parents that were "respectful of the foster parents' intelligence."[37]

The dubious, anecdotal methodologies that led to assertions like Charnley's were not unique to the studies of foster parents in this period but plagued child welfare research in general. Between 1955 and 1960, the Child Welfare League would set out to expand and update its volumes of *Standards* under the direction of Zitha Turitz and with funding from the Ittleson Foundation. Turitz, a graduate of the Simmons School of Social Work who first joined the Child Welfare League staff in 1940, noted in 1958 that it was clearly desirable that all social work practice be based on "tested knowledge." Yet in reality, she lamented, the child welfare profession was at a stage in which "few of the practices that we have called standards can boast the scientific validation that is required in other technical fields." Instead, standards were based on untested principles and assumptions that had been developed "out of experience and repeated observations in the field of social work, child welfare, adoption and other related disciplines." Although Turitz directed her comments specifically at adoption standards, they could just as easily have applied to foster care and related fields of child welfare.[38] As one professor of social work complained more generally, it was problematic that the league's various *Standards* publications were not based on empirical data, but unfortunately there was still little empirical research to draw on.[39] The league had been committed from its founding to establishing standards and best practices in order to help give the child welfare field professional legitimacy. But it had not yet conducted much of its own research by this point.

Although the field lacked good research on foster parents and foster children, anxiety about foster parents was widespread among leaders in the field. With changes in the foster child population and new therapeutic functions for foster care came new roles for foster parents, which brought important new responsibilities and new stresses. Charged with helping children whose birth families were found to be in some way dysfunctional, how could agencies be sure that the foster families to whom they entrusted those children did not also suffer from problems that could be harmful? How could they be sure that foster parents would work on behalf of agency goals? The aim was to select "normal families."[40] It was, of course, hard to know how to recognize a normal family, but there was a sense that it meant a family with a successful marriage that was able to meet "more than the ordinary stresses of life."[41] Thus, families needed to be both ordinary and extraordinary, normal and not normal.

Mothers were at the heart of these discussions. Foster mothers were ideally motivated, at least in part, by a maternal love that enabled them to embrace someone else's children as their own. But there was always the danger that they would take that love too far, as Mrs. Sanders did. Understanding foster care providers as analogous to "mothers," "fathers," or "parents" was probably the most accessible way for professionals, the wider community, and foster parents themselves to understand that role. Yet experts worried that if foster families overidentified with the parent analogy, they could not serve agency goals in working with birth parents or in readily surrendering the child when called upon to do so.

Courageous foster mothers were those who, after going through the daily struggles of child-rearing and at last seeing that "Johnny behaves more like a reasonable human being than a selfish little animal," would gracefully allow him to leave "for someone else to reap the harvest of good manners, some regard for others, and good health," despite the "acute" pain of separation.[42] Part of what enabled good foster mothers to have these characteristics was that they were innately loving and giving. A child in foster care because his own mother was mentally ill and unable to provide physical comfort could get that affection from a foster mother who had an "emotional need to 'cuddle' a child."[43] A group of Pittsburgh caseworkers in the late 1950s described typical foster mothers as earthy, giving women with "round bodies" and strong biological desires to be mothers that they "need[ed] to satisfy."[44]

These descriptions of foster mothers might seem sentimental, but deep suspicions lurked beneath. Precisely because their roles seemed so unnatural, foster parents' motivations were the subject of much scrutiny. And in an era in which (white) unwed pregnancy, infertility, and adoption were frequently explained as symbolic manifestations of various female neuroses, it is not surprising that foster mothering was discussed similarly.[45] Of little significance in the 1920s and 1930s, psychology and psychiatry's influence on social work, including adoption and foster care, "reached its zenith" in the postwar period, and Freudian theories were embraced by leaders in the field of social work and child welfare whose sway circulated through research, teaching, and training in the field. By midcentury, a third of social work graduate students in their second year had elected to specialize in psychiatric social work.[46] Such influence was found in a number of writings on the evaluation of foster mothers in the 1950s. The carefully trained home finder would know that the conscious motives articulated by applicants never revealed the whole story. It was the job of a trained professional to understand the unconscious motives at work. If this was done poorly, good homes might be rejected and inappropriate homes accepted.

What were the qualities, then, of women who were able to be loving foster parents with no real claim to the children in their care? What motivations were healthy and mature? Which were not? As two administrators from the Illinois Children's Home in Chicago put it in 1956, "Taking a child for foster care is never merely the expression of an altruistic impulse or any other single wish. It is an expression of a complex constellation of emotional needs." It was "unrealistic" to hope to find foster parents who were "entirely free of neurotic motivations," since the decision to pursue foster parenting was usually "the family's way of solving a conscious or unconscious problem."[47]

As evidence of the need to be on the lookout for the unconscious motives of prospective foster mothers, Dr. Irene Josselyn, a psychiatrist who also had training in social work, offered the case of a "Mrs. D" whose family, on the surface, seemed ideally suited to be foster care providers. The Ds had a comfortable home and two children, ages nine and twelve, who were well adjusted and eager to have another child to play with. The family had an extra room available, and all were comfortable with the uncertainties and temporary nature of foster care. "Superficial exploration" suggested that this would be an ideal foster home. But further investigation revealed a different picture. The problem lay in Mrs. D's past. When she was born, her parents already had two older children, ages nine and twelve. The siblings had resented Mrs. D's birth and had shown her great hostility. Now as an adult, Mrs. D was seeking a foster placement at precisely the moment her own children reached the ages her siblings had been when she was born. "Unconsciously the foster child would complete the picture of her childhood, but in this case she would be the master instead of the victim," Josselyn noted. This unconscious motivation would have "jeopardized the entire family balance."[48] The message was clear. The wise caseworker, who took the time to puzzle out the implications of the family's profile, would reject the Ds' home.

Analyzing the motivations of foster mothers was a subject rich with possibilities and one to which David Fanshel devoted much thought. Before moving to New York, Fanshel had spent two years at Family and Children's Service of Pittsburgh and later worked with contacts there to conduct his dissertation research.[49] His study asked Pittsburgh caseworkers to consider a list of possible reasons a woman might serve as a foster mother: Had the foster mother herself been "denied consistent mothering"? Did she need to be "fighting society" on behalf of a "cause"? Was she trying to save her marriage? Did she like to have children around because she needed to control and manipulate others? Was she seeking "prestige" from her neighbors? Was the mother "compensat[ing] for feelings of inadequacy about her femininity"?[50] This list betrayed considerable suspicion that potential foster mothers might be governed by questionable motives.

Caseworkers had to be able to distinguish between "mature" motivations and those that might hide neurotic impulses. Fanshel was particularly concerned about women who fit what he labeled "the Benefactress of Children" typology. These were foster mothers who, when asked to rank statements that best explained what they found rewarding about foster parenting, selected those such as "[I like] doing something for the community" or "I like helping the unfortunate down-trodden people," perhaps giving an "inflated picture" of a foster mother's "own virtues." Fanshel considered such answers to be potentially "pathogenic," especially if they were accompanied by disillusionment with society. His study found that African American foster mothers were especially likely to fit this problematic typology, which suggests that black foster mothers, in filling out Fanshel's surveys, may have been expressing broad understandings of family and community responsibility that were part of a long tradition but that appeared deviant to Fanshel and his team.[51]

Fanshel used a comparison between two descriptions of foster mothers offered by social workers to illustrate the pathological egotism of the "Benefactress of Children." "Mrs. A" (an ideal foster mother) was a "heavy-robust-looking woman" who was "given to hearty gales of laughter as she recounted the mischievous behavior of the foster children that had been placed in her care." Mrs. A emphasized the happiness the children provided to her family rather than any contribution she had made to the children. Meanwhile, her foil, "Mrs. P," was criticized for being "sanctimonious" and for noting that foster children could be difficult to love, thereby requiring "*special* kinds of people like herself" to care for them.[52]

Not all of the literature on home finding labeled a desire to help children as pathological. Indeed, one recruitment pamphlet explained that a way to cope with the pain of a foster child leaving was realizing that one had "helped a defenseless human being in great need."[53] But Fanshel's concern with the "Benefactress of Children" suggests his sense that because the desire to help needy children was *not* a reason for natural motherhood, it could be potentially problematic in an alternative caregiving role. Some desire to help children, such as that expressed by Aunt May at the opening of this chapter, was appropriate and necessary for foster mothers, but it should not be the sole or even the primary factor.

Interestingly, "helping the down-trodden" was the most common motivation selected by the men in Fanshel's study, but this was not a matter of concern, presumably because child placement workers believed husbands played only a minor role in the decision to become foster parents.[54] Although typically using the unsexed plural in their titles (*In Quest of Foster Parents, Foster Parenthood,* or *Selecting Foster Parents*), expert literature in the postwar years was overwhelmingly focused on foster *mothers*.[55] In developing a "science" of child placement, child welfare experts spilled much ink on the subject of the women who cared for foster children — their admirable qualities, their hidden pathologies. Certainly, a man's presence in a foster family was considered absolutely necessary. Indeed, while a few agencies continued to occasionally use female-headed households for some foster placements, it had become, by midcentury, a ubiquitous requirement that foster families be married couples; widows and unmarried women no longer made acceptable foster mothers (as they once had). In St. Paul, Minnesota, for example, 90 percent of foster families in the mid-1940s were "married people living together." Of the rest, 7.6 percent were widows and the remaining were single, separated, or divorced. (British practices, in the same period, were more accepting of single women serving as foster parents.)[56]

Single women and widows were "seldom acceptable" except in cases such as a trained infant nurse who might provide temporary care, according to the 1959 edition of the Child Welfare League's foster care *Standards*.⁵⁷ Single men were either so implausible or considered so profoundly unsuitable that I have found no mention of them in the literature in this period. Some agencies did suggest the need for a "less sweeping exclusion of single women and widows." Perhaps, proposed an employee of the Oregon State Public Welfare Department, a foster home headed by a single woman could be acceptable as a home for a "mentally deficient child" awaiting placement in an institution, so long as the child was of "sufficiently low mentality so that the absence of a father figure could not be vital."⁵⁸ For the vast majority of children not deemed "deficient," though, the presence of a father was essential.

Despite this consensus that modern foster homes needed to be headed by married couples, there was otherwise little discussion of men in the foster care system. For foster care to serve its therapeutic purposes, foster families needed to have two parents. Child welfare professionals developed ideals for both parents but in the end scrutinized women far more than men. Dorothy Hutchinson's influential 1943 book on home finding included a chapter titled "Introduction to a Foster Mother" but no separate chapter on foster fathers.⁵⁹ Hutchinson, a former caseworker, was a well-regarded professor at the New York School of Social Work and a much-sought-after speaker and consultant. Her book was considered a classic by those in the field, went through several reprintings, and, by 1959, was still the only book that focused exclusively on foster parents.⁶⁰ In the late 1950s and early 1960s, researchers such as David Fanshel and Martin Wolins would begin examining foster fathers more closely. Yet even in their studies, men's precise role in foster care remained decidedly undertheorized. There was no discussion of the "complex constellation of emotional needs" leading men to become foster fathers or of their potentially problematic neurotic impulses. In listing possible motivations for men seeking to become foster parents, Fanshel thought of two: a "need to assert his paternal role" and — that idea so often the stuff of period sitcom fodder —"merely going along with his wife."⁶¹ As Wolins put it, although professionals understood fathers to be essential to foster care, "it seems doubtful that the father as a person — aside from his role in the father-mother relationship — gets much attention in the decision about a foster home."⁶²

Josselyn, author of a number of books and articles about childhood and adolescence, suggested in a 1956 study that it was not surprising foster fathers were overlooked in the expert literature, given that society was dismissive of fathers' roles in child-rearing in general.[63] Yet Josselyn's statement was not exactly accurate. Popular ideas about fatherhood in the 1950s, in fact, stressed a new importance of the father figure, insisting that he provide a strong model of masculinity that would help both boys and girls develop into healthy, stable adults. In the years following the Second World War, Americans discovered fatherhood with enthusiasm. They began to celebrate Father's Day in earnest, and men were encouraged to embrace fatherhood to make their own lives more meaningful.[64]

Perhaps most important, experts settled on a view of engaged fatherhood as critical to healthy development in children.[65] New conceptions of fatherhood gained prominence in the postwar years, reflecting the hope that men would "play a more central role in the overall psychological development of their children."[66] Fathers' roles seemed particularly pressing given the intensified concerns about juvenile delinquency and homosexuality in boys and unwed pregnancy in girls. Child development expertise, suggesting that strong, involved fathers could be an antidote to excessive maternal care, trickled down to advice literature and magazine articles, urging fathers to become more involved with their children. Josselyn herself was one expert who promoted the view that American society was lamentably drifting toward a "social structure made up of he-women and she-men."[67] Yet foster fathers did not receive much attention in the expert discourse on foster parenting. As late as the early 1970s, a proposal for a foster parent training course noted that while it was "vital" that potential foster fathers be involved, "reality dictates that it will be the woman who will be most able to focus on the course."[68]

If one's understanding of foster care at midcentury were rooted in previous practice, this omission made sense. In the not-too-distant past, fathers had been, it is fair to say, largely insignificant to foster care. Nineteenth-century boarding mothers had often been widows. In those boarding homes with both a husband and a wife present, his primary role was wage earning. By the mid-twentieth century, the breadwinning role certainly remained important for foster fathers and was now more closely scrutinized through the Child Welfare League's promotion of standards and best practices for foster care that emphasized the need for foster families to have stable income. Yet while agencies spoke wistfully of their desire to recruit more middle-class foster parents, in reality most foster families were of modest means, headed by men who provided for their families through work at blue-collar jobs.[69] A 1946 survey of foster homes in St. Paul, Minnesota, found that 84.5 percent of foster parents owned their own home and had an average income of $2,640 per year (about $32,700 in 2016 dollars). Fanshel's study of Pittsburgh foster fathers found them to be good providers, not affluent but financially stable and reliable, about a quarter having worked at the same job for twenty-one years or more.[70]

While a man's breadwinning capacity served as a baseline measure of whether or not he and his wife could be considered as foster parents, one might expect the "science" of home finding to also have made nods toward new ideas about fatherhood in assessing prospective foster families. Expert and popular understandings of fatherhood in the 1950s no longer stressed the breadwinning role exclusively. The gender roles performed and modeled by fathers were celebrated in popular culture and by social science experts. Historian Elaine Tyler May describes the view that men needed to engage in physical activities with their children, for "without such masculine influence, children, especially boys, might become weak and dependent" from too much time with their mothers.[71] According to historian of fatherhood Robert L. Griswold, the experience of World War II had led to the wider acceptance of the views of psychologists — that nurturing, involved fathers who were "secure in their identities" could play a significant role in the healthy personality development of their children. A father should "help" his wife while retaining his place as the family's head. The "right blend of masculine sympathy and manly toughness" could help prepare children to resist the perceived dangers of the postwar world — authoritarianism, juvenile delinquency, homosexuality, out-of-wedlock pregnancy.[72] In other words, fathers needed to be securely masculine but not authoritarian. Yet despite the expert emphasis on the importance of the father to children, child welfare agencies seemed to be "generally reconciled to his playing a relatively minor role" in foster care.[73]

By the 1950s, developmental psychologists were also paying more attention to the quality of the marital relationship and its effects on children. The combination of a weak or passive husband and a strong and domineering wife was considered particularly toxic to children.[74] And indeed, some of this attention to marriages and parental gender roles was reflected in the literature on foster home finding. Foster families needed to be headed by a married couple that displayed a "warm, outgoing love between husband and wife." Such a bond would help show foster children, whose own family environment may have been troubled, what a rich marriage could be and would provide a model of healthy, gender-role-normative relationships.[75]

But did the relationships between foster parents actually live up to ideals of postwar marriage? Lurking beneath the surface in the expert writing on home finding were concerns that they did not. Before the late 1950s, most of the professional literature on foster parents was, as noted, impressionistic and anecdotal. The child welfare experts who wrote these works held particular assumptions about the relationships between what they considered to be "typical" foster mothers and fathers without having done much to methodically study the actual individuals serving in those roles. Foster mothers, according to common descriptions, usually were the dominant figure in their families and were married to passive men.[76] Some of this understanding of foster mothers as dominant stemmed from the fact that it was almost always women, not their husbands, who took the initiative in inquiring about fostering (which also appears to have been true for adoption).[77] Dorothy Hutchinson wrote that it was "usual as to be almost proverbial" that foster fathers stayed in the background of the home evaluation process. And when asked why they were interested in caring for foster children, they mostly spoke in terms of their "approval for their wife's plan" rather than of their own motivations to parent another's child.[78]

Yet the perception of foster mothers as dominant and fathers as passive went further. According to Jean Charnley, the typical foster father, although not a "weakling," was a man who found it "most comfortable to let his wife make many of the major decisions of the family." He is quiet, Charnley wrote, not a "fluent talker."[79] One agency staff member in Fanshel's study described the typical foster father as "almost a 'moon' who reflects the foster mother."[80] Hutchinson observed that foster families were "typical of the matriarchal family group," with the mother assuming the position of family head, organizer, and director.[81] Although Hutchinson did not mention race and while the foster families she and her colleagues had in mind seem to have mostly been white, this kind of argument — especially the invocation of matriarchy — calls to mind pernicious stereotypes about black families that would "grow into a full-blown racialized image" by the late 1960s and that would define black families as pathological for their "maternalist" structure.[82] In discussions of foster families in the 1940s and 1950s, "matriarchal" families were pathologized, although not yet necessarily fully racialized.

Foster families raised other concerns as well. The widely read postwar child-rearing manual *The Common Sense Book of Baby and Child Care* by Dr. Benjamin Spock advocated a turn away from authoritarian parenting styles of the

1920s in favor of a more conversational approach that encouraged mothers to be intensely engaged with their children and to follow the youngsters' lead.[83] Thus experts also worried that the working-class parents who made up the pool of foster families were focusing too much on instilling respect and obedience in their children. In other words, a problem with working-class foster families, according to the new post–World War II models for parenting, was their authoritarian child-rearing.[84] The alleged passivity of foster fathers mitigated that concern somewhat. Presumably a "passive" husband could take his authoritarianism only so far. Yet the dominance of the mother in these families made the foster parents poor role models for vulnerable children in other ways.

In other words, couples interested in foster parenting typically did not fit the idealized white middle-class model of family structure, parenting style, and gender relations that dominated the postwar literature on parenting and that were understood to lead to optimal personality development in children.[85] Indeed, social workers believed that the combination of a "manipulative mother and a passive father" was a "potent recipe" for premarital pregnancy in girls and homosexuality in boys.[86] This idea had been popularized by journalist Ferdinand Lundberg and psychiatrist Marynia Farnham in their book *Modern Woman: The Lost Sex,* published in 1947.[87] Lundberg and Farnham had described a "recipe" they considered harmful to children in general. But only in the case of adoption and foster placement were those who subscribed to this perspective (as many in the social work field did) presented with the opportunity, at least theoretically, to *select out* parents whose relationship seemed to match the risky combination Lundberg and Farnham described.

Given the therapeutic functions foster care was now expected to perform, could a home in which the husband was the "weaker partner" really be a suitable one for children who had "already suffered at the hands of inadequate parental figures"? This was an important question for professionals. But instead of producing calls to aggressively screen out families with "weak" fathers or "dominant" mothers (as adoption workers could do and did), authors of foster home-finding literature tended to finesse or overlook the issue. David Fanshel seems to have been more interested in understanding foster fathers than were most others in his field. Yet even he was limited in his approach to studying them. In constructing his own research project, Fanshel set up interviews with foster fathers that were only a little more than half the length of the planned interviews for their wives. This was done deliberately, partly because foster fathers were not considered as important to foster care as their wives but also because Fanshel expected that they would have "less tolerance for lengthy research interviews." And in fact, the refusal rate was higher among foster fathers (12 percent) than foster mothers (1 percent). Nonetheless, Fanshel found the participation of fathers to be relatively high given the reputation foster fathers had for not cooperating.[88]

In the 1950s and early 1960s, the description of foster fathers as weak and passive was akin to common knowledge among child welfare professionals. Indeed, Fanshel noted in 1966 that the limited picture of foster fathers in the literature — as passive men who relied on their "more energetic" wives for leadership in the family — was not very flattering. But, Fanshel went on to say, child welfare experts had to admit that they actually did not know all that much about foster fathers. Just because they were "passive at home" did not necessarily mean they were not "adequate performers in the masculine work world." Fanshel's own study of Pittsburgh foster parents found that, in fact, many foster fathers had leadership roles at their jobs (as foremen, for example) or performed work that "demanded physical strength and dexterity." And while child welfare experts may have questioned whether these men were good masculine role models for children, foster fathers themselves indicated that they took this aspect of their role seriously. Fanshel discovered that the foster fathers he studied (a third of whom indicated that fostering had turned out to be much more satisfying than originally expected) found opportunities to "provide a masculine role model for the foster child" to be among the main satisfactions of fostering.[89] Perhaps these men had understandings of masculinity that differed from those of the social workers who assessed them.

As working-class men — and, to a growing extent, men of color — foster fathers often embodied ideas about child-rearing, masculinity, and gender relations in the family that were not embraced by middle-class social workers and that were out of step with current expert thinking about fatherhood. Such fathers were at once too passive (in their relationships with their wives) and too authoritarian (in their approach to child-rearing). Agencies apparently expected little of foster fathers, and experts who studied foster care and foster parenting either paid little attention to them or glossed over their apparent inadequacies. Given the importance newly given to fathers' roles in the family, it is perhaps surprising how little attention child welfare professionals gave to the men who applied to become foster fathers. While experts gestured toward the new ideals of fatherhood, they seem to have concluded that there was little they could do to integrate those ideals into the foster care system.

Experts understood working-class foster fathers to embody different qualities than did adoptive fathers, whose ideal types were middle class. Despite efforts to recruit more middle-class foster parents, the families interested in fostering continued to come overwhelmingly from working-class backgrounds. And agencies were not always receptive to those families. As one Children's Bureau staff member acknowledged, agencies at times overlooked the "misspelled pencil letter from rural" women interested in fostering because agency employees held to a "'middle class mentality' when selecting foster parents" that was not always helpful.[90] Postwar middle-class ideals about fatherhood also conflicted with African American models, in which extended kin and fictive kin networks enabled families where men faced unemployment, underemployment, or racial discrimination in the job market to share resources and encouraged a sense of community responsibility for children.

That notion of fictive kin networks seems not to have been well understood or appreciated by leaders in the child welfare field, although it was at times acknowledged. Former Children's Bureau chief Katharine Lenroot suggested that part of the difficulty in recruiting middle-class foster parents was that successful foster parenting required an understanding of family relationships that seemed to be easier for "very simple people" who were used to caring for the children of relatives from time to time. Lenroot had in mind "the attitude of my Negro cleaning woman to her niece's children, for whom she has had to care at times because of a tubercular condition in the mother."[91] The qualities that Lenroot and others imagined made foster parenting *possible* were the qualities of "other" kinds of people, which only reinforced their suspicions of foster parents. (Becoming a licensed foster parent, of course, also meant inviting the government into one's home in ways that many Americans like Lenroot probably would have found intolerable.)

Anthropologist Judith Modell has described foster parents as "parents who are not supposed to act parental."[92] Although she was writing in 2002, this astute observation applies equally well to the earlier postwar professional understandings of foster parents (particularly foster mothers). The therapeutic benefits that postwar foster parents were to provide to dependent children in their care rested on them replicating a normal family life of love, nurture, and interpersonal relationships. But professionals recognized that most families would not be able to do this effectively, particularly due to the lack of permanency in the fostering relationship. The "science" of screening promised that prospective foster homes could be properly vetted to secure those parents who would remain committed to the goals of the agency while best meeting the needs of children at risk. The ideal foster parents, as understood by child welfare experts, embodied gender roles and marriage norms most likely found among middle-class people. Yet efforts to recruit foster parents from the middle classes were largely unsuccessful. One of the complications of foster parenting was that child welfare experts, having concluded that foster homes played a crucial, therapeutic role in the child welfare system, were now in the difficult position of expecting a great deal from people of whom they actually thought very little. This dilemma bolstered tensions over the need to also understand foster parents as workers who were compensated for the parenting tasks they performed (as will be discussed in chapter 6).

But this gap between ideals about fatherhood and motherhood and the reality of the homes in which children were placed also suggests another problem at the heart of the foster care system, one that was deeply entwined with issues of supply and demand. Children in foster care, coming overwhelmingly from poor (and increasingly non-white) backgrounds and who were perceived as suffering from numerous problems, were not as desirable as children who lived in intact families or who were available for adoption. Thus standards not only *had* to be compromised for pragmatic reasons but *could* be compromised because Americans as a whole simply did not value foster children in the same way as they did other children.

CHAPTER 5

THE HARD-TO-PLACE CHILD

Family Pathology, Race, and Poverty

In the postwar years, it became conventional wisdom among child welfare workers that the foster care population was far more damaged than in the past. This understanding affected perceptions of foster children, their biological parents, and their foster parents. Concepts like "hard-to-place" and "family pathology" entered the child welfare lexicon, starkly revealing the economics of child placement. By the late 1950s, these terms would become increasingly associated with race. Foster children were marked with undesirability, even as agencies began to try more aggressively than ever before to find permanent homes for them.

By the 1950s, a consensus developed that almost *all* foster children were in some way damaged. A number of factors were leading to this new view. One was the influence of British developmental psychologist John Bowlby, whose studies of attachment suggested that a period in foster care, separated from birth families, could, in and of itself, be profoundly harmful, leading to "stunt[ed] emotional growth." Bowlby's wartime studies, first published in the early 1950s, revealed that children separated from their parents (particularly their mothers) during early childhood experienced profound distress and disrupted development. Bowlby's ideas — known as "attachment theory" — had important consequences for foster care. Attachment theory suggested that a one- or three- or five-year stint in foster care while parents tried to work out their problems was not harmless to children.[1] Later studies would undermine the conclusion that foster care was inevitably detrimental to children and looked instead to what particular circumstances could mitigate the disruption of separation. But research such as Bowlby's contributed to a sense that foster children were inherently damaged.[2]

Family Pathology, Race, and Poverty

A 1960 report on child welfare noted that, in the past, when children were placed in foster care or orphanages, child welfare workers had found that the "outward results were satisfying — rosier cheeks, scrubbed bodies, clean clothes. But the inward results were often devastating." Only recently, the report continued, had experts come to understand what "deep-rooted damage" separation from family caused in children.[3] This contrast between past and present was exaggerated. The observation that children probably suffered when removed from their home was not entirely new. Progressive Era reformers had come to believe that children were best served by remaining with their families of origin and had advocated for mothers' pensions to that end. And already by the late 1930s, removal from one's home was suspected to be injurious enough that one report argued all foster children needed to undergo psychological evaluation, not just those who exhibited "overt behavior manifestations."[4] But not until after World War II did such conjecture about the harm of separation from parents develop into a full-blown theory, backed by the authority of influential scholarship from the fields of psychology and psychiatric social work.

One reason, then, that foster children in the postwar period *appeared* to be more damaged than those of the past was because the work of Bowlby and others enabled postwar child welfare professionals to identify disorders in children that they had not hitherto appreciated. It was not only that experts were able to see problems that had previously been invisible to them, however. They also became convinced there was something profoundly different about the children coming into care now when compared with the caseloads of as few as fifteen or twenty years earlier. For one thing, there were fewer orphans, diminishing the role that death of a parent played in leading an otherwise "normal" child to need out-of-home care.[5] Reformers also repeatedly traced the differences they saw in the foster care population to the successes of New Deal family security programs, which were widely believed to have transformed the foster care population and the very purpose of foster care.

Consider the enthusiastic words of the Reverend William Swaim, a Pennsylvania minister active in Presbyterian social services, speaking in 1945; "stupendous" was how he described the changes of the last decade. "At last we are able to say," Swaim declared confidently, "that poverty is no longer a cause for breaking up a family."[6] Similarly, the Child Welfare League explained in 1957 that today "economic want and death are no longer major factors" causing children to enter care.[7] Indeed, throughout the late 1940s and 1950s, not only Reverend

Swaim but also child welfare leaders in general repeatedly heralded survivor's benefits, workman's compensation, unemployment insurance, and Aid to Dependent Children as benefits of the New Deal welfare state that were helping keep families intact, thereby diminishing the need for foster care.[8]

The New Deal successes that Swaim celebrated meant that the child who still needed foster care services must be a very different kind of child indeed. In addition, Swaim noted that public conscience had now embraced foster care as the "ideal" for the "normal child."[9] For Swaim, these changes were complementary as together they ensured that children would not be placed in foster care simply because they were poor and that "normal" children in need of foster care would not be housed in institutions. Yet who exactly were those nonimpoverished yet "normal" children whom foster family care would now serve? The assumption that economic want no longer was responsible for children's placement meant that foster children were well on their way to being declared inherently *not normal* simply by virtue of their being in foster care.

Meanwhile, the population of children in foster family care was growing steadily—reaching almost 208,000 in 1965 (about double the number in 1933). Much of that increase had to do with the decline in institutional care over that same period.[10] Yet whether children were entering orphanages or foster family care, the question still remained: if poverty was *not* the main cause of children needing out-of-home placement, as reformers clearly believed, then what *were* the reasons? This question demanded an answer. Child welfare professionals concluded that children must be entering care for very different reasons than in the past. These reasons were encapsulated in the term "family pathology."

In the late 1930s and 1940s, the child welfare profession had depicted foster children as homeless "through no fault of their own" or as children whose "own homes [had] been broken by illness, death or the separation of parents."[11] In other words, children in need of foster care were mostly described as ordinary children whose families had simply hit a rough patch. By the postwar years, this older notion—of the "average" foster child from whom a small number of more difficult children deviated—was fading from view. The foster children of the day instead typically exhibited disturbing emotional and behavioral problems that presented serious challenges. Some agencies in the 1950s were reporting that 10 to 20 percent of placements were due to "psychosis of the mother," which could render the "ego development of the child ... endangered" or lead to distorted perceptions of reality.[12] One Tennessee worker reportedly "guessed" that about 95 percent of the children her agency was supervising had low IQs.[13] A major study of foster care conducted in the late 1950s found that in one of the communities under review, 55 percent of foster children had come into foster care with symptoms of psychological disturbance.[14] Indeed, one agency executive said of the new postwar foster care population that now "all our children are problem children" in that they all came from "disorganized families."[15]

Life with their problematic families of origin were said to render foster children far more troubled than in the past. "Disorganized" and "pathological" were catchall terms, more evocative than precisely descriptive. Alcoholism and violence plagued some of these families, but the main culprits, as experts seemed to understand it, were out-of-wedlock birth, divorce, and mental illness of a parent.[16] Such factors undoubtedly created challenges to raising children and could result in various forms of neglect and abuse. Parents in those circumstances were also likely to struggle financially, yet this fact often remained unacknowledged. The new "pathological" families were poor. But child welfare professionals suggested that it was their pathology, rather than their poverty, that shouldered the blame for family dissolution because New Deal measures supposedly assisted the more worthy poor. There seem to have been legitimate reasons for economic want (for which there were New Deal security and assistance programs) and less legitimate reasons for economic want tied to notions of immorality, pathology, and depravity (for which there was foster care). These understandings of pathology were often deeply gendered — a father who was an unreliable or half-hearted provider, a mother who engaged in premarital or interracial sex or who failed to remain married. Mental illness requiring child placement almost always involved the mother, the "psychotic mother" becoming something of a stock character in child welfare literature.[17]

As an institution now caring for "problem children" rather than orphaned and poor children, foster care increasingly took on therapeutic functions, which meant a significant change in the purpose of foster care from earlier in the century.[18] Of course, what occurred was not simply a transformation in the foster care population itself but a change in how an increasingly therapy-centered profession viewed that population. As the child welfare infrastructure was fleshed out and with the growing use of individualized casework, record keeping, and home-finding methods, foster children and their families were scrutinized in the postwar period far more closely than in the past. And this scrutiny came from professionals who were trained and prepared to understand children's difficulties in terms of emotional problems or personality disorders, as defects of the individual rather than as structural problems of society. This so-called residual perspective in social work assumes, in the words of Duncan Lindsey, that the "troubles of those families served by the child welfare system derive from shortcomings in the parents (that is, a moral, psychological, physiological, or some other personal failing) that must be addressed through casework."[19]

The expert view that erratic care from unstable parents can be traumatic for children continues to be supported by research and continues to inform best practices.[20] Yet as Linda Gordon has noted, "When caseworkers lack the resources to help clients materially, they may focus on psychological problems — which are usually present — because at least something can be done about them."[21] Child welfare workers' conviction that economic problems leading to child placement had largely been resolved, together with their training geared to address problems that were more psychological or emotional, meant that it was toward individual psychological problems that their attention would be directed.

In fact, poverty intersected with various forms of parental vulnerability in ways that could look like "family pathology" but that also made it impossible to fully untangle the reasons children came into care, as in the case of Virginia Dixon. In early 1946, the court took custody of two of her children, ages five and three, charging Dixon had neglected them after witnesses reported she was leaving the children alone at night while she went out. Dixon, a single mother receiving ADC who was now pregnant, was assailed by the judge for her "long record of promiscuous relations with men." She had been married to the father of one of her children but had left him, she said, because he had been abusing her. In May, the court threatened to take her infant as well. Dixon wrote to President Truman in desperation, acknowledging that she had made mistakes but insisting that she nonetheless deserved to mother her children. "There are so many young mothers that have given their children away," she wrote, "but I am one young mother that really wants my children."[22]

Like Dixon, Ruth Parker of southern Indiana claimed she was assaulted by her ex-husband, who then threw her out of the home along with three-month-old Susan. Parker and her daughter turned for a time to another man for shelter and later to the Salvation Army. Eventually, according to Parker, she was forced to stay in a Louisville mental hospital, at which point family services took custody of Susan. As Parker put it, "They tried to claim I was crazy." Between the winter of 1947 and the spring of 1950, Parker wrote numerous lengthy letters seeking the return of her child. According to Parker, she was unable to regain custody of her daughter because children's services wanted her to pay for Susan's clothes and other expenses, "which they make so heavy a poor person can't pay."[23] Dixon's and Parker's struggles occurred at a time when the field of social work had turned — particularly in the case of white women — to psychiatric explanations for unwed pregnancy, offering complex schematics of diagnostic categories such as "psychoneurosis," "psychopathic personality," and "adult maladjustment" to understand unmarried mothers. Indeed, as Regina Kunzel suggests, simply being an unmarried or divorced mother was to suggest the possibility that one suffered from poor mental health.[24]

And consider the case of Mrs. Bessie Clay of Georgia, who also experienced profound anguish over her children's placement. In Clay's case, the matter was intensified by race. She was an African American mother of five whose youngest had been placed in foster care. Clay was now being asked to pay part of the costs of board. She poignantly described her distress:

> I am so much worred about my child that to see whie people take collut peope an do them Like thay . . . and then call them crazy Beckose that they talk for what thears its mine an I shud Have it Back I ant ast no Body to take it the welfaire is to pay that Bill thay is the one made it now tryin make me pay it i am to get my child Back Home an on no charge no dear sure do this letter talk Like I lost eny since or crazy . . . (*I am so much worried about my child that to see white people take colored people and do them like that . . . and then call them crazy because they take for themselves what is mine . . . I should have it back. I ain't asked nobody to take [the child so] the welfare [department should] pay the bill. They is the one [that] made it [but are] now trying to make me pay. I am to get my child back home and at no charge [but] they talk like I lost any sense or [am] crazy.*)

Clay was acutely concerned about her baby's well-being, angry that local child welfare officials had intervened in her family, and resentful that she was now being asked to pay the costs of boarding. The chief of the Georgia State Department of Child Welfare, Loretta Chappell, initially insisted that Clay, who had four older children living with her, had consented to the boarding arrangement "as being so much better for the baby." After following up on the case with the local children's services director, however, Chappell noted that Clay's baby had been placed with relatives when Clay was sent to the notorious Milledgeville State Hospital "for mental illness."[25]

Clay framed her concerns in terms of race. Her baby was taken by an anonymous — white — child welfare system that then labeled her "crazy" when she complained. Chappell told a different story. The local office had provided Clay with a service she had requested and yet was now being irrationally criticized by a disturbed and difficult parent for having done so. Both scenarios are at least plausible, and absent additional records, it is impossible to state definitively which best describes the Clay case. Birth parents could feel quite powerless in the face of the child welfare system, as desperate letters to the Children's Bureau like Clay's attest. There was considerable social distance between caseworkers and clients, a distance compounded in this case by race.

The emphasis of child welfare services was still on voluntary placements. Indeed, understanding foster placements as mostly voluntary — willingly sought by distressed parents who were ready to accept help for themselves as well as for their children — was essential to the conception of foster care as a therapeutic service. Caseworkers did, however, steer parents toward requesting services as best for their children, leaving some of those parents later feeling they had been coerced. Yet to recognize that categories of neglect and abuse are not fixed and to acknowledge the roles that race, gender, class, and power have played in defining and policing those categories is not to say that children are never at risk. Some parents indeed were unfit to care for children. We do not know all of the facts in the cases of Dixon, Parker, and Clay. But certainly the individual "pathologies" and "disorganization" that child welfare workers saw in these families were deeply entwined with the broader structural challenges of poverty, lack of support for single parenthood, and racism. The pathologizing of unwed mothers together with the opposition to publicly funded day care put single mothers in a real bind. In 1954, Congress approved a tax deduction for childcare, but this measure mainly helped middle- and upper-income Americans, not families like those described here.[26]

It was not only families headed by unmarried women that appeared disorganized or pathological, as we see with the Hendricksons of Michigan, whose seven minor children first entered foster care in 1940. Fern Hendrickson had borne thirteen children, three of whom died in infancy. According to local officials, the Hendricksons used various aliases and moved over forty-three times in an attempt to avoid creditors. Landlords and neighbors complained that the parents constantly argued, used profane language, committed vandalism, and neglected their children. The schools reported that the children were frequently absent, performed poorly, and were "dirty and unkempt." On the visit that prompted the children's removal, the mother and seven youngest children were "all living and sleeping in one room."[27]

Jimmy Hendrickson, who wanted his children returned, certainly believed that their removal occurred for reasons of poverty. Local officials saw the situation differently. Undoubtedly the Hendricksons were poor. Indeed, the family had received public relief and charitable assistance off and on over the previous fifteen years. But this family had "always been extremely difficult to handle," according to a representative of the local juvenile court. The Hendricksons, it seems, were not suffering merely from poverty, but from broader kinds of dysfunction, including the parents' unwillingness to perform their conventional duties within the family. The Public Welfare Department had found wage work for Jimmy Hendrickson, but he turned the position down. He was referred for a WPA job but failed to report. Fern repeatedly kicked her husband out of the house.[28] In other words, he was a failed provider, she a failed dependent and caregiver.

When children from these backgrounds entered foster care in the postwar years, they were assumed to bring with them a kind of damage derived from their chaotic family lives — damage that modern experts believed had not been significant factors when children entered care simply because they were poor. Experts understood that damage to be compounded for many children by the very experience of being in out-of-home care. One effect of these ubiquitous references to pathology and damage was to potentially stigmatize all foster children simply because they were in foster care. To be sure, there were some dissenting voices. A representative of one Portland, Oregon, agency complained that the tone of some professional literature left the impression that "every child entering or living in a foster home is to be considered a sick child."[29]

This new emphasis on the ways in which foster children were damaged meant challenges for social workers trying to find temporary homes for them. It had been hard enough to recruit foster homes for "orphans of war" (as described in chapter 3). How much more challenging to find temporary homes for "problem" or "sick" children. Such challenges were quantified in the higher board rates that agencies paid to foster families willing to take children understood to be "hard-to-place." Under earlier models of the quasi-adoptive free homes, the average school-age child was assumed to have no problems, so the foster family "was rewarded largely by the satisfaction of rearing such a child." Some children, though, placed "unusual demands" on foster parents beyond the inherent pleasure of child-rearing. In addition, others were suspected of providing only limited satisfaction.[30] Thus, for the foster care field, the term "hard-to-place" was, on the one hand, descriptive of a practical problem — agencies had a responsibility to find temporary homes for dependent children, even those for whom it was especially difficult to do so.[31] Yet the term also reflected foster parents' and child welfare professionals' own understandings of which children were desirable and which were less so.

A series of board rate studies the Child Welfare League conducted in the 1940s and 1950s offer insight into the ways foster children were perceived. Beginning in 1941, the league sent questionnaires every few years to its member agencies specifically inquiring about the board payments agencies were providing to foster families. The results were compiled by league staffer Henrietta Gordon, who also provided analysis and commentary. As the league's director of publications until her death in 1960, Gordon not only worked on the board rate studies but also edited the league's journal, *Child Welfare*. The board rate studies, begun at a time when paying board was just beginning to be standard practice for most agencies, reveal the very practical considerations at play in establishing those board rates and help us to see the connections between those practical considerations and perceptions about the relative value of certain children.

By the 1940s (as will be discussed in chapter 6), local child welfare agencies were paying at least minimal board for most children. In 1941, 98 of 115 agencies surveyed reported that they were paying a standard board rate for the "average school child who presents no serious difficulties."[32] Those rates ranged from a low of $9.00 to a high of $26.00 per month ($148.00 to $427.00 in 2016 dollars). By 1954, those base rates had risen somewhat to an average range of $37.50 to $47.50 in the continental United States. Board rates increased dramatically during the war, when the chronic shortage of homes intensified, and regularly thereafter, primarily to address increases in the cost of living.[33]

The number of agencies paying above their base rate for certain categories of children rose over the years. The board rate studies from the forties and fifties reveal four basic categories of children for whom higher board rates were typically paid: those who were not school age (infants, preschoolers, and adolescents);

children with a range of physical "impairments" (including epilepsy, cardiac conditions, blindness, deafness, hemophilia, and "crippling" conditions), as well as those who were convalescing from illnesses; those with mental impairments (including those described as "mental defectives" or "retarded"); and those with disturbing behavioral problems (bed-wetting, aggression, or stealing, for example). A handful of agencies also reported paying higher rates for boys than girls, but this was not widespread.[34]

In the late 1950s, Gordon offered the following examples of cases in which agencies paid extra board: "An adolescent girl, bright, appealing and responsive, who is so deeply disturbed that there are times that she cannot control herself and acts out her hostile aggressions and frustrations in socially unacceptable behavior; ... a schizophrenic adolescent; a child with muscular dystrophy; a feebleminded child with terminal cancer; two children with spinal bifida, one of them paralyzed from the waist down, incontinent and having much destructive behavior; a child who is a double amputee; a child so disturbed that he sits in a chair for long periods of time speaking to no one."[35] In these examples behavioral problems, physical disabilities, chronic illness, mental illness, and cognitive disability are lumped together. What united these children, for Gordon, was that agencies found they had to pay more to place them.

Agencies at midcentury did not typically take children with physical or mental impairments for foster home care, yet this was changing. In the 1950s, there was a move to try placing physically disabled or convalescent children in private homes rather than in hospitals, creating a need for foster families willing to take such children.[36] By 1951, Henrietta Gordon noted that foster home care was being increasingly used for children with physical disabilities. Such children were typically placed under a higher board rate.[37] Average board rates for "physically handicapped" children tended to be more than 50 percent above average base rates. Yet rates for children with behavioral problems or who were "mental defectives" could be even higher.[38]

The official justifications for payments above the basic board rates were the greater costs involved (such as special diets, equipment, or modifications to the home) or the greater time involved in caring for an infant or a convalescing child. Because babies in foster care would have typically been on their way to an adoptive home, the intense care that infants require was perhaps less rewarding when there was no expectation of a long-term relationship. But these higher rates also suggested the difficulty in finding families ready to take on what were perceived to be quite challenging children. The 1941 study noted that "variations in board rate should cover not only additional expenses but additional responsibilities, or *where the returns in 'pleasure' will be less*, as for the instance, in the care of the infant, the care of the sick child, the care of the physically and emotionally disturbed child."[39]

Henrietta Gordon acknowledged in 1946 that higher rates for "hard-to-place" children amounted to a "service fee" (similar to a salary) because these rates typically went above and beyond differences in the costs of raising such children and were, therefore, "offered in an attempt to overcome the reluctance of foster parents to care for these children."[40] (Paying a service fee to foster mothers was a practice supported by professionals, but that was controversial and not widely implemented, as will be discussed in chapter 6.) In explaining the especially high rates paid for "mental defectives" in 1951, Gordon speculated that such high rates were paid because these children were seen to offer the "least sense of reward."[41]

The scenarios professionals seem to have been most comfortable with were those in which higher rates were tied directly to material costs associated with care. But the real challenges of finding homes often led caseworkers to more ambiguous reasons for raising rates. For a child with behavioral problems, the agency could justify additional payments because of "wear and tear on household furnishings," although the real reason for the need might have been more intangible.[42] An incontinent child or one who raged unpredictably took a toll on foster parents in ways that went beyond damage to furniture. Many agencies seem to have seen the board rate as a "casework tool" that could help to persuade individual families to take in certain children. As one agency described in 1941, the present shortage of foster homes "especially for babies" made it necessary to pay $15 per week per child ($246 per week in 2016 dollars). "This is not because they are receiving any special care but because the only home available is conducted by a trained nurse who has made this her special price."[43] What we see here is recognition (or perhaps an assumption) that certain children would be hard to find homes for because they — even infants — were the kinds of children that society found troublesome. As Gordon, referring to board rate differences based on age, put it, "Experience shows that these children do make unusual demands on a family that must be compensated for, if homes are to be found for them."[44]

Increases in board rates reveal a process of negotiation and demonstrate how practice was created through interplay between law, policy, elite professionals, social workers in the field, and families themselves. Agencies found they could not recruit and retain the necessary number of families; flexible board rates were believed to help. Responses collected for the 1954 board rate report indicated that "dissatisfaction of the boarding home parent was the major reason for changing the base board rate."[45] Thus different board rates for special cases suggest a certain amount of bargaining power on the part of foster parents as agencies found it necessary to "pay any amount" to find homes for certain children.[46]

One method of finding foster homes for hard-to-place children, then, was to pay higher board rates for their care. This was not the case, though, in addressing the difficulty in securing foster homes for black children. If anything, foster parents of black children had traditionally been paid lower rates than those of white children, as was the practice of some agencies in the 1930s and 1940s. These practices were based on long-standing assumptions of some private agency boards, particularly in the South, that African American families could support themselves on less money, despite the opinion of professionals that there was "no evidence that the price of consumers' goods is less for a Negro family than for a white family."[47] By 1951, this practice was on its way out; no Child Welfare League member agencies were still reporting lower rates for black children.[48]

In fact, African American children had not initially been identified as "hard to place," because so few agencies were really trying to place them. Children of color instead were likely to have their family problems go unnoticed altogether by child welfare workers. Black families lived below the radar of public concern. Annie Lee Sandusky, an African American social service specialist who did consulting work for the Children's Bureau, wrote in her comments on a draft of new standards for protective services that communities might generally agree on what home conditions were minimally acceptable for children yet "at the same time feel the conditions that may be deplorable [for some] are all right for others." This was particularly the case, Sandusky continued, for "Indian children, Negro children, etc."[49] Representatives of the National Urban League worried that "neglected or dependent Negro children are 'turned down' more frequently than white children by child welfare agencies" because the agencies faced a shortage of suitable homes for them.[50]

To learn of these fears that child welfare organizations in the 1950s were overlooking black children can be disorienting for those familiar with the current racial politics of foster care. Recent critics rightfully deplore the overrepresentation of black children among the foster care population, arguing that the child welfare system intervenes disproportionately in black communities and families. Dorothy Roberts, writing in 2002, pulls no punches in describing this racial disparity: "If you came with no preconceptions about the purpose of the child welfare system, you would have to conclude that it is an institution designed to monitor, regulate, and punish poor black families."[51] By contrast, civil rights advocates in the postwar period identified a *lack* of foster care services for black children as a problem of discrimination in need of remedy. This perspective indicates the prevalence of the view, even among black leaders, that midcentury foster care was a potentially positive service to families rather than an intrusion.[52] Nelson Jackson, who served as director of community services for the National Urban League and as an officer in the National Association of Social Workers, cautioned in 1954, for example, that the dearth of African American foster homes meant dependent black children were denied access to the stabilizing and nurturing benefits of family life provided by foster care and therefore, in the long run, had fewer opportunities than did white children to develop "normal, integrated personalities."[53]

This was a national problem, one with regional dimensions. At midcentury, foster care services in general had long been lacking in the South, but the problem was particularly acute in the case of black children, for whom services were "extremely poor or almost non-existent."[54] The National Urban League's Nelson Jackson, noted in 1947 that Child Welfare League executive director Howard Hopkirk recognized these problems as well. Hopkirk reportedly observed that it was "almost impossible" to secure social workers in much of the south due to "certain customs and traditions which seem to be present in the region toward the employment of Negro workers." Black social workers could not obtain training placements or jobs. The lack of services meant situations such as in Fort Worth, Texas, where black children ended up housed in jails because the area lacked childcare, foster home care, and detention facilities for black children.[55] In the urban North, dependency among black children became more visible after the war, as ongoing migration of African Americans coincided with growing affluence for white Americans. Together, these factors meant that in northern cities, "increasing proportions of poor children [were] black children." Yet the child welfare services available to them were often of very low quality or nonexistent altogether.[56] Black children in need of foster care typically experienced delays, long waits in shelters or hospitals, or inadequate homes. Too often, dependent black children were treated as delinquent because there was nowhere for them to go.[57]

As the child welfare field expanded in a postwar climate of greater racial liberalism, organizations like the National Urban League, the Children's Bureau, and the Child Welfare League began calling for efforts to secure more foster homes for black children, often working hand-in-hand with local agencies in major cities. In the mid-1950s, an executive from one agency noted that the problem was "critical as well as appalling," insisting that the agency did not have a single adequate foster home for black children at that time. The homes it did have suffered from a "poor emotional atmosphere" as well as the "highly questionable motives" of the parents applying for a license.[58] Those concerned about the shortage of adequate foster homes pointed to a number of factors in black communities affecting foster parent recruitment, including lack of adequate housing, low economic status, and the number of women employed outside the home.[59] Similarly, in the case of indigenous families, requirements concerning square footage and individual rooms for children, as well as prevailing stereotypes about Native American depravity, "prevented many Indians from being licensed as foster parents."[60]

Perhaps obstacles such as these could have been addressed by the strategy used to find foster homes for other "hard-to-place" children — that is, by paying higher board rates to better meet the needs of the families that agencies were targeting. But such a move would have gone against the deeply held view that foster care should not be a significant source of income for a family and that families needing additional income from board payments were, by definition, poor candidates for fostering. Indeed, it is certainly likely that the "highly questionable motives" mentioned above referred to black families expressing too much interest in board payments. Experts considered it acceptable to pay higher board in exchange for "wear and tear on furnishings" or even because certain children brought less "sense of reward" but not to address income issues that might prevent some families from fostering.

Difficulties in finding placements for black children would not be addressed by higher board payments but by other means — ones that suggest the varying ways different advocates understood race to impact child dependency, child welfare, and the responsibilities of the state. Although rarely required by law, standard practices advised that black children be placed with black families. Thus the primary strategy for expanding the availability of foster care to black children would be targeted home-finding campaigns—in other words, concerted efforts to recruit foster parents in minority communities. The National Urban League worked together with the Children's Bureau, the Child Welfare League, and local agencies on such home-finding projects in the late 1940s and 1950s.[61] These campaigns employed tactics designed to go beyond "ordinary home finding methods."[62] Typically the agencies interested in the project would appoint a separate committee, which would include both white and black members who would determine the particular methods to use, such as working through ministers and other community leaders in efforts to persuade more black families to foster. In 1957, the Child Welfare League published *Finding Foster Homes*, a booklet focused particularly on locating homes for black children authored by Cornelia Ougheltree, a white woman who served as president of New York's Federation of Protestant Welfare Agencies.[63] Yet, as Andrew Billingsley and Jeanne Giovannoni note, home-finding projects were not typically done in equal collaboration, and white social workers and other experts did not always listen to the Urban League.[64]

For impoverished indigenous children, child welfare experts came to support a strikingly different approach to placement and race. The scaling back of government's existing obligations to indigenous peoples coincided with "purportedly color-blind liberalism," Margaret Jacobs argues, to make placement of indigenous children in non-indigenous homes appear to be both a practical and a humane way to promote the welfare of indigenous children.[65] A similar trajectory occurred in Canada and Australia. In the United States, beginning in the late 1950s, the Child Welfare League worked together with the Bureau of Indian Affairs to launch the Indian Adoption Project. This project sought white parents to adopt Native American children and worked to persuade Native mothers to relinquish newborns. For Jacobs, many of the "problems" that the experts were trying to solve through foster care and adoption were in fact invented by those same experts. By constructing indigenous children as unwanted and their families and communities as hopelessly impoverished and deviant, they helped nourish a powerful desire among liberal white Americans to "rescue" these children as a way to address the "plight" of the Indian.[66]

Meanwhile, white experts remained committed to placing black children in black families. Although apparently sincere in their desire to provide services to black children, white experts did not always see the problem in the same way that African American activists did. White professionals committed to

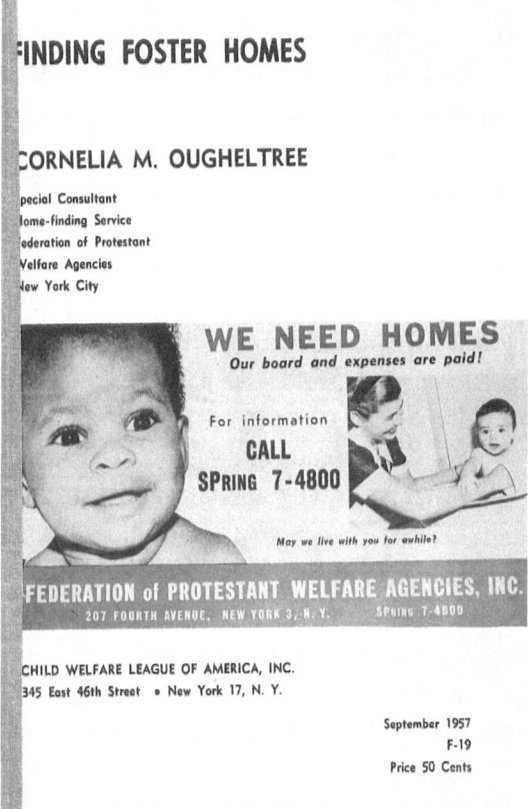

"We Need Homes." Cornelia Ougheltree's *Finding Foster Homes* detailed strategies for recruiting African American foster families.

home-finding projects were certainly aware that inadequate housing and income affected the number of black families that could "open their homes to children." African American families, after all, often lived in parts of town that agencies found undesirable and where homes were not up to Child Welfare League standards. Experts generally seem to have concluded, however, as Milwaukee's Negro Foster Home Finding Committee did, that addressing such problems lay "outside the limits of the committee's assignment." In the Milwaukee case, the committee instead chose to focus on factors they were more confident they could affect, including the sometimes rigid standards of placement agencies.[67] Thus one approach to finding foster homes for black children was to encourage agencies to relax requirements banning foster mothers from having outside employment so that more black families would qualify to be foster parents.

But how were agencies to get black families interested in fostering in the first place? Here there were "cultural problems" to tackle. One such factor seemed to stem from black communities' "lack of knowledge and acceptance" of foster care and other welfare services.[68] The organizers of a home-finding project in Michigan suggested that population changes during and after the war affected the dynamics of foster care services around Flint. Large numbers of southern, rural blacks moving into the area in the early 1950s brought with them their own suspicions of child welfare agencies. Due to the "established cultural pattern of southern Negroes to take care of their own homeless children," the absence of child welfare services for black children in the South, and the lack of experience with "interracial participation and cooperation in the solution of social problems," recent black migrants were left "distrustful" of the established programs in the Flint area and uninterested in becoming foster parents.[69] Thus home finders in a number of cities embarked on special recruitment campaigns intended to overcome black resistance to child welfare services in general and foster care in particular.[70]

"Cultural factors," then, could refer to the theory that black families' backgrounds made it difficult for them to appreciate the benefits of foster care and thus needed better information. At other times, "cultural factors" referred more openly to insensitivity within white agencies. When Margie Friend of the Kentucky Department of Child Welfare asked for help in finding homes for black and mixed-race children, the Urban League's Jeweldean Jones replied tersely: "We have found that many social workers have little understanding of the cultural and value factors affecting the Negro's use of agency services." If agencies wanted to begin serving minority children, Jones suggested, they needed to establish training programs with their staff to "sensitize them to these concerns."[71] Was the problem, then, one of educating black families or of educating white social workers? Indeed, the emphases of the Child Welfare League on the one hand and those of the Urban League on the other indicate that child welfare organizations and civil rights organizations did not always understand the dynamics of foster care for black children in the same way. Billingsley and Giovannoni argue that whites typically saw the problem primarily in terms of persuading more (and allegedly "better") black families to foster, while black civil rights organizations were more apt to emphasize broader structural inequalities.[72]

Among the systemic inequalities limiting the number of black foster homes were poverty and racism inherent in both policy and custom. Income inequality and segregation contributed to living conditions and family arrangements that meant many black families did not meet agency requirements for fostering (hence the idea of "relaxing standards" in order to recruit black foster families). Furthermore, Urban League officials pointed out that the problem of illegitimate birth — which was rising among both whites and blacks — affected black children differently because of the lack of adoptive homes available for black children.[73] Yet there was also overt discrimination within the child welfare field itself to contend with. In New York, where almost all child welfare services were sectarian, religious matching laws required that children be placed with families of their own religion. Yet in the late 1930s, 80 percent of Protestant agencies practiced racial exclusion and did not work with black children. Since most black children were Protestant, there were few agencies to serve them. In 1942 the city outlawed segregation in residential child-caring facilities receiving public monies, but implementation and compliance were slow to be achieved. Furthermore, African Americans were sorely underrepresented among child welfare administrators and as caseworkers, contributing to the social distance between child welfare agencies and black families.[74]

Through the early decades of the twentieth century, foster care was generally seen as a "service" assisting primarily a white population. But by the early 1960s, the number of minority children in foster care had become higher than their proportion in the general population: children of color were 29 percent of all children in public foster care in 1964. This was up from 14 percent in 1945 and from 27 percent in 1961. Along with this increase, there remained an acute shortage of foster homes and institutions serving minority children. By 1964, the Child Welfare League was calling the need to expand such services "one of the major problems facing agencies today."[75]

The modern, midcentury foster care system of standards, professional home finding, and scrutiny through casework was one designed with white families as the norm. Black families were located on the periphery of this system — sometimes overlooked, sometimes formally excluded. There were also other ways in which the white and black foster care populations were different. The child welfare profession had persuaded itself that poverty was no longer a significant factor causing children to enter foster care, and thus the children in care were more damaged than in the past. Yet there was evidence that this pattern perhaps did not apply to black children. Helen Jeter, a sociologist who conducted research for the Child Welfare League in the 1960s, noted in 1963 that black children in foster care were less frequently reported to have emotional and behavioral problems than were white children. Her colleagues at the Child Welfare League speculated that this difference might be because relationships between black foster children and their parents were "less disturbed" than those in the white foster care population. Although there were various possible explanations for this finding, Child Welfare League researchers hypothesized that African American children might now be coming into care for the kinds of reasons that occurred "among white foster placement cases several decades ago"—financial need or family emergencies. In other words, African American families were being excluded from New Deal programs designed to provide family security, and thus black children who were otherwise "normal" were entering foster care because services and programs to keep families intact were not available. Perhaps, Child Welfare League staff suggested, it was not foster care that these minority families needed but supplemental services such as day care, homemaker services, or even financial support.[76] Similarly, Bureau of Indian Affairs bureaucrats and child welfare experts turned to child removal for Native American children because they were unable to imagine solutions for Native children that involved supporting children's own families and promoting economic and educational opportunity closer to home.[77]

Indeed, sunny assertions (like Reverend William Swaim's) that children no longer entered foster care because of poverty did not hold up once researchers began studying the foster care population more systematically. Instead, researchers found that children in foster care came overwhelmingly from families of low income.[78] A study of foster care in New Mexico—a state that had among the highest percentage of Hispanics and Native Americans in its population—found in 1955 that low ADC rates, set at 80 percent of need, were forcing children into foster care. "A goodly number of babies," this disturbing report revealed, were being referred by pediatricians for temporary foster home care to "build them up until they are able to withstand" the impoverished conditions in their own homes.[79]

In discussing the results of a major study of foster care released in the late 1950s, the Children's Bureau new chief, Katherine Oettinger, pointed to what was, for her, one of the study's problematic conclusions. While marital breakdown was found to be the "single most important cause" of children entering foster care, "much foster placement was still associated with poor parental health, low income, unemployment, and inadequate housing."[80] It might be unfortunate to have to remove children from divorced families, her comments suggest, but to do so seemed to be *tolerable* in a way that removing children for reasons of poverty was not. Divorced or separated parents often had great difficulty both financially supporting and caring for their children, but their economic difficulties were not the kinds that New Deal programs had been intended to alleviate. They were instead examples of family disruption or pathology and marked the children of these families as damaged goods, as "hard-to-place," or even as "handicapped."

Joseph Reid, who served as the Child Welfare League's executive director for twenty-five years beginning in 1953, would help steer the league to do far more to address the needs of "hard-to-place" children. In 1970, he noted that the term "handicapped" referred not only to children with physical disabilities. The "handicapped child," Reid maintained, was any child for whom agencies had difficulty finding a home. This included "the child who is born into a large family, the older child, the nonwhite child or the child of mixed race. It is the child who is emotionally disturbed, the child who is not appealing." He went on to say that, in his view, people were typically more open to physically handicapped children, for whom they felt admiration and sympathy. It proved to not be so difficult to find homes for such children once agencies began to try. Far more challenging to place was "the child whose problems and whose handicaps are not that appealing, the child who is different from us, the child whose emotional disturbance may stem from the fact he has been deserted time and time again by his own parents and placed in a number of foster homes, who can't quite give up his parents or accept adoption. Any child that we find is staying on unnecessarily in foster care, whether it be foster homes or institutions, is a handicapped child, moreover, every day that he is not placed he becomes more severely handicapped."[81] Powerful advocates of finding permanent homes for such children, as Reid had become when he made this statement, recognized that the very fact of being in foster care at all seemed to render children "hard-to-place."

The American system of foster care was certainly transformed — in terms of its scope, its methods, its philosophy, and its challenges — by the New Deal as well as by World War II. Eligibility for social insurance programs "ballooned" in the 1950s.[82] In this regard, Reverend Swaim and his colleagues were correct. Title V, part 3, of the Social Security Act had pushed states to establish public child welfare services. The war had further accelerated the development of child welfare infrastructure and guidelines for best practices and also highlighted the need to reimburse foster parents adequately. Meanwhile, the family security programs of the New Deal began to address many of the problems families had long faced, problems that had previously brought children into out-of-home placement. In the mid-1950s, more than 60 percent of children whose father was deceased were receiving benefits through social insurance or through veterans' benefits; another 10 percent of paternal orphans received ADC.[83] These were families that in the past might have collapsed under financial strain, fating their children to become public charges.

Yet many struggling families remained outside the scope of the nascent welfare state. New Deal programs, which were supposedly keeping children out of foster care, did not reach all families, despite the hopes of reformers. Deserted women, for example, could have applied for ADC, although many states required an onerous process of determining an alleged desertion, mandating that a wife show she had done everything possible to track down her husband and file support complaints against him. In 1952, only 10 to 20 percent of deserted mothers reportedly received ADC or other public assistance.[84] For widowers or men with incapacitated wives it would have been unlikely (although not unheard of) to receive ADC. In 1948, less than 2 percent of ADC families gained assistance because of the death or incapacity of the mother.[85] Professional homemaker services were sometimes touted as a resource for single fathers, but those services remained only thinly available.[86] Like foster mothers, professional "homemakers" provided, under the auspices of child welfare agencies, physical care and emotional support to children who were not theirs biologically. Often an ill or otherwise incapacitated mother was also in the home, and the duties of the homemaker (sometimes called a "mother's aid") could include caring for the mother as well as performing housework.[87] Homemaker services emerged in the early twentieth century and were implemented as public work relief in the 1930s. They began expanding as a child welfare service in the 1950s, although this strategy for allowing children to remain in their homes was never adequately developed.[88] Federally supported day care might have helped many families, but it was controversial, offered only during the war in some cities to meet the demands of mothers working in war industries, and ended with the war itself. Thus, many families were not enjoying the family security promised by New Deal programs. Prominent among them were families of color, who were overrepresented in occupations exempted from social insurance, such as agriculture and domestic service, and who were subject to "suitable home provisions" often designed to keep unmarried black and Hispanic mothers off the ADC roles.

Poverty, then, remained entwined with foster care even as child welfare experts persisted in their conviction that postwar foster children were more damaged than the impoverished orphans that out-of-home placement had served in the past. Expert consensus by midcentury held that it was no longer the case that "just any charitable family" could provide an acceptable foster home. This consensus was driven not only by new understandings of childhood, child development, and child psychology but also by the professionalization and specialization of social work. Perceived changes in the foster care population meant important new responsibilities and new stresses requiring that foster parents possess "special skills and qualities."[89]

A foster home was not merely a place where dependent children would be physically cared for but where, ideally, foster mothers (like "Aunt May," whom we met in chapter 4) would help facilitate the precarious process of healthy child development in children increasingly seen as damaged goods. And yet foster parents had to do all of this without the satisfaction derived from a permanent relationship with the children in their care. Foster families were to provide therapeutic benefits to damaged children. They also served as an arm of the welfare state, in that they provided the housing, the board, and the physical and emotional care to children who, for whatever reasons, had become the public's responsibility. Child welfare professionals would come to insist that foster parents needed to be compensated for the difficult and important work they did. The challenge would be to somehow reconcile the idea of *payment* with the idea of *family*.

CHAPTER 6

COMPENSATED MOTHERHOOD AND THE STATE

Foster Parents as Workers

U nder modern understandings of childhood, children were not to be a source of income for families — neither through their own labor (a principle reflected in the 1938 Fair Labor Standards Act, which banned labor of children under age fourteen) nor by bringing payment to those who cared for them.[1] Therefore, well into the twentieth century, many child welfare professionals remained wary of the motives and qualifications of boarding mothers, even while coming to reject other alternatives for caring for dependent children such orphanages and free homes. The role of foster parents was indeed ambiguous. Were they most like parents? Or more like employees? Or was there perhaps another way of understanding them altogether that might reconcile their multiple roles?[2] And, finally, what part should foster parents themselves play in defining that role?

In 1940, a New York woman named Pearl Jacobs explained, in a letter to Eleanor Roosevelt, what she understood to be the situation of foster mothers like herself. "Who are our foster mothers?" she asked.

> Not the idle rich, for they can't take care of their very own. No but the widows who with perhaps 3 or 4 children takes one or two of these little ones, so that this *lousy* measly 24 dollars a month will help her keep her own loved ones with her.... [Or] the woman of middle age, who wants to live at home who still loves children [and] is lonesome after her loved ones have left..., so she takes one or two of these little ones and gives them... a mother's love and devotion for only can mothers like these do this.

Jacobs went on to further describe the intense bonds of "everlasting love" that could develop between foster mothers and foster children in their care. But, she emphasized, "remember this, ... these women need this money in spite of everything."³ Indeed, after lives devoted to raising their own children, women like Jacobs often felt that fostering was among the only forms of paid work they were qualified to do.

Pearl Jacobs's letter suggests the historical links between foster parenting and women's "home work," work that had been so important to working-class and widowed households in the nineteenth century. A number of women interested in taking in children continued to see fostering in the context of this tradition of women's domestic home work well into the twentieth century. Many of the letters that found their way to the offices of the Children's Bureau in the 1930s, the 1940s, and even the 1950s reflected that view. But it was a view increasingly at odds with a developing child welfare system whose leaders were busy transforming child placing into a state-monitored service and a scientifically based profession driven by new concepts of child development. Indeed, Agnes Hanna, the Children's Bureau's Social Services director, while acknowledging that funds for board were limited, responded to Jacobs in a way that showed little appreciation for her perspective. "Fortunately," Hanna wrote, "there are many homes in which service to children is gladly given by the foster parents because of their love for children."⁴ Other women who penned similar letters were typically told by Hanna that foster care was not a "business from which financial returns may be realized."⁵ It was instead to be done by those who were motivated solely by a desire to help children. Despite such protestations, though, women's paid care work would, in fact, have a central place in this new child welfare system, a reality that never rested entirely well with professionals.

Agencies and professionals, then, were left with an uneasy tension between their discomfort at paying for care and their recognition that agencies nonetheless had to do so. This contradiction would be mediated by a number of strategies that helped child welfare professionals build a public child welfare system that relied on compensated substitute motherhood. These strategies included the appeals to patriotism of the World War II era and, in the postwar years, celebrations of love between foster parents and children. The most ambitious strategy, though, involved attempts to develop foster parenting into a quasi-profession. These strategies were intended to help transform the crass economic role of *boarding mother*, which still had a lingering hold, into the specialized role of certified *foster family care provider*.

The crux of the difficulty in resolving these tensions lay in the persistent unease at viewing foster mothering as a job, as Jacobs did. The Child Welfare League recognized that "'mothering' is definitely something which one would like to think should not be paid for."[6] The subject of board payments remained a delicate one. Although most experts would come to believe they were necessary, many lay people feared that children placed in boarding homes would be "exploited for financial gain."[7] The families of children in care could also be skeptical. The children of Lillian Walters, who was separated from her husband, a World War II veteran, were placed in foster care in 1951. The children's grandparents Mr. and Mrs. Carlo Accurso wanted to care for the children themselves and questioned the decision to place the girls in foster care. "Can strangers love these children like their own blood?" Mrs. Accurso wondered. She went on to complain that the foster parents were receiving thirty dollars per week, yet when she went to visit them, the children "looked unwashed and very ill looking and cry they want to come home to Grandmother."[8] Noted author and adoption proponent Pearl Buck probably spoke for many when she assailed the "evil effects" of foster homes because foster parents "frankly take a child for money."[9] Yet as early as the late 1930s, but especially after the disruptions of World War II, child welfare professionals had concluded that families taking in children needed to be at least minimally reimbursed for their expenses in feeding, housing, and clothing their charges. Such care was not intended to be charity, after all. Indeed, one reason why an earlier generation of child placers had switched from free rural homes to paid boarding homes was to protect children from exploitation.

To what degree, though, was it acceptable for foster mothers to be motivated by the remuneration they received for their care of dependent children? Simply put, did that desire for adequate pay, expressed by Mrs. Jacobs, indicate that she and others with similar needs were incapable of providing good care?[10] Part of the mistrust directed toward foster mothers derived from their working-class status. Turn-of-the-century middle-class child savers had assumed that the ties of the working classes to their own children were apt to be mercenary rather than properly emotional. Viviana Zelizer has addressed this point in relation to the class conflict over child labor. Opponents of child labor during the Progressive Era came to dismiss the critical importance of working-class youths' wages to family survival and to insist that if children "produced money, they were not being properly loved."[11] These same class tensions, I would suggest, influenced child welfare professionals' views of foster parents, who came primarily from the working classes. When held up to a model of middle-class parenthood in which women did not "have to" work to help support their families, many prospective boarding mothers not only fell short but even raised suspicions.

For Henrietta Gordon, compiler and editor of the Child Welfare League's board rate studies, the necessity of board payments derived in part from changes in the purpose of foster care. She noted that "years ago" foster placement was more like informal adoption. But by midcentury, there was more need for temporary placements, and it was the job of agencies to help children return to their own families. Children who could not be returned to their homes, it was hoped, would be placed in adoptive homes. "So the foster home service becomes something of a job which members of the community must undertake in the interest of children," Gordon explained. "Those who are willing to give that service [foster parents] ought not be asked in addition to bear the major burden of the cost of that service."[12] The results of the Child Welfare League's board rate studies reflected this grudging approval of at least minimal board payments by the 1940s.

Wartime conditions contributed to this growing acceptance of board payments. The increased cost of living during the war and the movement of women into the workforce meant pressure from foster mothers for higher board rates. Furthermore, the wartime slippage between "day care" and "foster care" pointed to the fact that women providing foster care were home care workers, providing services in their homes for compensation. By framing foster mothers as patriotic war workers rather than as self-interested economic actors, home finders developed a way out of their conundrum over the role of board payments. But this resolution was only temporary.

The ambivalence would return. While experts acknowledged the need for board payments, it was important that prospective foster mothers not appear too concerned with them. What agencies needed were not the boarding homes of the past but what were coming to be called foster family homes. This transformation in naming from "boarding" to "fostering" suggests a shift in how foster care providers were seen — from the turn-of-the century role of wage earner to the midcentury role of substitute mother. *Boarding* was an economic activity that had its analogy in women's traditional home work and was seen as potentially at odds with modern views of child-rearing; *fostering* emphasized a caring, maternal relationship that had only recently been nearly synonymous with "adoption." The parenting analogy, though, had its own pitfalls (as described in chapter 4), and expert literature was steeped in cautions about foster mothers who became too attached to their charges.

Although love between foster mothers and foster children could be viewed as potentially problematic in its own right, emphasizing such love was also critical to rehabilitating the idea of boarding homes. According to Zelizer (discussing an earlier period), an "emotional tie between boarding mother and child 'cleansed' board payments."[13] Columbia social work professor Dorothy Hutchinson wrote in 1943 that foster mothers deserved praise for their "gift for mothering" and the "acceptance of themselves as truly maternal women."[14] But how did one distinguish Hutchinson's idealized, selfless *foster* mother from the self-interested, mercenary *boarding* mother? To ensure that love trumped money required professional, up-do-date social work. Home studies, casework, and state licensing could provide a safeguard against foster families with incorrect motivations and inadequate qualifications. Agnes Hanna, who was quick to admonish potential foster mothers who saw boarding as a possible source of income, was just as ready to correct those who condemned board payments altogether: "The fact that a child is boarded in a home," she replied to one critic, "does not mean that his care is undertaken with the thought of profit. A good child-placing agency exerts the greatest care to select homes where the basic motive for taking a child is love of children and interest in their development."[15]

By the postwar years, increasingly honed standards helped mitigate discomfort with board payments, at least among child welfare professionals. Under these new standards, child-placing arrangements were no longer private ones between a biological parent and a boarding mother (although such practices still occurred). Child welfare professionals continued to make the case that independent boarding (like independent adoption) was risky for all. They instead promoted child placing as part of a burgeoning child welfare system that was developing best practices based on the latest thinking by experts. In the 1930s and 1940s, the Child Welfare League of America published standards for foster care that laid out principles along these lines. So too did state agencies and the Children's Bureau. And the 1940s and 1950s saw the publication of books on home finding that further helped solidify the science and art of finding foster families. Ideal foster parents, under these developing standards, would be quasi-professionals who provided the proper kind of love and care, along with housing, clothing, and food, according to up-to-date professional expertise.

The principles laid out in the Child Welfare League's *Standards* and other professional literature represented a general consensus about best practices. What actually occurred on the ground in real child welfare offices and in real homes often deviated considerably from these standards due to funding problems, peculiarities of state and local law, the size and makeup of case loads, the training of child welfare workers, or the size of the foster parent pool, among other factors. In her review of the 1959 update of the Child Welfare League's *Standards for Foster Family Care Service*, Helen Ripple, supervisor of Foster Home Services for North Carolina, noted with understatement that "there has been a big gap between what is considered good practice and actual practice."[16] But setting particular standards was a crucial part of reimagining foster family care as a sound, therapeutic, modern system of delivering services to dependent children, in which children would be *treated*, not exploited.

Certainly those standards of good practice included vetting potential foster families for the structural features of the home, certification of the parents' good health, and letters of reference. But standards also included critical matters of family makeup that in some ways mirrored the new standards for adoptive placements. Since the 1920s, adoption workers had been developing policies and practices of "matching" they hoped would create adoptive families in which children's appearance, culture, talents, and potential would be "as if begotten." By mimicking biological kinship, adoption could be made "safe," and adoptive families, as Ellen Herman describes, "might approximate normality through intelligent design."[17] As Herman, Barbara Melosh, and Julie Berebitsky have further argued, adoption experts also hoped, by stressing the importance of "matching," to enhance their own status as the expert professionals best able to facilitate scientific, safe adoptions.[18]

The foster care professionals who developed midcentury best practices for selecting *foster* parents certainly shared many of these concerns. Yet unlike adoption workers, foster care caseworkers and professionals were not trying to create permanent new homes for children. Agencies typically practiced broad matching for race, although it was not as crucial that foster families be matched for subtle factors of appearance and intelligence as it was for adoptive families.

It was important to experts, though, that foster families adhere to certain structural qualities that made them seem close enough to a "real" family. Such standards for foster families, it seems, could help mitigate the ambivalence child welfare professionals continued to have about paying for "mothering."

Foster family care was allegedly superior to both orphanages and older models of boarding homes because of the foster family's resemblance, as much as possible, to a "normal" modern family. Under the coalescing standards, foster parents, first of all, needed to be a married couple whose age made them plausible parents to the children in their care, thus excluding the widows and older couples of the past from fostering. Such insistence that only nuclear families could provide a "normal" home environment led one regional staff development group to consider even a grandparent living in the home to be a "danger signal" when evaluating prospective foster families. Second, the household was not to contain more children than would allow for the individualized attention considered necessary under modern child-rearing techniques.[19] Adhering to this standard meant excluding many of the large rural families of the type that had previously taken in children and incorporated them into a life in which cash was scarce but food was not and in which older children could help care for younger ones.[20]

Mrs. Annette Alderink of northern Minnesota illustrated the disconnection between modern ideals held by professionals and the understandings of some prospective foster parents, understandings that were holdovers from earlier conceptions of boarding care. In 1947, Annette was thirty-seven years old, her much older husband sixty-five. The couple had ten children at home (as well as two older ones residing elsewhere) and lived in a small house in the country with cows, chickens, and a garden. Mr. Alderink received government assistance, and Mrs. Alderink was a housewife. She wondered if she could "get a job for the Government" taking care of "poor little ones that need care." Three of her older daughters would be able to help her. "I would like to do something and try to make my owen [sic] living this way if it works," she wrote. Such a home as this one was problematic to modern child welfare experts for many reasons. Mildred Arnold, the Children's Bureau's director of Child Welfare Services, balked at what Alderink saw as an asset (her large family that could help take care of young children): "Because you already have such a large number of children to care for," Arnold replied gently, "we do not believe it would be possible, even with the help of the three oldest girls, for you to give the kind of individual care needed to additional children and particularly babies. They need very special care and individual attention." Arnold also noted, as was standard in such replies, that the care of children was "not a money-making business."[21]

By setting standards like these, professionals promoted foster families that would look more like modern, as-if-begotten ones, in which children appeared to be part of a naturally occurring family and not a commercial enterprise. The Child Welfare League itself, by the early 1940s, had already settled on the position that board rates needed to be high enough to attract "families of average income" who were interested in "mothering" a child but were also interested in earning money. But the payments should "not be so high as to attract applications from families" that were interested only in the money. Therefore, professional standards also held that foster parents needed to be financially independent, since board payments were scarcely enough to cover costs associated with caring for a child. Board rates in 1941 were in some places as low as nine dollars per month.[22] Standards relating to household income, whether or not this was their explicit purpose, helped mask the financial elements of foster care.

These financial elements could not be entirely obscured, however. By far, the greatest difficulty with this endeavor was that the families most likely to express interest in receiving placements typically were those of modest income for whom the costs associated with caring for an additional child were not easily absorbed and in which a wife's earnings were, in fact, needed to supplement the husband's income.[23] Attempts to recruit middle-class families were not as successful as agencies hoped. A study of foster homes in St. Paul, Minnesota, found that "many desirable neighborhoods do not contain any boarding homes available to the County Welfare Board."[24] And Pearl Jacobs was certainly correct in her assertion that the "idle rich" were not lining up outside the offices of child placement agencies in hopes of becoming foster parents. David Fanshel speculated that there was something about modern, middle-class families' insularity that made them less "open to perfect strangers" than were the families that willingly accommodated not only foster children but also caseworkers and birth parents into their lives. In other words, foster families were "very different from the families he knew."[25]

Never entirely free of their suspicions of foster mothers, child welfare professionals tried to strike a precarious balance between understanding them as mothers and as workers. Providing foster care could mean extra dollars for the foster mother to include in "planning her monthly budget," as well as offering her meaningful work.²⁶ This was the model Evelyn Felker followed when she decided to become a foster parent. Once her children were in school, she tried going back to paid work but decided it was not worth the compensation; she tried volunteer work but found much of it to be "'busy' work"; and she had no particular educational goals to pursue. "Foster care seemed an opportunity to use my time in worthwhile ways," she later wrote in a guidebook for other foster parents, "and my responsibilities in the home could be tied into these new responsibilities in a way that would benefit my family."²⁷

A piece in the Child Welfare League's March 1945 *Bulletin* spoke to the complexity of the foster parent role. Foster parents, the author noted, had their performance evaluated, and the use of their home could be discontinued if they failed to meet certain requirements and standards. In this sense, they were "employees of the agency" who happened to have "perhaps the most important part" in the foster care program. But board payments that barely covered the cost of care alone "were in effect a denial of this." At the same time, the "well-worn" argument that "'mother love cannot be measured in money'" remained in play and could be seen as a way of "rationalizing our need to keep the foster home program inexpensive." Paying board over the cost of care, the *Bulletin* suggested, could help to identify foster care more properly as "a service rather than a charity."²⁸ Because prospective foster mothers were rarely affluent, professionals had to come to terms with the financial realities of families who desired to take in foster children. Similarly, Jean Charnley suggested in her 1955 book on child placing that if, "as a repayment for laundering mountains of sheets cheerfully and without complaint for a child who wets the bed every night, a farmer's wife can swell her egg money to the point at which the family can have a television set before the snows set in[,] my only concern is that she has had to work so long and hard to save so little money."²⁹ In Charnley's view, financial motivations for fostering were acceptable as long as the payments were intended to help the wife build up her pin money and were not crucial to a family's survival.

Like Charnley, psychiatrist Irene Josselyn also came to accept a connection between fostering and compensation and was untroubled by it. Josselyn noted in 1952 that it "is an accepted part of our culture that a person who works earns financial returns." This is the case "no matter how emotionally gratifying the work experience may be." Thus, if a mother wanted to supplement family income, this motivation should not be automatically ruled out but scrutinized for the reasons why she would rather foster than seek part-time work outside the home.[30] Another pamphlet, targeted at potential foster mothers rather than home finders, emphasized that remuneration did not compensate for all that foster parents put into foster care. "However," the pamphlet stated, "if your income is adequate, and your husband has no objection to your earning money," and if the potential foster mother felt foster parenting would be more satisfying than a part-time job, then payment could be a "legitimate consideration" in deciding to become a foster parent.[31] Certainly mothers looking to earn additional income had more options to consider than in the past. Between 1940 and 1960, the proportion of married working mothers rose by 400 percent.[32] One way child welfare professionals responded to this reality was to present foster parenting as a caring profession that shared aspects in common with parenting but was not parenting per se.

Expert discussions of professional homemaker services contained little of this anxiety. Like foster care, public homemaker services were arranged by social welfare agencies in an effort to help struggling families stay together. Homemakers received training and were typically replacing or supplementing the work of the mother, whether she was ill or absent. Families receiving the services of a homemaker would ideally, according to their ability, pay a fee to the agency, which would in turn make up the difference in paying for the homemaker. The homemaker was unambiguously understood to be an "employee of a social agency" without the hand-wringing about whether or not she was also a potentially neurotic woman seeking a child to fulfill her own emotional needs. Whereas foster mothers needed to be of an age plausible for her to be the children's mother, the Child Welfare League set the ideal age range for professional housekeepers at forty to fifty-five, or the "usual age range of grandmothers in the families they serve."[33] The age qualifications seem to have been a gesture toward propriety, so that she would not appear to be a sexual interest of the husband and so to alleviate an ill mother's fears that she was being "replaced by another woman" as both a mother and a wife.[34] While foster mothers needed to be of the same race as her foster children, professional housekeepers were often women of color.[35] Although among her important qualifications were interest in and experience with children, there was no doubt that she was an employee. While her wages were not high, she was not viewed with suspicion for the mere fact that she received them. Indeed, public homemaker services were developed in the mid-1930s under the WPA as a form of work relief to needy women, and the role of homemaker was often confused with that of domestic servant. This program proved to be one of the more significant forms of relief for black women. Agencies providing homemaker services, as Eileen Boris and Jennifer Klein emphasize, recruited women "directly from public assistance rolls."[36]

Although child welfare professionals seemed less conflicted about the women serving as homemakers, these services were never widely implemented. The development of homemaker services was hindered by high costs and limited personnel.[37] Meanwhile, the conception of homemaker services gradually evolved from in-home care of children whose mothers were unavailable into the home health care profession serving primarily elderly or disabled adults.[38]

If the homemaker role was less troubling than that of foster mother, perhaps a move to "professionalizing" foster parenting could help with the ambiguity. Postwar talk of "professionalizing" foster parents also reflected the widely accepted view that children were now coming into care for very different reasons than in the past, as described in chapter 5. The foster care caseloads were now allegedly made up of children who were there due not merely to poverty but because of family pathology. Therefore, foster care was no longer a place where dependent children would be simply cared for physically. Instead, it was one where, ideally, foster mothers would also help facilitate the precarious process of child development. Foster parents were "ordinarily not equipped to be therapists," yet they were to address the needs of children increasingly understood to be disturbed in some way.[39]

In an effort to recruit more foster mothers who were appropriately qualified for these new tasks, some child welfare experts would begin promoting foster mothering as a quasi-professional service "similar to the services of a housemother in a boarding school, a nurse, or a teacher."[40] Along with this view came the argument some made that foster mothers should be paid a "service fee," beyond the costs of board, that would cover the care work of the foster mother herself. Utah, an early adopter, began this practice in the late 1940s, when state funds became available for payment of a service fee of up to fifteen dollars on a case-by-case basis, depending on individual circumstances. Payment of service fees, while not common in practice, was found in "some of the better child welfare agencies."[41] In arguing for higher board rates and even service fees, the Child Welfare League framed the issue in terms of its long history of protecting children. Paying at least something toward foster care helped to "end a common abuse of past years" in the form of the free home where even young children had to perform hard labor and were too often denied the opportunity to attend school.[42] By 1959, the league was advocating payment of service fees in the new update of its *Standards for Foster Family Care Service*. The *Standards* stated that service payments were a "realistic and valid" way for foster mothers to get "additional satisfaction from performing service for children, and it reflects the agency's recognition of the value of the service to the welfare of the community."[43] One representative of a South Carolina agency, however, objected that some foster parents saw their work purely as a voluntary, sometimes religiously motivated service, and therefore payment would be "unnecessary and inappropriate."[44]

There was an unintended consequence of such calls to pay foster parents for their service. If foster care was a "job," then a foster home could be seen as a "commercial enterprise" and subject to restrictive zoning. In the early 1960s, New Jersey agencies reported that some communities were developing zoning laws to bar families living in "desirable middle-class neighborhoods" from taking foster children.[45] When foster parents in Los Angeles worked in the late 1960s to change a local ordinance that prohibited foster homes in areas zoned for single families, they were reportedly opposed by realtors, property owners, and members of the city council. In appealing to the city council to change the zoning, the Child Welfare Services Department and foster parents found themselves up against negative stereotypes about foster parents and foster children and arguments that "allowing people to take in foster children ruins the sanctity of the single-family dwelling."[46] Bans on illegitimate children in housing units were another way some communities restricted foster parenting in certain neighborhoods, as many foster children were born to unmarried parents. The problems for foster families raised by zoning issues and illegitimate birth became common enough that the Child Welfare League included questions about both issues on a survey it conducted in 1966.[47]

Despite such potential drawbacks to board payments, by the late 1950s there was a general consensus among child welfare experts that board rates needed to be higher and that foster care was a quasi-professional service meriting additional service pay or, at least, higher board rates. Such reforms would have required a public commitment that was not forthcoming. State budgets were strapped, and efforts to increase federal expenditures for foster care failed repeatedly. Board rates remained very low, only a negligible number of jurisdictions paid a service fee to foster mothers, and agencies continued over the decades to bemoan the lack of high-quality foster homes. The Child Welfare League despaired that the many children needing good foster homes would not get them "until foster mothers are better paid."[48] Jeanette Harris of the Children's Bureau wrote in 1958 that most agencies agreed that low rates "definitely affect the type of parents who can be attracted to the program."[49] A decade later, consultant Gertrude Layden noted that one often heard of women who wanted to be foster mothers but unfortunately had to work outside the home to supplement their husbands' wages. "Were adequate board rates and supportive services available, some of these families might well be attracted to foster parenthood."[50]

Such attention to foster mothers' pay loomed large as it became increasingly clear that working mothers were not a temporary anomaly.[51] During the 1950s, one-third of women worked outside of the home, and half of them worked full-time.[52] New opportunities in the workforce were offering compelling options to women who might, in decades previous, have elected to become foster mothers. This shift was undermining the quality of the foster parent pool, according to one observer. In a 1964 typescript fragment found in the Child Welfare League records, a person identified by the initials "EEG" was particularly frank. Agencies across the county, EEG stated, were reporting that "the quality of the families who apply to be foster parents is decreasing and there is evidence of considerable pathology in many applicants." EEG urged that more agencies begin taking steps to give status to foster parenthood and to pay for foster care services according to terms that might be competitive with jobs for women outside the home.[53]

Furthermore, the field's "best practices" standards did not reflect the changing roles of women in the workplace and family. Into the 1960s, agencies continued to require (at least on the books) that foster homes be two-parent families in which the wife was a full-time mother. Such policies, which were based on the Child Welfare League's *Standards*, were the same as what was required of adoptive families in the period. Experts agreed that two-parent families were necessary to facilitate "maximum opportunities for personality development" in children.[54] Foster care differed from adoption, however, in that potential foster families were in short supply, whereas potential adoptive families were not. Foster care home finders were forced to recognize, as Layden did, that their efforts to recruit foster families were in increasing competition with part-time jobs for women. Adoption workers, meanwhile, had less reason to accommodate families with working mothers because the high demand for adoptable white infants made it unnecessary for caseworkers to question their own insistence that adoptive mothers be full-time caregivers. Indeed, a working woman hoping to adopt typically had to quit her job months before the screening process began in order to demonstrate her commitment and for the couple to adjust to living on one income.[55]

Foster home finders simply could not be so choosy. Instead, foster home finders found that they frequently needed to modify or ease agency standards in order to increase the pool of potential foster parents. In 1965, Barbara Fillmore, a prospective foster mother, was frustrated that she and her husband had been repeatedly turned down for a placement because she was a "working mother." She complained that the state's rules were "'old-fashioned'" and were preventing hundreds of older children, who did not require a stay-at-home mother, from the "love and care of a *normal American* home" like hers. She noted proudly that her own mother had worked and that she herself had worked since her youngest entered first grade without ill effects. The Children's Bureau in its response, while acknowledging that more mothers were now in the workforce, insisted that "there is a trend, also, toward greater maladjustment in the children who need foster care," rendering it unlikely that they would be able to thrive without "full-time mothering and guidance."[56]

Yet, in fact, the requirement that foster mothers be in the home full time was one about which agencies often showed great flexibility.[57] Such requirements were believed to contribute to the "severe problem" many agencies in large cities faced in finding homes for minority children, especially those who were African American.[58] Although more agencies were trying to recruit black foster families by the late 1950s, those families typically did not look like the picture established in the Child Welfare League's *Standards*. One way in which this was true was that women in black families typically worked outside the home or were heads of household.[59]

Despite so much discussion about the need to think of foster parents as quasi-professionals, to treat them with respect, and to compensate them adequately, foster parents remained decidedly junior partners in a child welfare regime imagined and implemented by psychologists, university professors, and social work professionals who made the rules and set the standards. One agency representative (identified only as "E. H.") acknowledged in 1958 that foster parents were not always treated as full members of the professional child welfare team. "Personally," E. H. noted, "I know of only two or three manuals for foster parents that are respectful of the foster parents' intelligence, most of these being sentimental, lacking in a statement of the agency's philosophy of foster care, the foster parents' responsibility, and simple, useful information of a factual nature."[60] Ten years later Mary Daly, director of the Child Welfare Department of a Catholic organization in St. Louis, noted with dismay at a major conference on foster care the tendency of agency staff to view foster parents as clients themselves rather than as partners.[61]

Indeed, recognized foster care experts, for all their interest in improving the delivery of foster care services, rarely consulted foster parents as part of these efforts. Social workers, developmental psychologists, child welfare professionals, and the like had become increasingly interested in foster care by the 1950s and early 1960s. The Child Welfare League began sponsoring important research projects, and by the early 1960s the Children's Bureau had secured a budget for awarding research grants on child welfare and directed some of those funds to foster care research. In the fall of 1967 the Child Welfare League (with financial support from the Children's Bureau and the New York Fund for Charities) sponsored a National Conference on Foster Care, held in New Orleans. The conference, the first of its kind, hoped to look at foster care in its broadest context by bringing in the expertise of sociology, law, medicine, psychology, psychiatry, and social work. The list of speakers included former Child Welfare League researchers David Fanshel and Bernice Boehm (at this point, professors of social work at Columbia University and Rutgers University, respectively), professor of sociology Marvin B. Sussman (Case Western), Boston area psychiatrist Irving Kaufman, and Halbert B. Robinson, who was director of the Child Development Laboratory at the University of Washington. Tellingly, however, the conference did not hear much from those most directly involved with the implementation of foster care. Only two foster parents were invited to present, and their participation was described as a novelty.[62] And no one spoke representing individuals who had spent time in foster care or parents whose children had been placed in care.

Meanwhile, in the 1960s, foster parents began to make themselves heard. In numerous ways foster parents would challenge the role that professionals had promoted for them within the midcentury system of child welfare services. This role was an uncomfortable hybrid of parent and worker, and foster parents ran afoul of agency expectations when they overidentified with either aspect of their role. Yet foster parents did so nonetheless, challenging the idea that they had to simply accept the authority and the terms of social workers, agencies, and courts.

One way they did this, as we saw in chapter 4, was by trying to adopt their foster children. In a number of well-publicized cases in the late 1950s and 1960s, foster parents sued when they were turned down for adoption by the agencies for various reasons: a child had lived with foster parents, the Sanders, for four years but had not been relinquished by her mother, as discussed earlier; another child was too intelligent to be adopted by the foster parents, who were not well educated and who liked to watch television; or a child's "blond, blue eyed and... fair complexion" did not match that of her Italian American foster parents.[63] In each of these cases, the foster parents and agencies disagreed profoundly over the definition of family and the role of the foster parent. Sometimes courts sided with agencies, sometimes with foster parents, but whatever the outcome, the lawsuits suggested that foster parents had their own understandings of what constituted a family. They rejected agency insistence that professional staff knew better than foster parents themselves what was best for the children whom they had come to know intimately through the day-to-day acts of parenting.

Foster care providers troubled the system when they overidentified with the role of "parent" and tried to make permanent claims on the children in their care. Yet they also challenged foster care practices when they took seriously the rhetoric of professionalization and insisted that they had expertise and interests that agencies needed to respect. We see this type of challenge in the emergence of independent foster parent organizations. Early examples include the efforts of sixty black and white foster parents in Montgomery County, Maryland, who came together in 1957 in an attempt to obtain higher board rates from the Montgomery County Public Welfare Department.[64] The number of such organizations began to expand in the late 1960s with the formation of groups such as Community Assistance to Homeless Youngsters (known as CATHY) in Los Angeles, formed in 1967, and Michigan's Christopher Street Society, established in 1969. In 1971, the Child Welfare League was aware of only thirty foster parent organizations nationally; by 1974, that number had jumped to three hundred.[65]

Foster parents were forming these organizations at a time when poor communities and communities of color were growing more assertive and increasingly critical of their position in American society. Welfare rights organizations, for example, agitated for a guaranteed income, for the rights to due process and appeals, and for curbs on the discretionary power of caseworkers.⁶⁶ In their own organizing, what foster parents seem to have wanted above all was for agencies to treat them as full partners and for their standing in the public eye to be improved. Ruby Kennedy, a foster parent organizer from CATHY, put it this way: "Many foster parents do not feel respected; they feel 'used.'" They "sometimes feel that their knowledge and day-to-day experience are not accepted as valuable." At the same time, Kennedy reported that most foster parents in her area also wanted better training, through contact with experienced foster parents and workshops where foster parents and social workers would "train together" rather than from social workers providing training to parents.⁶⁷

Foster parents did not unanimously support salaries or service fees, however. Indeed, the idea of paying foster mothers a service fee made some foster parents decidedly uncomfortable. In two admittedly unscientific surveys of several hundred foster parents in Los Angeles and Nebraska, respondents in 1967 overwhelmingly agreed that board payments were inadequate to meet children's needs. Like child welfare professionals, they supported higher rates. Yet most found the idea of a salary (or even training) for foster parents to be — according to the Nebraska report — "repugnant." These foster parents insisted that foster care was, in fact, "a natural expression of love," which a person either had or did not have.⁶⁸ They saw their role in contrast to the professional agency staff, who performed their part in the child welfare system as a job, who favored book learning over the knowledge gained from parenting experience, and who were professional rather than loving.

Others worried about the potential side effects of a salary — the agency might feel it "owned" the foster homes, there might be more red tape, and parents might have less choice about the children in their homes. Notably, skeptics worried that a salary would attract "people who wanted to do it just for money."⁶⁹ Foster parents in this survey were asserting the view that "mothering" was an innate skill that good foster parents possessed. Like "real" mothering, it could not be quantified in terms of salary. And a salary might, therefore, attract unqualified people. If child welfare professionals seemed suspicious of the motivations of potential foster parents, it appears that foster parents themselves were not necessarily any less so.

Foster parent organizing achieved a new visibility in May 1971 when Eugene Glynn, head of Michigan's recently formed Christopher Street Society, decided to hold a national conference for foster parents.⁷⁰ Organizers of the conference were enthusiastic. The Child Welfare League was more wary. Recent trends in social work theory were critical of past condescension toward clients and foster parents. In the midst of this cultural pivot, the league was not going to openly fight an effort by foster parents to meet and discuss common interests. Yet staff members were clearly concerned. Were foster parents perhaps trying to unionize? How could they be assured that such groups would remain committed to children and not "become self-serving"? The league looked into the plans for the conference and its organizers and reassured itself that the foster parents involved simply wanted to be in a position to offer better care to children. And it concluded the conference could be a positive development if the league's own staff got involved.[71] The league offered its resources and expertise to the group, ensuring that professionals would have a hand in whatever organization emerged from the conference. Indeed, in 1971, the Child Welfare League secured a three-year grant from the Department of Health, Education, and Welfare (HEW) to set up what became known as the National Foster Parent Association, along with additional supplemental funding in 1974.[72]

The NFPA's first conference was held in Chicago and was attended by around eight hundred foster parents and social workers. Although tensions between these two groups were evident, attendees were encouraged to focus on their shared goal of improving foster care services to children. Among the main themes of the conference were the needs to improve relations between foster parents and social workers, to promote more positive public images of foster parents, to pursue legal and tax reforms to protect foster parents, to develop and promote better foster parent training, and to improve board rates and reimbursement for other expenses.[73]

Thus, much of the NFPA program rested on the idea that foster care services to children could be improved through supporting the status of foster parents themselves. The NFPA wanted foster parents to have the right to attend court hearings involving the children in their care and for states to provide liability coverage for foster parents.[74] It hired a public relations firm, which developed a public relations kit of sample editorials, press releases, and other materials.[75] The NFPA called on foster parents to send in clippings of newspaper articles "detrimental to the foster care program" so that the NFPA could respond.[76] And it developed new recruitment materials it hoped would improve and expand the pool of foster parents. (One might imagine, though, that its recruitment poster

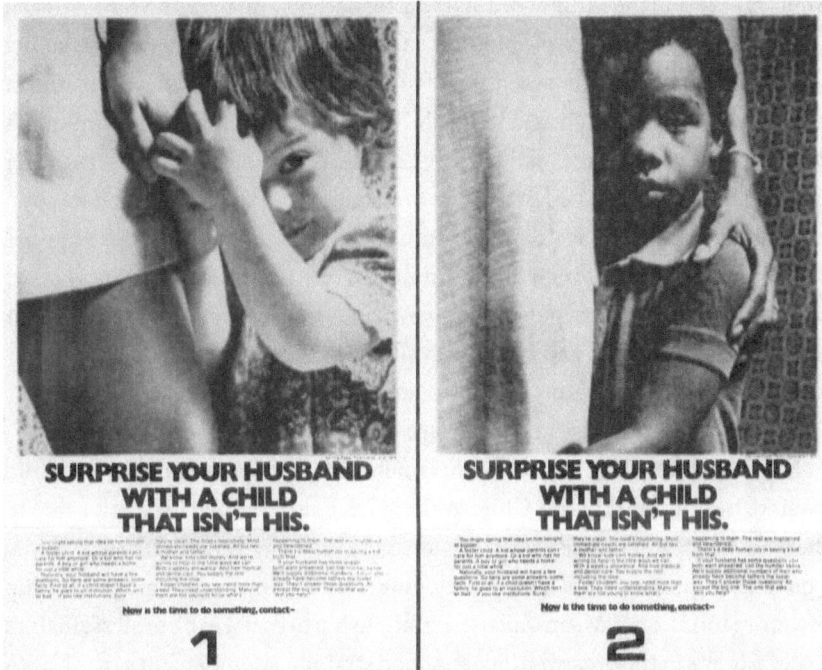

"Surprise Your Husband with a Child That Isn't His." The National Foster Parent Association in the 1970s tried novel approaches for recruiting foster parents. ("Surprise Your Husband with a Child That Isn't His," undated, ca. 1975, NFPA [5], box 62, CWLA records. Used with permission from the National Foster Parent Association.)

suggesting to women interested in foster parenting that they "surprise your husband with a child that isn't his," while witty and transgressive, might have been counterproductive).[77]

One of the NFPA's biggest achievements was in the area of training. A consistent complaint from foster parents was the lack of adequate preparation for the demands of their role.[78] The state of foster parent training was indeed dismal in the early 1970s. Despite the constant emphasis on the challenges of foster parenting and the damage suffered by those children coming into care, despite the considerable attention given to the process of *selecting* foster parents, very few foster parents were receiving any training in addressing the needs of abused and neglected children. As the NFPA put it, in many cases foster parents had become "paraprofessional and voluntary practitioners" in providing care that went "far beyond the skills of ordinary foster parents." In 1972, the NFPA began collecting resource materials for foster parents on a number of different training areas, including the foster parenting of disabled children, of adolescents, and of children who had been abused.[79] The NFPA, under a grant from the Children's Bureau, worked with the Child Welfare League to develop national curricula for training foster parents, which became available by the late 1970s.[80] Before 1973, no state mandated any foster parent training. By 1981, nineteen states required some kind of training for all foster families, while two others plus the District of Columbia made it compulsory for parents taking "special needs children." A number of other states had training available but did not yet require that parents participate. (As of 2014, all but six states — Alaska, Connecticut, Hawai'i, Pennsylvania, Tennessee, and Vermont — required preservice training.)[81]

Many of the NFPA's projects were conducted in cooperation with the Child Welfare League. In 1973, the Child Welfare League described its relationship to the NFPA as one of providing facilitation more than anything else, being "by design" only minimally involved in policy, programming organization, or leadership of the organization.[82] Meanwhile, the relationship of social work professionals to foster parents in the organization remained strained. Membership in the NFPA was open to social work professionals as well as foster parents. Yet, the by-laws initially denied professionals any vote, except to those who held a chairmanship of a standing committee.[83] There were contentious confrontations at the early foster parent conferences over this issue, revealing deep distrust between these two groups. And the NFPA board continued to complain that too many agencies were sending social workers as delegates to the NFPA conference rather than foster parents.[84]

Of the 926 foster parents who attended the second NFPA conference, around a third were foster fathers.[85] Although data is not available on race, photographs from some of the early conferences indicate a largely — thought not exclusively — white group. Many foster parents participated as couples, and foster fathers — overlooked for so long — took on a number of important leadership roles. Indeed, men appear to have been overrepresented in leadership positions and seem to have been especially assertive in those positions. An early NFPA brochure even featured a man holding hands with a young boy on its cover, a complete break with long-standing assumptions that the most important foster parent was the mother.[86] Thus, foster parents formed a national organization,

Foster fathers. This 1970s pamphlet from the National Foster Parent Association was noteworthy for its depiction of a foster father. Fathers had long been only minor characters in foster parent recruitment and casework. (*National Foster Parent Association* [brochure], undated, National Foster Parent Association [3], box 62, CWLA records. Used with permission from the National Foster Parent Association.)

but it was one dominated by foster fathers and social workers. Meanwhile, foster mothers (and women of color) remained somewhat on the sidelines.

In 1969, the Child Welfare League's executive director, Joseph Reid, addressed a gathering of foster parents. His description of those who cared for the nation's foster children was not sentimental. "Foster parents, generally speaking[,] are not the high status people," he pointed out. "They are not the bankers of the community, they are not the well paid lawyers, they are not the businessmen who head corporations. They tend to belong to the middle or lower middle class and hold jobs that are usually modest in pay. They are not people, in other words, who individually have a lot of power in the community."[87] Reid might also have mentioned — although he did not — that the people providing foster care were overwhelmingly women and that more and more of them were non-white. These indeed were not the "high status people." Yet they played an essential role in the American welfare state, providing care in private homes —

as both "parents" and as "workers"—for the nation's dependent and neglected children.

By the mid-1970s, foster parents—who had often been ignored or condescended to by child welfare professionals—were acting to shape their role and to define their legal rights. Through the courts they challenged agency definitions of family, asserting that the emotional ties between themselves and foster children should have legal standing. While individual foster families won some of these cases, the Supreme Court would rule in 1977 that foster "families" were not families before the law. In the case known as *Smith v. OFFER*, the Court reversed a lower court decision stating that foster parents were entitled to a hearing before a foster child was removed from their home. In its reversal, the Supreme Court noted that foster parents and children undoubtedly had emotional attachments and could not be dismissed as a "mere collection of unrelated individuals." Yet the fact that the foster family was defined by "state law and contractual arrangements" meant that they were not true families with a "liberty interest" protecting them from government interference under the Fourteenth Amendment.[88]

Through foster parent organizations and the drive for professionalization, foster parents insisted that they too had expertise in the field of child welfare that should be developed and respected. Despite the efforts to professionalize foster parenting in the 1960s, despite all of the arguments in favor of paying foster parents higher board rates or even a service fee, by the early 1970s rates were still inadequate. Rates remained lower for public agencies, which were the agencies that were now serving the majority of all foster children, as well as the majority of black children in particular. According to one league researcher, it was especially disturbing that agencies seemed unconcerned about the impact that low rates would have on the ability to attract quality foster parents, even though it was widely recognized by those in the field that that board rates did not cover the full costs of caring for foster children.[89] This was an old refrain. Agencies lacked resources to compensate foster parents adequately. But they also continued to struggle with the very notion of paying for parenting. This reluctance left foster families literally subsidizing the care of the nation's dependent children.

CHAPTER 7

POVERTY, PUNISHMENT, AND PUBLIC ASSISTANCE

Reorienting Foster Family Care

Child welfare experts prescribed a largely untenable role for foster parents. In the 1960s and 1970s, foster parents increasingly pushed back. Meanwhile, other features of the midcentury conception of foster care were unraveling as well. The tenuous vision of therapeutic child welfare — one that was paid for by the public but provided by individual families — would be further challenged in the 1960s as the state role became stronger and more coercive. Foster care could not become the welcomed service envisioned by professionals as long as adequate resources were not forthcoming. In the 1960s, federal money would finally be made available for foster care. Yet federal funding came in ways that made the system more punitive and coercive. Although child welfare professionals were able to predict some of the negative consequences that followed, they were blindsided by others. Child welfare experts worked within a policy landscape during the sixties that would end up codifying unsatisfactory answers to the complex problems that had always been at the heart of foster care.

Foster care from the beginning had been linked in the public mind to assistance for the poor. This association dated back to efforts to find new homes for urban street children in the mid- to late nineteenth century. In the midtwentieth century, as foster care programs received more public funds, lay people at times referred to foster children as "government" or "welfare" children. But that was not what foster care's architects envisioned. Modern foster care was not supposed to be a welfare program for impoverished children. In the 1930s, child welfare reformers had looked forward to something more holistic, optimistically predicting that New Deal family security programs would so drastically reduce poverty among families that foster care would find its place as one of a number of individualized "other child welfare services" used temporarily — and sought willingly — by families dealing with problems not necessarily linked to poverty, such as marital problems or disability. By the late 1950s, once researchers began studying foster care more systematically, it became clear that important parts of this vision simply had not materialized. And over the next decade, as reformers and their congressional allies attempted to increase the nation's commitment to dependent children and improve foster care services, changes to federal law would make foster care more punitive and even more clearly a program for poor children, shoring up its association with "welfare" and — not incidentally — with children of color.

The profession's perspective on foster care would be utterly upended by the 1959 publication of a 462-page book titled *Children in Need of Parents*, which thoroughly and systematically exposed many of the depressing realities of American foster care. As early as the war years, some individual states such as Arizona had conducted studies of their foster care populations, but *Children in Need of Parents* was the first such study executed on a large scale.[1] Its genesis lay with the Child Welfare League's Zelma "Buzz" Felten. Felten had joined the Child Welfare League in 1955 as an adoption specialist. Motivated by a desire to find adoptive homes for more children, Felten proposed in early 1957 a systematic examination of foster care in one city, New Haven, Connecticut.[2] This pilot project led the league to embark on a larger study, which was directed by Henry S. Maas, associate professor of social work at Berkeley, and sociologist Richard E. Engler. Maas and Engler are typically listed as the main authors of *Children in Need of Parents*, but the associate director of the study was Felten, who coordinated the work of a staff of researchers, including social workers in the field and sociologists.[3] The study examined nine U.S. communities, seeking balance between regions and between rural and urban areas. Thus the study highlighted the "widespread variation" in how communities understood the problems facing dependent children and the types of services communities provided.[4] Before the release of this study, foster care had occupied a peripheral place among the concerns of child welfare professionals. The journals of the U.S. Children's Bureau and the Child Welfare League between the late 1930s and the late 1960s show only occasional discussion of foster care before 1959.[5] *Children in Need of Parents* would be a powerful wake-up call.

The study exploded important myths about modern foster care. Two of these myths in particular stand out — that foster care was temporary and that it was not a poverty program. In the 1950s, social workers had understood foster care to be one part of a total treatment program but not "an end in itself."[6] This "temporary" nature was part of what so starkly separated modern foster care from adoption in this era. Unlike Charles Loring Brace's "placing out," which had been akin to informal adoption, foster placements were not intended to be permanent. A stay in foster care would be a mere interlude, during which children could enjoy the therapeutic benefits of family life in a foster home while their parents received rehabilitative services geared toward their children's eventual return home. In other words, modern foster care would not mean the permanent rupture of families that had occurred in the nineteenth century.

Children in Need of Parents destroyed that myth. The study found that, in fact, around 250,000 children were lingering in foster care or institutions for years at a time, neither with hope of returning to their biological families nor with prospects of being adopted. Most experienced multiple placements.[7] Indeed, one researcher involved in the project would suggest that the idea of foster care as temporary was nothing but "wishful thinking."[8] The broader array of services to parents that child welfare advocates had foreseen as helping reunify families simply failed to materialize in a climate in which money for child welfare services was so limited. For most foster children, Maas and Engler emphasized, "the foster care experience will stretch across months, even years, of a crucial period in their lives."[9] The study's authors labeled this problem "foster care drift." It is astonishing that professionals needed Maas and Engler to alert them to this problem, which surely was apparent to anyone working on the ground. That this discovery of foster care drift proved so explosive offers a powerful example of how the realities of foster care often bore little relation to the ideals of its theoreticians.

The spotlight on foster care drift remains perhaps the best-known result of the Maas and Engler study. More than fifty years after its publication, *Children in Need of Parents* is still heralded for having "illuminated the plight of children who drifted aimlessly in foster care without a case plan for their permanent care" and for having focused public attention on the need to find permanent homes for children in foster care, often through adoption.[10] Out of this concern about foster care drift developed the "permanency movement" of the 1970s, which included large-scale efforts to find adoptive homes for children considered "hard-to-place" (later known as "special needs").

Less well remembered was the way *Children in Need of Parents* undermined stubbornly persistent assumptions about the success of the social safety net in keeping children out of foster care. Zelma Felten highlighted the reasons why this finding was especially troubling. "We have said for many years," she wrote in 1960, that "children are no longer placed because of economic need because we now have the social insurances, good public assistance programs, and so on." While most children were indeed placed because of "neglect or abandonment by their parents," *Children in Need of Parents* reached the sobering conclusion that one-fourth of children were placed in foster care initially "for reasons which should not require placement," that is, death, illness, and/or economic hardship. Furthermore, the communities with the highest percentages of children placed for such reasons were also "at the bottom in ranking of the amount of their public assistance grants."[11]

New Deal family security and public assistance programs should have helped these families, yet many parents did not qualify for such programs because they worked in fields exempted from survivor's insurance or unemployment insurance. Furthermore, the more meager Aid to Dependent Children was intended only for single-parent families, was only rarely used to support single fathers, and allowed states to systematically exclude large groups of families because the mothers who headed them were deemed morally wanting. Even for those who qualified for ADC, the very low levels of support led to charges that inadequate ADC was to blame for children coming into foster care who "otherwise would not need to."[12] The data from *Children in Need of Parents* showed that the communities in the study with the highest percentage of children placed for reasons Felten considered preventable were in southern communities "where the level of public assistance grants is extremely low."[13]

Because New Deal family security programs — for all the help they did provide — failed to reach all Americans, foster care continued to be an essential service for agencies trying to assist poor children. It remained an underdeveloped service, however. In 1960 Mildred Arnold, the Children's Bureau's director of Child Welfare Services, complained that in too many instances, public child welfare programs as a whole were still "poorly financed," especially in rural areas.[14] The Children's Bureau was supposed to help. During the decade, the amount of federal grant money flowing to the states "grew astronomically."[15] And indeed, the Children's Bureau was now administering $46 million in federal grants-in-aid, assisting states in launching new programs and in revamping existing ones. Yet, it did this with a skeletal staff of individuals who did not always have the specialized training most relevant to their duties. Seven of the bureau's nine regions in 1960 had only one child welfare representative who was supposed to oversee child welfare services across an entire region of four to eight states.[16]

The child welfare infrastructure problems went well beyond the staffing needs of the Children's Bureau. By the end of the 1950s, only half of all counties in the United States had even one caseworker assigned full-time to child welfare.[17] More than half of child welfare workers had no professional training at all.[18] And there were "practically no protective agencies outside of the major cities."[19] Inadequate financing meant not enough workers, too many staff without appropriate skills, high turnover, and limited preventive services. And it also meant "low board rates for children in foster care," a factor, as we have seen, that made it challenging to recruit the kind of foster parents who met the profession's own high standards.[20]

Many in the field had for years bemoaned the lack of federal money available to pay the costs of child placement or delivery of other services such as homemaker and mental health services. According to the original 1935 Social Security Act, its child welfare funds could be used only for expanding child welfare infrastructure and providing training. The ban on using Title V, part 3, funds for board payments was due in large part to the public/private mix of boarding-out services. The original architects of Title V had been reluctant to allow federal money to go to private and sectarian agencies that arranged so many placements. By 1965, though, 78 percent of children in foster family care were under the care of publicly funded agencies.[21] And already by the mid-1940s, advocates began proposing various revisions to the Social Security Act to make federal money available to pay more directly for foster care.[22]

When Congress finally did authorize federal dollars for board payments, however, it would not be through child welfare funds but through the public assistance stream. Specifically, the federal money that became available in the 1960s for foster care (as part of a broader Social Security reform package) would be linked to a child's eligibility for ADC (renamed Aid to Families with Dependent Children, or AFDC, in 1962). Supporters of what was called AFDC–Foster Care touted this reform as one that would right a wrong by allowing federal funds to assist children in need of out-of-home placement.

Yet staff at the Children's Bureau and the Child Welfare League were wary of AFDC–Foster Care. To understand their concerns, we need to look more closely at the uneasy relationship between public assistance and child welfare. This distinction was of great importance to child welfare professionals who had long argued that foster care was not a poverty program but a service (one among a theoretical many) to promote the well-being of all children. As Katharine Lenroot had put it, attempts to integrate child welfare services and public assistance programs had "presented many problems because of differences in concept, function, and method."[23] The Children's Bureau had from its earliest years advocated for a "whole child" approach to government programs addressing the needs of children, believing, for example, that children's health services, protective services, and services to dependent children should all be overseen by one department staffed by people with special training in the unique needs of children and a mandate to advocate for them. At the federal level, that department would be the Children's Bureau; at the state level, public children's services departments would meet the need. Critics resisted the Children's Bureau's insistence on this point, and in 1935 the newly created ADC program was placed outside the bureau's jurisdiction. The Social Security Act created other new federal programs for children, though, such as child welfare services and maternal and infant health, which were given oversight by the Children's Bureau.

The bureau and its allies believed that services to children should involve carefully administered, individualized casework and child placement training. State public assistance departments, which administered the federal ADC program, did not have staff with specialized training and did not necessarily use child welfare methodology. Thus child welfare experts feared from the beginning that the development of AFDC–Foster Care had the potential to undermine many of their chief goals for child welfare services and to narrow their scope.

Why did child welfare professionals invest so much in this distinction? To understand, we need to be mindful not only of their commitment to the belief that children's needs were best addressed separately and holistically but also of the marginalized status within the federal government of the Children's Bureau — an agency whose staff was made up of mostly women, who one former director recalled were treated like a "huge corps of clerical workers" despite their training in diverse fields. Some critics found it inefficient and redundant for the Children's Bureau to be responsible for all federal programs pertaining to children, separate from other social services. They argued that it made more sense to have a single federal agency responsible for overseeing all social welfare programs. And in fact, efforts to reorganize the Children's Bureau and reassign some of its functions had begun already in the 1930s; by 1946, a "bureaucratic reshuffle" put an end to the bureau as a "largely self-governing federal enclave for children's interests," limiting its authority to "research and reporting functions."[24] Was the creation of AFDC–Foster Care possibly another sign of the bureau's deteriorating influence?

The creation of AFDC–Foster Care was part of an effort to reform ADC. The program had been designed to provide single mothers with assistance to enable them to care for their children in their own homes. Its funds were issued to mothers on behalf of their children, and thus mothers were scrutinized as to whether or not they (and as a result their children) were deserving of assistance. ADC, although a federal program, allowed states to pass individual criteria for eligibility that continued to prevent many poor children from receiving assistance because local administrators considered their mothers to be unworthy. In the 1940s and 1950s, several southern and southwestern states passed laws restricting ADC eligibility to homes considered "suitable."[25] This was a major means by which black women were kept from qualifying for ADC.

These suitable-home provisions came under scrutiny in the late fifties and early sixties. In 1960, Louisiana passed a particularly draconian measure that denied ADC benefits to children born out of wedlock. The law quickly became notorious as it led to twenty-three thousand children being removed from the ADC caseload within a matter of months. Some 80 to 90 percent of the households affected were headed by African American women.[26] Child welfare advocates assailed restrictions like Louisiana's because children were being deprived of public assistance through no fault of their own. Arthur Flemming, President Eisenhower's secretary of the Department of Health, Education, and Welfare, which oversaw ADC, held hearings on the Louisiana law. Civil liberties, civil rights, and child welfare advocates testified in opposition to the Louisiana policy. In the end, Flemming ruled in late 1960 that states could not remove children from ADC eligibility because a home was not "suitable" unless states provided services intended to improve the home or provided for the child *in some other way*.[27] Foster care would be one means of supplying such other provision. The so-called Flemming rule allowed more children of color to receive welfare support, but by separating the interests of children from those of their parents, critics have argued, it also "diminished the focus on supporting the family."[28] The implementation of AFDC–Foster Care was one way that occurred.

As Flemming was throwing out suitable home provisions, Congress was considering a number of modifications to the Social Security Act that would include changes to both ADC *and* foster care funding. The Public Assistance Amendments reflected recommendations made by experts on both public assistance and child welfare who sat on two separate advisory councils created by Congress in 1958.[29] Each advisory council explored ideas that would later be reflected in AFDC–Foster Care. The Advisory Council on Child Welfare Services tried to clarify in its first report in 1959 what the often invoked but rarely defined "child welfare services" actually entailed. Child welfare services, it concluded, were services that "supplement, or substitute for, parental care and supervision" in order to ensure that children were not neglected, exploited, or abused. When needed, child welfare services included providing "adequate care for children and youth away from their own homes." The twelve-member advisory council was made up mostly of representatives of public and private welfare organizations. It included the Child Welfare League's executive director Joseph Reid and received staff support from the Children's Bureau. The council's report, reflecting members' commitment to distinguishing child welfare from public assistance, insisted that it was imperative that such services be available to address "any social problem" affecting child welfare, not just poverty.[30]

The Advisory Council on Child Welfare Services identified funding (both the amount and the restrictions placed on it) as a critical problem — namely that Title V funds could be used only to stimulate the development of child welfare services, not for delivery of the services themselves. The advisory council wanted the federal role extended, recommending that federal money be made available through open-ended matching grants to pay part of the costs of public child welfare programs, including money for "broad social welfare services" as well as to help "bear the heavy cost" of care outside the children's own home.[31] In other words, the council advocated allocating federal money to help states cover the cost of finally implementing a broader conception of child welfare services, including — though not limited to — board payments sufficient to help ensure high-quality out-of-home care.

The Advisory Council on Child Welfare Services contrasted the limitations placed on federal support for foster care with what was available to other children under ADC. ADC funds, unlike child welfare funds, went directly to support children in their homes. By not paying anything to help board foster children, the council concluded, the federal government was actually discriminating against those dependent and neglected children unable to live with their parents.[32] Meanwhile, the Advisory Council on Public Assistance was recommending that the Social Security Act be amended to allow public assistance to cover more needy people. Of particular relevance, it noted that ADC at present explicitly excluded from support children living with two able-bodied parents and children in foster homes.[33]

Revisions to the Social Security Act in the early 1960s would address these concerns that foster children were not currently receiving federal support (although the child welfare council's endorsement of open-ended matching grants to the states for child welfare services was not to be). The revisions were part of a welfare reform package intended to better serve needy families. Under the revisions, it was hoped that more children could receive protection, families could be rehabilitated, and children could be quickly returned to a better environment. One measure, initially passed in 1961, allowed states to temporarily grant AFDC to children in two-parent families whose need was due to the father's unemployment (AFDC–Unemployed Parent). This change would enable poor families who had not previously been eligible to qualify for support. AFDC–Unemployed Parent was adopted by fewer than half the states, but it was innovative in its acceptance that there "could be such a thing as a deserving, able-bodied male."[34]

The Public Assistance Amendments of 1962 notably shifted AFDC to a new emphasis on moving single mothers into the workforce.[35] It also created AFDC–Foster Care. AFDC–Foster Care allowed federal funds for the first time to be spent directly on foster care for some children. Under the 1962 amendments, certain foster children who had been receiving AFDC when they were still living in their own home could now have part of the costs of their foster care paid out of Title IV AFDC funds. One advantage of AFDC–Foster Care was that it at last provided federal money that could go directly to support board payments for foster children. The hope was that abused and neglected children living in poor families could be removed to qualified foster homes, the parents would receive services aimed at rehabilitation, and children would quickly be returned home to improved circumstances.

Child welfare professionals at the Children's Bureau and the Child Welfare

League, who had been clamoring for years for federal money for foster care, had deep reservations about AFDC–Foster Care. Some of their opposition centered on fears that the Children's Bureau would lose even more authority and responsibilities to the Bureau of Public Assistance. And indeed, the leadership at the Department of Health, Education, and Welfare had unsuccessfully sought to reorganize the Children's Bureau as part of an effort to modernize the delivery of social services. These critics found the Children's Bureau's approach old-fashioned and the separate emphasis on children's services to be inefficient. The Children's Bureau, the Child Welfare League, and their allies, on the other hand, understood child placement to be a precise and subtle practice that required "skilled casework services," unique to their own field, which was necessary to prevent children from being "permanently damaged emotionally."[36] Part of their resistance to AFDC–Foster Care certainly reflected fears that the program was intended to undermine the Children's Bureau by administratively combining child welfare programs with public assistance programs.[37] Yet officials at the Children's Bureau and Child Welfare League were also troubled by issues that went beyond the territorial and that spoke directly to their ideal of holistic child welfare services — their notion of foster care as only "one tool among many."[38]

The Children's Bureau, complaining that the public persisted in understanding boarding home care as a service exclusively for the "economically underprivileged," continued to promote a vision of foster care and other child welfare services as ideally available to all children who might need them regardless of "economic status."[39] So did the staff of the Child Welfare League, which took on a greater advocacy role in the sixties in relation to other welfare programs like AFDC and whose executive director, Joseph Reid, expressed serious doubts about tying child welfare funding to public assistance grants.[40] Although they did not say so openly, these advocates surely also recognized that foster care's public image might fare better if child welfare agencies could, as Duncan Lindsey suggests, separate themselves in the public mind from increasingly "unpopular poverty programs."[41] Indeed, such an association between publicly funded childcare and welfare does seem to have worked to stigmatize proposals for universal day care around the same time. In the 1960s, the Child Welfare League was at last coming to see the role that day care could play in preventing child placement. Reid would testify before Congress in 1962 that "day care is one of the least developed and most necessary child welfare services," noting that due to "lack of day care, children are frequently placed in 24-hour foster care at much greater expense to the community."[42] When federal money did became available for child care in the 1960s (for the first time since the World War II Lanham Act), those funds were limited to poor and low-income families, cementing a link between public child care and poverty, as Sonya Michel argues, that "precluded the possibility of developing a universal system."[43]

Being so adamant about distinguishing child welfare services from public assistance, child welfare professionals were decidedly uneasy about AFDC–Foster Care. They worried not because some number of additional children would now receive foster care through AFDC funds. The fear was that foster care services would end up being substantially rearranged and reoriented in order to access that funding—reoriented in ways that would be anathema to the philosophy of the child welfare profession. And indeed, some of their concerns were borne out by a number of the practical issues raised by implementing AFDC–Foster Care. Early reports from the field suggested that too often the plan for a particular child was being determined more by the practical circumstances resulting from separate and different funding streams than from what was in the best interests of that child. Right away some states were reporting a tendency to have child welfare workers devote almost all of their time to AFDC–Foster Care cases, which made it difficult to also carry a regular child welfare caseload.[44] In the late 1960s, federal matching for AFDC could be as high as 85 percent, whereas matching for child welfare services averaged only about 10 percent and could not cover board. Therefore the "pressure [was] great" on states to provide foster care through the AFDC program.[45]

Modifications to the program only accelerated this shift to AFDC funding of foster care. At the time of its passage, AFDC–Foster Care was intended to serve only a very small number of children, with the bulk of foster care caseloads still supported by state funds. By June 1965, only twenty-three states had elected to make use of AFDC–Foster Care (serving a total of 5,779 children).[46] In 1967, eligibility for the program was expanded to include not just children currently receiving AFDC but also children who were AFDC-eligible.[47] The Child Welfare League continued to oppose "any administration of such foster care funds through AFDC channels."[48] But in 1969, state participation in AFDC–Foster Care was made mandatory. By 1972, 79,527 children, or one-quarter of all children in publicly funded foster care, were now covered through the AFDC–Foster Care program. In at least one state, 62 percent of all children in foster care were supported by AFDC–Foster Care.[49]

In other words, foster care had become, as critics had feared, increasingly linked to public assistance — in terms of funding, implementation, and public perception. These links would limit the scope and spirit of foster family care. Part of the problem was rooted in the unintended effects of one of the successful efforts to improve the original program. Some child welfare advocates had worried initially that AFDC–Foster Care might be used punitively. With the Flemming rule in place, it was now a violation of policy to deny AFDC to a child because the state did not like the behavior of his mother. But under AFDC–Foster Care, the state could remove the child from the home for the same kinds of reasons, place him in a foster home, and help pay the costs with AFDC funds. In foster care, the child was technically still receiving the funds, but the "unsuitable" mother could be sidestepped. Thus those who worried that AFDC–Foster Care might be used punitively against single mothers had pushed for what they considered a safeguard — a requirement that in order for a child to receive AFDC–Foster Care, a judge would first have to determine that conditions in the child's own home were actually harmful due to a parent's "immoral or negligent" behavior.[50] This clause was intended to ensure that rogue caseworkers would not remove children from their homes simply to punish poor mothers for applying for AFDC in the first place.

This safeguard, though, had the potential to undermine something else held dear by child welfare professionals — the tradition of voluntarism. The voluntary nature of foster placements was essential to the conception of foster care as a therapeutic service. A belief that families voluntarily sought foster care services had been a large part of the vision that had inspired professionals at midcentury. Voluntarism was what made foster care benign. It helped families stay together instead of tearing them apart. Foster care did not really become a "system" until it came to emphasize the element of coercion, which occurred with the decline of voluntary placement.

Child welfare professionals in the early sixties still championed foster care as a service for parents who needed temporary help caring for their children but who had not been accused by the state of neglecting or harming them.[51] In other words, child welfare services were different from child protective services, although both could result in out-of-home placement. Referrals to protective services "ordinarily [came] from someone other than the parent" (or from a noncustodial parent) in the form of a report of suspected neglect or abuse.[52] Local jurisdictions also had various provisions allowing removal of children due to morals concerns, including cases where children were exposed to alcohol, to pool halls, or to persons known to be fornicating.[53] Child welfare services, on the other hand, were requested by families themselves.

Maas and Engler had found that even by the late 1950s, more than half of foster children in the communities they studied were in care because their mothers or fathers had gone to child welfare agencies and *voluntarily* asked that their children be placed. In the largest city studied, that figure was 66 percent.[54] Yet the lines between protective services and other child welfare services, if they had ever been as stark as some maintained, were certainly quite fuzzy by the 1950s. More and more often, agencies were taking the initiative with families even before (or whether) help was requested. As Annie Sandusky put it, "We are trying to make a distinction between casework services in relation to the problem of neglect of children and casework services to children in relation to other problems, and the distinction *does not exist*."[55] There was also a racial dynamic at play. Black families were much less likely than white families to request voluntary services, suggesting that "the voluntary agency [was] still regarded by the [black] community at large and the [black] client in need of services as providing service primarily for the white child."[56]

"Voluntary" placements could at times be quite coercive, as parents who turned to agencies for help were sometimes steered to placement even if they were looking for some other kind of support. It was difficult for parents to keep control of their relationship with social workers, and thus they did not always get the particular assistance they sought even when they initiated contact themselves.[57] But the "voluntary" nature of placements nonetheless set the tone for a more productive working relationship with agencies than did involuntary child removal. Child welfare experts thought highly of voluntary placement, because they believed that when children were placed voluntarily, their parents were more likely to stay involved with their children and more inclined to develop a working relationship (rather than an adversarial one) with the agency.[58] Under voluntary placements, parents at least theoretically had the right to have their child returned upon request. When children were placed voluntarily, they were more likely to return home or be relinquished for adoption than if they were committed by the court. Indeed, court removal of a child from her family tended to be associated with that child remaining in care.[59]

It was also the case under voluntary placements that parents were expected to pay something toward the cost of board, although they often struggled to do so. When families could not or did not pay, agencies still had to compensate the foster families with whom they contracted. Children in protective custody, however, were often eligible for public funding. The 1959 foster care *Standards* stated that it was not acceptable to terminate or limit parental rights "solely for the purpose of receiving public funds for support of the child, or for the convenience of the agency."[60] Yet clearly this practice occurred. In some states it was possible to use public funds for child placement only if the child were placed under jurisdiction of the court. This varied from state to state, with some states, such as Missouri, placing the majority of foster children through juvenile court commitment.[61] Thus in the 1950s, despite the continued preference among professionals for voluntary placement, many states were already requiring court commitment to use funds for foster care. Child welfare professionals described such policies, though, as "a destructive approach in trying to help the family work out their problems," not one to be emulated at the federal level.[62] Yet this is precisely what AFDC–Foster Care would do, requiring a finding of neglect by a court in order for federal funds to be used.

Under AFDC–Foster Care, states could not avail themselves of AFDC resources to pay the board of children who entered foster care under voluntary plans or who were not AFDC-eligible. Thus AFDC–Foster Care seemed to create a disturbing incentive to shift the focus of foster care services away from voluntary placements by a range of different kinds of families to children under court commitment whose families were eligible for AFDC (and thereby poor and female-headed). The financial stakes in shifting away from voluntary placements were significant; already in 1965, some child welfare professionals noticed that an effect of the 1962 amendments was to transfer "professional personnel from child welfare services to public assistance simply because federal matching was available."[63]

The court commitment provision had been intended as a protection for families. And yet professionals would discover that in practice the provision meant foster care would now be used punitively against particular AFDC mothers who local agencies believed fell short of local standards of propriety "without regard to the interests of the child."⁶⁴ There were reports that agencies in some states were threatening families applying for AFDC—particularly those headed by women whose children had been born out of wedlock who were only recently eligible under the Flemming rule—that if they did apply, the public agency would scrutinize their child-rearing practices and possibly remove their children if those practices were not satisfactory. Elizabeth Wickenden, a New Dealer now working with the Department of Health, Education, and Welfare, was told by a woman from the local welfare rights group in West Virginia of a nineteen-year-old white mother of a toddler and a three-month-old who was still nursing. The mother was reportedly told by her caseworker that "if she did not go to work cleaning the restrooms in the court house her assistance would be discontinued and her children placed in foster homes." Wickenden explained to her informant that only the court (and not the caseworker) had the power to remove children from the care of their parents. Although this was but one anecdote, Wickenden saw it as "an excellent example" of the way new policy had "open[ed] the door to intimidation and discriminatory actions ... by individual workers."⁶⁵ Furthermore, this shift occurred at precisely the moment when increasing numbers of black women were becoming eligible for AFDC.

Ten years after the creation of AFDC–Foster Care, in the early 1970s, Winford Oliphant, who was the director of New York State's Department of Social Welfare, began investigating the impact of AFDC–Foster Care, first in Minnesota and then more broadly. Working under the auspices of the Child Welfare League and with a grant from the Field Foundation, he found that the judicial determination clause had indeed led to the undesirable effects many had feared. Since other monies for foster care were not increasing, there was an incentive at the local level to move dependent children into AFDC–Foster Care. This meant that even in cases in which parents were not neglecting their children but were turning to agencies for help, agencies were frequently going to court to obtain a judicial determination of neglect in order to have AFDC pay for the child's foster care. In eight of the eleven states Oliphant studied, voluntary agreements with parents as the basis for providing foster care had been "curtailed." In some cases, officials simply stopped accepting children by voluntary agreement altogether. One Minneapolis agency expressed dismay at this development, insisting that a basic necessity for providing child welfare services (apart from child protective services) was the agency's "voluntary relationship" with the parent; "resort[ing] to the court disturbs the relationship with families." Agencies also reported that AFDC–Foster Care was making it harder to obtain services for children equally in need but who did not qualify for AFDC.[66]

Oliphant found further problems and collaborated with the Child Welfare League in documenting them. Supporters of AFDC–Foster Care had originally hoped the ability to remove children from AFDC homes where parenting was inadequate would allow a range of services to be offered to the family (not just foster care). Lack of such services, after all, was one factor that had contributed to foster care drift.[67] Ten years later, most states in his study reported that this hoped-for effect had not occurred. AFDC–Foster Care funds were to be used only for sharing costs of providing foster care — not for help with costs of other social services to children and parents. An additional problem, Oliphant argued, was that once children were removed from AFDC homes, mothers were no longer eligible for public assistance. Agencies reported that mothers then began moving from place to place in an effort to support themselves, and "contact with children declines." Agencies would thus often lose track of parents, and children remained in foster care.[68] In 1978, the Children's Defense Fund would denounce AFDC–Foster Care funding patterns as actually "encourag[ing] the break-up of families."[69]

In Oliphant's view, foster care was not serving children well, and recent changes associated with AFDC–Foster Care were making a troubling situation worse. Although the problems Oliphant identified applied to all foster children, it was becoming harder to ignore the fact that black children were disproportionately affected. Around the time that Oliphant was finishing his report on AFDC–Foster Care, Andrew Billingsley and Jeanne Giovannoni published their influential critique of the role that race played in the child welfare system. Titled *Children of the Storm: Black Children and American Child Welfare*, the book argued that racism had "extensive and intensive effects" on delivery of child welfare services to black children. The authors, a black sociologist and a white professor of social work, concluded that contemporary child welfare services for black children in American cities consisted "of 'rescuing' them from [so-called] inadequate parents and herding them into large, impersonal institutions or shelters until they can be placed in more adequate homes," homes that were allegedly nearly impossible to find due to what prevailing ideology assumed to be a "pervasive internal pathology" within black communities.[70]

If Oliphant was aware of Billingsley and Giovannoni's work, he did not indicate so in his report. But the child welfare profession as a whole was being rocked by these kinds of critiques. By the early seventies, in a context of increased black discontent and growing black nationalism, the politics of race and child welfare became particularly charged, making it impossible to continue overlooking black families, black children, and black social workers. The National Welfare Rights Organization, whose members were predominantly black women on public assistance, was founded in 1966 to demand welfare as a right and to insist that recipients be treated with respect.[71] In 1968, a group of African Americans broke away from the major professional social work organization to form the National Association of Black Social Workers and to orient their social service work to black liberation goals.[72] The NABSW would become well known among adoption professionals for its 1972 statement unequivocally opposing transracial adoption and foster placement, describing the practice as harmful to black children as individuals and destructive to black culture more broadly.[73] In the spring of 1969, welfare rights advocates, including members of the National Welfare Rights Organization and what one bewildered journalist referred to as "dashiki-clad" black nationalists, disrupted the National Conference on Social Work in New York. They insisted that the voices of welfare recipients be heard and that black social workers have greater representation within the organization.[74] For her part, Katharine Lenroot, now in her late seventies, was appalled to read in the paper of the "obscenities and contemptuous abuse" uttered by the demonstrators as well as by the way the conference president, Arthur Flemming, appeared to "appease" them.[75]

A few years later, indigenous activists, including social workers and former foster parents, followed suit. They formed the Association of American Indian and Alaskan Native Social Workers and denounced the negative cultural stereotypes inherent in the pro-adoption rhetoric of programs like the Indian Adoption Project.[76] Their activism helped spur a reevaluation of Indian child welfare policy, culminating in the Indian Child Welfare Act of 1978, which sought to prevent placement of indigenous children in non-indigenous communities.[77]

Black social work activists turned their sights specifically on the child welfare field as well. In 1970, at a meeting of the Child Welfare League's executive directors in Miami, one of the few black child welfare administrators in attendance interrupted the proceedings to call attention to the dearth of African Americans in management positions at league agencies and to highlight the deficiencies in the services for black children. Out of that moment was born the Black Administrators in Child Welfare, whose first meeting was held in Philadelphia in May 1971. The intent of the organization was to serve as a support network to help other African Americans move into leadership roles in the profession and to provide a forum to advocate for issues affecting minority children and families.[78]

African American critics were increasingly blunt about their views that the American child welfare system was uniquely harmful to black children. Critics complained that many children were not receiving appropriate services due to racial prejudice and that welfare programs, including foster care, were destroying black family life. Many white social work professionals were sympathetic, in keeping with the social justice orientation of their field in the sixties. Yet, the child welfare establishment as a whole was at times slow to recognize how serious these criticisms were. For members of a helping profession, it was uncomfortable to learn that those they had committed their careers to serving frequently saw them as part of the problem. And ideas about race and child welfare were changing so rapidly that it could be challenging to keep pace. As recently as the late fifties, black civil rights organizations and white racial liberals had bemoaned the lack of access to foster care for black children and had worked together — albeit in uneasy alliance — on home-finding campaigns. After extensive efforts to find adoptive homes for black children, the National Urban League had concluded that transracial adoption should be considered. By the late 1960s and early 1970s, however, the problem had been completely reconfigured. Black children were now tragically overrepresented in foster care, and even the Urban League (never a radical voice like the National Association of Black Social Workers) had backed off its support for transracial placements.[79]

In 1968, the Child Welfare League acknowledged that there were still "severe gaps in services for certain children" and stated that it was "gravely concerned" that the child welfare field was unable to help "countless children" due to racial prejudice.[80] Addressing the prejudices of white agencies was one thing. But if the child welfare system were to adequately serve black children, critics argued, it also needed to have a "Black perspective," one based on the historical experiences of black children and black communities. One group of critics agreed that the "anger of the Blacks is related to the worker's perception and interpretation of Black behavior. Many workers have a mind set which determines what happens to the family's application if the family is classified by this. It may be that workers as well as total agencies... use false standards of behavior, language, and so forth."[81] When faced with lower income black families — whose cultural practices and conception of family and kin were often not those of middle-class whites — too many social workers, critics suggested, saw neglect or family pathology because they did not understand or appreciate the strengths of black families. This disconnect was compounded by the fact that few agencies had fully integrated staffs and only a handful of African Americans nationwide served as child welfare administrators.[82] There was also a legal dimension to this problem: Title VI of the 1964 Civil Rights Act now prohibited discrimination or denial of benefits on account of race, color, or national origin in "any program or activity receiving federal financial assistance."[83] Under Title VI, all state agencies administering public assistance and child welfare services would have to demonstrate their efforts to achieve compliance.[84]

African American critics of foster care decried the potential destruction of black families implied by the overrepresentation of black children in foster care. They insisted that updated standards needed to strongly promote practices intended to protect the rights of biological parents and emphasize reunification with birth families as the main goal of foster care. They had other suggestions, as well. Once placed in foster care, an African American child deserved to have caseworkers who could recognize that his family was "more encompassing than the biological family."[85] Foster children needed to have their dress, hair, and food preferences accepted as well as "figures and manners of speech which are peculiar to the Black child." Others noted that agencies should be doing everything from offering specific health information about sickle-cell anemia to confronting the special challenges in the "development of the identity of the Black child." The field needed a change in perspective. Such shifts could not happen without more African Americans working at all levels of the profession. Agency administrators, board members, and caseworkers needed to be able to communicate and work with black children and their families. Currently, the overwhelming majority of those positions were filled by whites. To secure more black child welfare workers, agencies would need to be willing, when hiring, to give as much weight to an "ability to communicate and work effectively with black children and their families" as they gave to the academic qualifications that served as gatekeepers in the field.[86]

The Child Welfare League did respond to many of these criticisms, revising its *Standards,* pushing for nondiscriminatory practices, and passing resolutions requiring that member agencies demonstrate a commitment to nondiscrimination (as now required by Title VI).[87] And the league also became increasingly involved in lobbying, trying — mostly unsuccessfully — to persuade Congress to enact social welfare reforms it believed would better support families in general (such as a guaranteed income) and trying to prevent the further erosion of child welfare services.[88] But these were not the directions that child welfare was headed.

In 1909, the White House Conference on the Care of Dependent Children had famously established the principle that no child should be separated from his or her family for reasons of poverty alone. Yet by 1970, Child Welfare League researcher Bernice Boehm concluded that the "thread of poverty, nonetheless, is woven throughout the foster care system."[89] Foster care in coming decades would drift even further from its idealized place as part of a full range of child welfare services available to any child in order to keep families intact. It would become instead an "auxiliary arm of public assistance" provided to children for whom, many would conclude, the best hope lay in permanently severing ties to their birth families.[90]

Foster care caseloads would come to be disproportionately made up of children of color. Like other welfare programs, as foster care became more accessible to African Americans, it also became more punitive and more disparaged. Its link to increasingly beleaguered and unpopular public assistance programs, together with a new emphasis on the role of child protective services, propelled foster care in directions that early twentieth-century reformers would have found difficult to imagine. Reformers in the 1930s had been optimistic that the Social Security Act and other New Deal measures would so drastically reduce poverty among families that foster care would find its place as one of a number of "other child welfare services," used temporarily to aid a family in dealing with problems other than poverty. By the end of the 1960s, that vision — always an unworkable one — had completely broken down.

CONCLUSION

"Foster family care" was meant to evoke a nurturing alternative to orphanages, in which children unfortunate enough to need to spend a temporary period away from their own parents would be provided love and care in a normal family setting. Anthropologist Judith Modell is blunt in her assessment of how that meaning of fostering has changed: "The roots of the word in nurture and in sustenance are missing for the participants in the process. Children who are fostered are not seen to be blessed with a generous and nurturing environment. Instead, 'foster' evokes provisional maintenance, detrimental to the child."[1]

The midcentury vision of foster care promoted by child welfare experts was a flawed one. It was more idealized than reality-based. It contained tensions that were destabilizing, such as the impossibly ambiguous foster parent role and the presentation of children as simultaneously innocent and deeply damaged. It was a vision dependent on social workers having all the answers and on policy makers, birth parents, and foster parents (not to mention children) accepting, endorsing, and facilitating those solutions. It was a vision whose parameters were shaped by assumptions increasingly out-of-step with a changing society, a vision that was hostile toward unmarried mothers; that was stubbornly resistant to accommodating working mothers; that dragged its heels on embracing day care as a service that could help families stay together; and that waited too long to acknowledge the centrality of race in the child welfare system.

Still, advocates got many things right, including their eventual (if at times grudging) conclusion that it was in the best interests of children for foster parents to be better treated and better compensated and their assumption (if not always acted upon) that children's interests could not be served without attention to the needs of their birth parents. Yet on the whole, it was an unrealistic vision in a late twentieth-century environment of changing understandings of gender roles, work, and family; Americans' skepticism toward public welfare provision; and intractable racial inequality.

One of the most persistent limitations of the child welfare vision was its ambivalence about care work. The uncomfortable discussions about compensated motherhood surrounding mid-twentieth-century foster mothering are part of the history of discomfort with paid female care work more broadly, complicated further by the fact that foster mothers' remuneration came from public funds. Modell has noted that "foster parents are cheap labor; foster parents are low paid and they lack collective bargaining rights."[2] Indeed the cheapness of that labor is a large part of what makes foster care so much less expensive than institutional care. While critics of adequate board rates may have feared that foster mothers were "doing it for the money," the reality was that foster families were being allowed (or asked) to shoulder a significant part of what was supposed to be a public obligation.[3] "We actually pay a foster parent nothing for her time and skill," wrote the director of Georgia's Division for Children and Youth in 1966. "Our boarding rate doesn't completely cover expenses for the child, and her time, energy, and skill ... [are] a donation to the public, that has asked her to help it rehabilitate a damaged child."[4] A 1958 Child Welfare League pamphlet called it an "abuse of foster mothers" to not pay them adequate board.[5] A consultant to the Child Welfare League noted that there were potential foster parents "who actually cannot afford" to be foster parents, since board rates out of step with the high cost of living prevented them from "'subsidizing' agencies as many foster parents have often done."[6] As one Children's Bureau employee argued in 1960, the bureau needed to face the fact that reimbursement rates were so disconnected from the true costs of caring for children that "often the foster family is literally subsidizing the maintenance of children who are public responsibilities."[7]

This "subsidy," although it might appear accidental, was actually critical to a privately implemented form of public welfare provision such as foster care. Why would communities have relied on private citizens to subsidize public services in this way? The answer is connected to both the low wages historically paid to female care workers and to the association of foster care with the unpopular term "welfare." The suspicion that foster mothers were "doing it for the money" relates to ongoing anxieties about all people working in "caring" occupations (nursing home attendants, day care workers, elementary school teachers, home health care aids). The fear is that if care work is properly compensated it will attract the wrong kinds of people—individuals who are motivated by "self-interest" rather than by "care." There is a level of discomfort with any attachment of monetary value to the labor of caring, especially for children. Sociologists and feminist economists have demonstrated that care workers suffer from low status and low pay because of these concerns.[8] While most care workers are poorly paid relative to their skills and training, the poor pay is assumed to somehow be a safeguard to ensure that only loving, caring individuals are attracted to the job. Indeed, low-wage home caregivers themselves often reject the idea that they are "workers," seeing their labor as akin to a "calling infused with spirituality" and demonstrating commitment to their clients far beyond what is expected according to their contracts.[9]

Perhaps because the role of foster mother is so close to that of "mother," the subject of compensation has been especially troublesome. The care work performed by foster mothers has been undervalued in terms of what taxpayers and lawmakers have been historically willing to support. So, too, has the care work performed by low-income birth mothers been undervalued. These facts are related. The Social Security Act and other New Deal reforms were supposed to eliminate (or at least sharply reduce) the need for foster care, so that poverty would no longer be a reason for placement. And yet Aid to Dependent Children rates, like mothers' pensions before them, were rarely enough to adequately support a family. Although foster care had only a minor place in the Social Security Act, the foster care system would continue serving hundreds of thousands children each year. A considerable number of these children were poor (hence the common reference to foster children as "welfare children").

As a result of the unwillingness to adequately value and support the caregiving of poor, unmarried biological mothers, states instead had to rely on foster mothers, whose status, while probably higher than that of ADC recipients, remained quite low. Both Aid to Families with Dependent Children homes and foster homes were subject to ongoing supervision. In the case of both low-income women on "welfare" and foster mothers, their parenting was suspect partly because they were "paid" by taxpayers to do something that other parents did for free. As historian Ellen Herman notes, the assumption was that "true parents" were those who took "full financial responsibility for children."[10] Low ADC payments reflected concerns about female dependency; low board payments to foster mothers reflected doubts about paying for care work. Both indicated a general, and ongoing, political problem—the difficulty that advocates had in persuading legislators to commit significant funds to adequately support poor children, particularly when their caregivers were low-status women. Not coincidentally, professional child welfare workers — those who investigate complaints about child neglect and abuse and who manage placement cases — are also overwhelmingly women. Those employed in this field today earn lower salaries than employees in comparable professions.[11]

As Ethan Sribnick argues, by the 1980s the United States had neither the truly effective family security that some had hoped for nor the individualized, nurturing system of temporary foster care that midcentury child welfare professionals had advocated. The United States was left with the "worst of both worlds," Sribnick concludes, "a fragmented and under-supported system of social services for children and families without preventive programs to support families."[12] Duncan Lindsey points to another important factor altering the nature of foster care — the mandatory child abuse reporting laws that most states had passed by the 1980s. The understandable and admirable concern of child advocates for children's safety led to more control and monitoring of families receiving services. "Threat of investigation and blame," Lindsey argues, "became the central characteristics of the new system." Lindsey further observes that foster care is a system that merely responds "to the most egregious problems" that result from wider social problems, including the feminization of poverty. The major child welfare program available to too many disadvantaged children, he concludes gloomily, is "removal from their family and placement in foster care."[13] In such a climate, adoption would come to be seen as the most promising alternative for many foster children. Judith Modell puts it this way: "As long as American society maintains a restricted and often punitive welfare system, adoption becomes an alternative to offering services to drug-addicted or otherwise dysfunctional parents."[14]

In August 2005, a woman known as "wantingtobond" posted a query to a discussion board that supports adoptive mothers hoping to breastfeed their adopted infants: "Is 9 months too old [to start breastfeeding]?" she asked. "I'm ... worried about anyone finding out because I know most people would think it's weird.... I tried to get him to rest near my brea[s]t today but he wanted [no] thing to do with it. Where do I start?"[15] Wantingtobond's concerns were similar to those of adoptive mothers hoping to induce lactation in order to promote both good health and mother-infant bonding. What was somewhat surprising in this case was that wantingtobond was referring not to an adoptive child but to a foster child recently placed with her. This is noteworthy because it suggests a desire to form an intimate bond with a child in a manner that goes against the understandings of foster parenting that dominated for much of the mid-twentieth century — as *temporary* caregiving en route to a child's placement in an adoptive home or return to biological family. Wantingtobond's desire to mimic a biological relationship with her foster child through breastfeeding (although illegal in many states) is in keeping with a new configuration of foster parenting — as a path to adoption — that has emerged in recent decades.

What had happened by the beginning of the twenty-first century to so completely reconfigure the role of foster parents and foster care? In the 1960s, with foster care more deeply entwined with poverty than ever, concerns about the lack of support for poor families dovetailed with another transformation in foster care — one that emerged directly from Henry Maas and Richard Engler's findings in *Children in Need of Parents*. This resulting "permanency movement" would be part of the story of how the institutions of foster care and adoption, so radically separated in the mid-twentieth century, would again come to overlap.

In announcing that the Child Welfare League was embarking on the study that would become *Children in Need of Parents*, executive director Joseph Reid had noted that less than 3 percent of the 255,000 children in foster care or institutions were "full orphans." A large proportion of the children were "older children, or children of minority races," so were not typical of those currently being sought by potential adoptive parents. Yet Reid pointed to surveys from a few years earlier in New York and Los Angeles indicating that between 12 and 21 percent of the children in foster homes or institutions could be considered adoptable.[16] The preliminary New Haven pilot study showed that as children got older it was harder to find adoptive homes for them. Many of these children thus grew up in an "unsettling succession" of foster homes and institutions, which led to "emotional problems" that made the prospects of adoptive placement even dimmer.[17] The study found a correlation between symptoms of emotional disturbance and number of moves, which made a much bigger difference than the length of time in care. In other words, long-term care with one foster family was better than many moves. Unfortunately, 25 percent of the children in the study had moved four or more times. Some had moved as many as fourteen times.[18]

The permanency movement sought to provide all children with a family they could call their own. Proponents insisted that "the child's biological family [was] preferred for this purpose," but if return to birth families proved impossible — if the birth family could not or would not provide proper parenting — "then society should provide him with another legal family."[19] One path to permanency involved intensive family preservation efforts, which became popular in the 1970s, designed to target at-risk families and offer in-depth casework to prevent child removal. These efforts had strong supporters but also earned criticism when, in some high-profile instances, a commitment to family preservation appeared to have led to severe abuse or even death.[20] And, as law professor Elizabeth Bartholet notes, while American society "espouses family preservation as the goal, we have failed to provide the resources to really make it work."[21]

If family preservation provided one means of achieving permanency for children in foster care, adoption offered another. But this strategy involved unavoidable challenges. Who exactly would be interested in adopting children from foster care? The adoptive families of the past, whom experts had long considered to be superior to the foster parent pool, were not the most likely candidates. Traditional adopters — the "young middle-class couple just informed they are 'infertile'" — preferred healthy white infants to the children available through public adoptions who were typically older, members of racial minorities, and/or classified as "special needs." Betsy Cole, who headed the Child Welfare League's special needs adoption project(known as ARENA), estimated in 1977 that around 100,000 children needed to be adopted. More than half of these children were African American, many were older than age six, and a number were members of large sibling groups or had physical, emotional, or intellectual disabilities.[22]

In many cases, the most likely candidates to adopt foster children were those who already knew them well, loved them, and were deeply committed to them — that is, the people already serving as their foster parents. Adoption workers, though, were accustomed to finding the people serving as foster parents to be "alarmingly different and very frequently 'unacceptable.'" Thus they had to overcome grave doubts.[23]

Yet even when they learned to see foster parents as adoptive resources (at least for children who lacked other options), adoption workers encountered another complication. If parents adopted a child they were fostering, they would lose whatever board payments they were currently receiving. Because foster parents tended to have lower incomes than more traditional adoptive parents, this loss of board payment was a real barrier to securing permanent homes for special needs children.[24] Thus, child welfare professionals, having only recently overcome their skepticism of board payments to foster parents, would begin to support payment to adoptive parents as well. By the late 1970s, most states had begun subsidizing adoption, and Congress was considering a federal subsidy as well. Adoption subsidies removed one of the disincentives for the couples most likely to be willing to adopt foster children.[25] There was a "secondary benefit" to subsidized adoption, however. The costs associated with foster placements were actually rising in the 1970s, and the federal government was paying a greater share. By 1978, federal funding for AFDC–Foster Care had grown to $205 million per year. Adoption, even subsidized adoption, proved cheaper than foster care or institutional placement.[26] In 1980, Congress would pass the Adoption Assistance and Child Welfare Act. The act replaced the problematic AFDC–Foster Care with the Title IV-E Foster Care Program, which continued to provide federal money for foster care of income-eligible children but now linked the program more closely to child welfare services and provided federal money for prevention and rehabilitation services. And the new act also included federal adoption subsidies among its provisions.[27]

Subsidized adoption, then, helped overcome one obstacle to the adoption of children from foster care. Most children in care, though, were not available for adoption because their parents retained legal rights to them. Some parents of children in foster care voluntarily relinquished their children for adoption, but most did not. If an agency wanted to seek an adoptive home for children in long-term foster care, it had to take the parents to court and persuade a judge to sever the rights of the birth parents in a process known as TPR (termination of parental rights). This was a very serious action that was supposed to be taken only when it was in the best interests of the child. It was a rare practice for most of the twentieth century, and TPR court cases were often lengthy, complex, and costly. Maas and Engler found that some jurisdictions had no provision for it at all.[28] For many children, foster care meant living in "legal limbo."[29]

Such high barriers to termination reflected the courts' understanding that parents' right to their children was fundamental. This view, that every child has a right to be raised in the home of her biological parents except under extreme circumstances, was one long advanced by the child welfare profession, dating back to the 1909 White House Conference on the Care of Dependent

Children. It is a principle also echoed in the 1959 United Nations Declaration of the Rights of the Child, which states that children "shall, wherever possible, grow up in the care and under the responsibility of his parents" and that a "child of tender years shall not, save in exceptional circumstances, be separated from his mother."[30] Yet many in the profession would come to see barriers to termination not as protecting families but as hindering permanency for children. For Maas and Engler, "a situation should not be permitted to exist wherein parents may essentially abandon their children in foster care and yet retain legal control over them." They advocated terminating parental rights in any case in which it was "obvious" that the parents would never again take responsibility for their child.[31] The Child Welfare League in 1960 noted that it was trying to "untangle the outdated, often cruel, laws and lack of laws that still deprive so many children" of permanent homes and tie them instead to "parents who have[,] in effect, abandoned them."[32] Additional obstacles to permanency, then, were the legal rights of birth parents.

By the 1990s, agencies were experimenting with "fost-adopt" placements in which some foster children were placed in homes of trained foster parents who were also cleared for possible adoption (as was the case with the child in wantingtobond's home). In 1997, such programs received a major boost when Congress passed the Adoption and Safe Families Act (or ASFA). The very title of the act indicated that the pendulum had firmly swung away from family rehabilitation and reunification as paths to permanency. Congress seemed to have given up on birth families.

Together with the 1994 Multiethnic Placement Act, which banned agencies from preventing adoption of minority children by white parents, ASFA marked a radical change in essentially advocating and encouraging adoption as the best solution for children who come into care. Under ASFA, after fifteen out of twenty-two months in foster care, as long as "reasonable efforts" were being made to work with birth parents, the child welfare agency was required to file a TPR petition. States were encouraged to double the number of children adopted annually and were rewarded financially for increasing the number of foster children adopted from year to year. Although resources for family preservation services were expanded under ASFA, there were no financial incentives to states when children were reunited with birth parents.[33] Although ASFA advocated permanency planning (which could mean a number of things, including reunification), its emphasis was now on adoption via TPR.

ASFA seems to many to be a commonsense way of addressing the tragedy of foster care drift. For Harvard law professor Elizabeth Bartholet, a longtime opponent of racial matching policies and a skeptic of what she saw as an unreasonable commitment to family preservation, ASFA was a potential godsend for children stuck in the tragic limbo of foster care drift by offering them the promise of a permanent loving home.[34] Yet ASFA has been sharply criticized by, among others, legal scholar Dorothy Roberts for the ways in which it marginalizes the rights and interests of biological parents (who are usually poor and frequently non-white). Roberts finds ASFA to be draconian in its intent and racially biased in its effects. She argues that black families suffer particular harm from ASFA. A system that rewards states for finding adoptive homes for children but does not reward them for facilitating reunification is bound to harm black families, as black children are disproportionately represented in foster care. By favoring adoption, ASFA seems to assume that permanency cannot be achieved through reunification with a child's birth family. And many of the older black children who are "freed" for adoption will never find adoptive families, leaving them in a state of legal orphanhood.[35]

It is not a coincidence that ASFA was passed in the climate of the bitter battle of the 1990s over welfare reform. That battle culminated in the passage of the Personal Responsibility and Work Opportunity Act of 1996, which ended AFDC. Some at the time, including Representative Newt Gingrich (R-Ga.), were suggesting a return to orphanages as an alternative to AFDC payments to single mothers.[36] Adoption could be seen as another such alternative, returning that practice to its late nineteenth- and early twentieth-century associations with social provision and the "rescue" of poor children.

As foster parenting is increasingly seen as a path to adoption (and a far less expensive path than international or domestic private adoption), foster parenting is currently attracting more couples and individuals who are explicitly interested in adoption. This may be good for many children for whom return to birth parents is highly unlikely, but it sets up a potentially adversarial relationship between foster parents and biological parents. Foster parents are asked to simultaneously serve two roles within the child welfare system: a public one, that of "professional team member" whose job is to support reunification with biological parents, but also a private one, that of "prospective adoptive parent" whose role is to foster healthy attachments and emotional bonding. The idea that foster care can be an avenue to eventual adoption raises questions about whether these new foster parents will have a commitment to the idea of temporary foster parenting itself. The emphasis on permanency establishes foster care as the antithesis of permanency, as a problem that has to be solved.[37]

Yet temporary foster care still performs an important role within our deeply flawed child welfare system in keeping children temporarily safe until parents can get the help they need. The fost-adopt role is, in many ways, more comprehensible than the foster parenting role of the mid-twentieth century because it presents fostering as a pathway to the legal, stable, more easily understood status of permanent adoptive relationship. This role might be easier to understand, but it is not without its problems and not without its own ambiguities. And it is a role that exists because the broader social supports that midcentury child welfare advocates hoped would render foster care unnecessary have not yet materialized.

APPENDIX

The following are two examples of the kinds of contracts foster parents and agencies entered into in the postwar period.

Jewish Child Care Association

On consideration of being accepted as foster parents by the Jewish Child Care Association [hereinafter referred to as the Agency], we agree as follows:

1. The child placed with us will be accepted by us as a member of our family, and will receive our affection and care as foster parents. The Agency will furnish a monthly board payment, payable at the end of each month. At the time of placement, we will be notified of the specific rate for the child placed with us.

The Agency will provide for the child's clothing, medical and dental expenses.

We will be reimbursed for certain other expenditures made, as described in the Foster Parents' Manual, provided they have been previously authorized by the Agency.

2. We will notify the Agency of any change or plans for change in our own life, which may affect the child placed with us. This will include, but is not limited to, vacation plans, illnesses, job changes, moving, and any change in the composition of our family.

3. We will notify the Agency immediately if the child placed with us becomes ill, and we will comply with the Agency's arrangements for medical and dental care.

4. We are aware that the Agency has the responsibility for making plans with regard to the child's relationship with his or her own relatives. We will cooperate with the arrangements made by the Agency worker for visits between the child and his or her own relatives.

5. We acknowledge that we are accepting the child placed with us for an indeterminate period, depending on the needs of the child and his family situation. We are aware that the legal responsibility for the foster child remains with the Agency, and we will accept and comply with any plans the Agency makes for the child. This includes the right to determine when and how the child leaves us, and we agree to cooperate with arrangements made toward that end.

6. Should we find ourselves unable to continue giving foster care to the child placed with us, we will notify the Agency promptly, and will cooperate with the Agency in making the change of placement as easy as possible. For this reason, we will give the Agency as much time to make such change as is needed, unless our situation is emergent.

Date _____

Signature of Foster Mother _____

Signature of Foster Father _____

Countersigned:

Agency Social Worker[1] _____

State of Tennessee

Tennessee implemented contracts in 1959. The Tennessee agreements were retroactive. Workers were instructed to get all existing foster parents to sign the new contract. The two-page contract contained the following language:

We agree to consider the child as a member of the family, and to provide care and training as we would for a child in our family.

We understand that this child is not and will not be available to us for adoption, and we agree that we will not attempt to adopt, file a petition to adopt, or to take any steps whatsoever leading to the adoption of this child.

Should we desire to apply to the Department for consideration as adoptive applicants under the Department's adoption program, instead of continuing under the temporary boarding home program, we understand that this agreement in no way makes us ineligible to apply.

We agree that the Department has the right to remove this child from our home at any time.[2]

NOTES

Abbreviations Used in the Notes

CB   Children's Bureau
CWLA Child Welfare League of America
NUL   National Urban League

Introduction

1. "Each Holiday Season, an Ex-foster Child Searches for Her Siblings," *Los Angeles Times*, December 24, 2012.

2. In the United States in 2014 there were more than 415,000 children in foster care, 22 percent of whom were Hispanic, 24 percent black, and 42 percent white. U.S. Department of Health and Human Services, *AFCARS Report*.

3. For uses of the phrase "foster care industrial complex," see the website of the National Coalition for Child Protection Reform, https://nccpr.info, accessed August 15, 2016.

4. "Statistics Suggest Bleak Futures for Children Who Grow Up in Foster Care," *Amarillo (Tex.) Globe-News*, June 24, 2012.

5. Wexler, "Take the Child and Run," 137–38.

6. CWLA, "Youth after Foster Care Statistics."

7. J. Doyle, "Child Protection and Adult Crime," 747.

8. Kutz, *HHS Guidance Could Help States Improve Oversight of Psychotropic Prescriptions*, 7.

9. Fessler, "Foster Kids Face Tough Times after Age 18."

10. U.S. Government Accountability Office, *African American Children in Foster Care*.

11. Bartholet, *Nobody's Children*; Roberts, *Shattered Bonds*; Lindsey, *Welfare of Children*; Wexler, *Wounded Innocents*.

12. Carstens, "Child Welfare Services," 64.

13. As a point of contrast, by 1970 the Child Welfare League was defining foster family homes as homes that (a) were approved by an agency, (b) provided twenty-four-hour care, (c) were supervised by an agency, and (d) were reimbursed by the agency for care provided. Specifically excluded from this definition were pre-adoptive homes, homes of relatives, free homes, work and wage homes, and family group homes. Lucille J. Grow to Executives of CWLA Member Agencies, June 18, 1970, folder 3, box 19, Records of

the Child Welfare League of America, Social Welfare History Archives, Minneapolis, Minn. (hereafter CWLA records).

14. Smith, "Bring Back the Orphanages?," table 1, 110.

15. Hacsi, *Second Home*, 1; Carp, "Orphanages vs. Adoption," 126.

16. Canaday, *Straight State*, 5.

17. Balogh, *Associational State*, 8, 10–11. See also Boris and Klein, *Caring for America*, 13–14.

18. On Canada, see Strong-Boag, *Fostering Nation?*

19. For overviews of foster care systems in twenty-one countries (including brief histories), see Colton and Williams, *World of Foster Care*.

20. For works that do include sustained discussion of foster care in the twentieth century, see Hacsi, "From Indenture to Family Foster Care"; Birk, *Fostering on the Farm*; Sribnick, "Rehabilitating Child Welfare"; and Ashby, *Endangered Children*.

21. Gerstle, *Liberty and Coercion*; Balogh, *Associational State*.

22. Modell, *Sealed and Secret Kinship*, 81.

23. "Adoption triad" is a phrase commonly used within the adoption community to acknowledge the significance of child, adoptive parents, and biological parents to adoption.

24. Fraser and Gordon, "Genealogy of Dependency," 320–21.

25. E. Lundberg, *Unto the Least of These*, 281. For example, the term "dependent child" or "neglected child" was defined by the State of Vermont in 1947 as a child under age sixteen who was "dependent upon the public for support, or who is homeless, destitute or abandoned; or who has not proper parental care or guardianship; or who begs or receives alms; or who is found living in a house of ill fame or with a vicious or disreputable person; or whose home by reason of neglect, cruelty, or depravity on the part of his parents, guardian or other person in whose care he may be, is an unfit place for such child; or whose environment is such as to warrant the state, in the interests of the child, in assuming his guardianship." Draft of the manual on foster home placements from the State of Vermont, June 1947, 7-3-3-2 Foster Home Care ... Placing Out September 1, 1947, box 156, CB Central File 1945–1948, Records of the U.S. Children's Bureau, National Archives, College Park, Md. (hereafter CB Central File).

26. Hacsi, "From Indenture to Family Foster Care," 163.

27. E. Lundberg, *Unto the Least of These*, 281.

28. Swift, "Outrage to Common Decency," 75–76.

29. Gordon, *Heroes of Their Own Lives*, 171.

30. Lindsey, *Welfare of Children*, 5.

31. Gordon, *Women, the State, and Welfare*; Muncy, *Creating a Female Dominion*; Gordon, *Pitied but Not Entitled*; Mink, *Wages of Motherhood*; Mittelstadt, *From Welfare to Workfare*; Quadagno, *Color of Poverty*; Chappell, *War on Welfare*; Kessler-Harris, *In Pursuit of Equity*; Michel, *Children's Interests/Mothers' Rights*; Boris and Klein, *Caring for America*; Fox, *Three Worlds of Relief*.

32. Boris and Klein, *Caring for America*, 10.

33. Michel, *Children's Interests/Mothers' Rights*, 4–5, 9.

34. For an overview of this scholarship, see Boris, "On the Importance of Naming," especially 75–82.

35. Andrew Morris provides a valuable discussion of the relationship of private agencies to the development of public social services in *Limits of Volunteerism*. Morris focuses on Family Services agencies, which were different in important ways from Children's Services agencies. Private child welfare agencies, for example, were more likely to be faith-based than were their family service counterparts and were in a somewhat stronger financial position in the 1930s.

36. Hacsi, *Second Home*, 9.

37. Carp, *Family Matters*; Berebitsky, *Like Our Very Own*; Solinger, *Beggars and Choosers*; Melosh, *Strangers and Kin*; Herman, *Kinship by Design*; Balcom, *Traffic in Babies*; Briggs, *Somebody's Children*; Oh, *To Save the Children of Korea*.

38. Roberts, *Shattered Bonds*; Briggs, *Somebody's Children*; Jacobs, *Generation Removed*.

39. This definition is taken from England, Budig, and Folbre, "Wages of Virtue," 455.

40. Fox, *Three Worlds of Relief*, 3.

41. I base my assessment of the network's general views on my readings of published articles, correspondence, speeches, best practices manuals, and other writings. For a more thoroughgoing examination of this network and its ideas after World War II, see Sribnick, "Rehabilitating Child Welfare."

42. Bernstein, *Lost Children of Wilder*; Toth, *Orphans of the Living*; Harrison, *Another Place at the Table*; Beam, *To the End of June*.

Chapter 1

1. Dorothy Hodgson to I. Evelyn Smith, January 20, 1949, 7-3-3-2 Foster Home Care Child Placing 1949–1952, box 449, CB Central File 1949–1952.

2. Hacsi, *Second Home*, 9.

3. *National Foster Parent Association*, undated pamphlet, ca. 1974, National Foster Parent Association [3], box 62, CWLA records. Since the NFPA first claimed him in the early 1970s, Benjamin has become something of a fixture in foster parenting literature. The NFPA set up a "Benjamin Eaton Scholarship Fund" for foster youth in 1975. Foster parent training materials often include a brief reference to the boy. Eaton appears in scores of web resources and foster parent blogs, the continual spawning of referrals to him as the "nation's first foster child" the result, undoubtedly, of numerous not particularly probing yet easily conducted Google searches. Many references incorrectly locate him in Jamestown. He is even referred to in several academic articles (although none by historians). David T. Evans to James S. Dwight Jr., May 3, 1975, 5th National Conference of Foster Parents, 1975, box 62, CWLA records; Colorado State University–Pueblo Continuing Education, *Foster Parent Core Training*, 7; Lacrosse County [Wisc.] Human Services Department, "Connections"; Sommer, "Empowering Children," 1200; Kingan, "Barriers to Recruitment." Robert Geiser makes reference to Eaton but refers to him, more accurately, as an indentured servant rather than as a foster child. Geiser, *Illusion of Caring*, 147.

4. Shurtleff, *Records of the Colony of New Plymouth*, 36–37; "Pilgrim Village Families Sketch: Francis Eaton," 609.

5. Grossberg, *Governing the Hearth*, 259.

6. Askeland, "Informal Adoption," 7–9; Ramsey and Abrams, *Children and the Law*, 8–10.

7. Hacsi, *Second Home*, 16.

8. Massachusetts Court of Assistants, *Colonial Laws of Massachusetts*, 26.

9. Zelizer, *Pricing the Priceless Child*, 5.

10. O'Connor, *Orphan Trains*, 37, 95; Trattner, *From Poor Law to Welfare State*, 112; Billingsley and Giovannoni, *Children of the Storm*, 34.

11. Hacsi, *Second Home*, 2, 11–12, 13.

12. Billingsley and Giovannoni, *Children of the Storm*, 51–54; Hacsi, *Second Home*, 26, 35.

13. Hacsi, *Second Home*, 242n63, 34–35.

14. Carp, "Orphanages vs. Adoption," 127.

15. On nineteenth-century institutional options for children with disabilities, see Nielsen, *Disability History of the United States*, 68, 72.

16. Smith, "Bring Back the Orphanages?," 117.

17. Abbott, *Dependent and the Delinquent Child*, 10. Laws banning the placement of children in almshouses did not bring an immediate end to the practice. In 1923, there were still 1,896 children living in almshouses (down from 8,885 in 1880.) The worst offenders were Massachusetts with 367 and Pennsylvania with 181, two states that had banned the practice decades earlier. Abbott, *Dependent and the Delinquent Child*, 10n3, 15.

18. Billingsley and Giovannoni, *Children of the Storm*, 65.

19. Abbott, *Dependent and the Delinquent Child*, 7–13.

20. Smith, "Bring Back the Orphanages?," 115–17.

21. Billingsley and Giovannoni, *Children of the Storm*, 77–78.

22. Abbott, *Dependent and the Delinquent Child*, 15.

23. O'Connor, *Orphan Trains*, 38–39; Holt, *Orphan Trains*, 45–47.

24. Hacsi, "From Indenture to Family Foster Care," 159; Zelizer, *Pricing the Priceless Child*, 172–73.

25. On the orphan trains, see Holt, *Orphan Trains*; O'Connor, *Orphan Trains*; Gordon, *Great Arizona Orphan Abduction*. Something similar occurred, albeit on a larger geographic scale, north of the border. Between 1886 and 1923, roughly seventy-seven thousand impoverished children were brought from Britain to Canada ostensibly to improve their lives through placement in Canadian homes. Swift, "An Outrage to Common Decency," 73.

26. Zelizer, *Pricing the Priceless Child*, 173; Holt, *Orphan Trains*, 47–48.

27. Hacsi, *Second Home*, 159; Gordon, *Great Arizona Orphan Abduction*, 10–11.

28. Trattner, *From Poor Law to Welfare State*, 118.

29. O'Connor, *Orphan Trains*, 251–54; Hacsi, "From Indenture to Family Foster Care," 161; Holt, *Orphan Trains*, 53.

30. Holt, *Orphan Trains*, 49–51, 63–64; Zelizer, *Pricing the Priceless Child*, 172–73.

31. Birk, *Fostering on the Farm*, 3.
32. See, for example, Pasztor and Barbell, "United States of America," 251; O'Connor, *Orphan Trains*, xviii, 312; Lindsey, *Welfare of Children*, 13. Lindsey implies that Brace was responsible for the "invention" of foster care.
33. Holt, *Orphan Trains*, 80–117; Gordon, *Great Arizona Orphan Abduction*, 14–15; O'Connor, *Orphan Trains*, 171–72.
34. Holt, *Orphan Trains*, 62; O'Connor, *Orphan Trains*, 150.
35. Zelizer, *Pricing the Priceless Child*, 170, 171.
36. Birk, *Fostering on the Farm*, 8.
37. Holt, *Orphan Trains*; O'Connor, *Orphan Trains*; Gordon, *Great Arizona Orphan Abduction*; Hacsi, *Second Home*; Cmiel, *Home of Another Kind*.
38. On boarding out, see Hacsi, "From Indenture to Family Foster Care," 163–67.
39. For a discussion of such practices in Brazil, see Fonseca, "Circulation of Children."
40. On industrial home work, see Boris, *Home to Work*.
41. Zelizer, *Pricing the Priceless Child*, 184–85; Riis, *How the Other Half Lives*, 146.
42. Birk, *Fostering on the Farm*, 16, 80, 103, 137, 145. Quotation is from 103.
43. Zelizer, *Pricing the Priceless Child*, 187.
44. Brace, "'Placing Out' Plan for Homeless and Vagrant Children," 144.
45. Riis, *How the Other Half Lives*, 146.
46. Hacsi, "From Indenture to Family Foster Care," 165.
47. Murphy, "Conserving the Child's Parental Home," 26.
48. Cited in Zelizer, *Pricing the Priceless Child*, 189.
49. Carstens, "Child Welfare Services," 67.
50. *Marshall (Mo.) Weekly Democrat*, August 21, 1924.
51. The nation's first adoption statute was enacted by Massachusetts in 1851. See "An Act to Provide for the Adoption of Children," 815–16.
52. Quoted in Grossberg, *Governing the Hearth*, 273.
53. On the *Delineator*'s "Child-Rescue Campaign," see Berebitsky, *Like Our Very Own*, 51–74.
54. Berebitsky, *Like Our Very Own*, 59.
55. Creagh, "Science, Social Work, and Bureaucracy," 31.
56. On the notion of "sentimental" adoption, see Zelizer, *Pricing the Priceless Child*, 189–95.
57. Herman, *Kinship by Design*, 1.
58. The process by which adoption became more widely accepted as a legitimate means of family formation in this period has been explored with great nuance by a number of historians. See Carp, *Family Matters*; Berebitsky, *Like Our Very Own*; Herman, *Kinship by Design*; and Melosh, *Strangers and Kin*.
59. Falconer, "Child and Youth Protection," 63.
60. CWLA, *Standards for Child Protective Service*, 7–9; Gordon, *Heroes of Their Own Lives*, 20, 60–61; "Proposal for a Coordinated Research Program in Foster Care," April 1964, folder 8, box 20, CWLA records.
61. Lindenmeyer, *"Right to Childhood,"* 2–3; Muncy, *Creating a Female Dominion*, xii–xv.

62. Hacsi, *Second Home*, 37.
63. Fox, *Three Worlds of Relief*, 95–96.
64. Lindenmeyer, "Right to Childhood," 19–21.
65. Mitchell, "Remarks," 49–50.
66. Billingsley and Giovannoni, *Children of the Storm*, 81–82; Fox, *Three Worlds of Relief*, 54.
67. Conference on the Care of Dependent Children, *Proceedings of the Conference on the Care of Dependent Children*, 5; Hart, "Development of Child Placing," 12–15.
68. Lindenmeyer, "Right to Childhood," 19.
69. Gordon, *Great Arizona Orphan Abduction*, 309.
70. Holt, "Adoption Reform," 27. The transition from evangelical amateur to scientific expert has been especially well explored by Kunzel in the area of services to out-of-wedlock mothers, a field dominated by women. Kunzel, *Fallen Women*. This transition within the child welfare field is not quite as stark, as the field was not so exclusively a female one.
71. Muncy, *Creating a Female Dominion*, xv.
72. Issues of women and professionalization are explored in depth in Kunzel, *Fallen Women*; and Muncy, *Creating a Female Dominion*.
73. Kunzel, *Fallen Women*, 38–39.
74. Ibid., 41–42.
75. On the origins of the Children's Bureau, see Muncy, *Creating a Female Dominion*, 38–47; and Lindenmeyer, "Right to Childhood," 9–29.
76. Grace Abbott quoted in Lindenmeyer, "Right to Childhood," 168.
77. Quoted in ibid., 1.
78. Muncy, *Creating a Female Dominion*, xii.
79. Tiffin, *In Whose Best Interest?*, 275–76; E. Lundberg, "C. C. Carstens."
80. Muncy, *Creating a Female Dominion*, 50–51, 56–57, 90–91.
81. Hart, "Development of Child Placing," 10–11.
82. R. H. Collacott, "Public Welfare Agencies and the Child Welfare League of America," March 1963, folder 13, box 43, CWLA records.
83. CWLA, *Standards for Foster Family Care Service*, viii.
84. Carstens, "Child Welfare Services," 64.
85. Billingsley and Giovannoni, *Children of the Storm*, 33; Holt, *Orphan Trains*, 71; O'Connor, *Orphan Trains*, 215; Hacsi, *Second Home*, 25, 121–23.
86. Birk, *Fostering on the Farm*, 59–60.
87. Billingsley and Giovannoni, *Children of the Storm*, 80.
88. Ibid., 23.
89. Hine, *Shining Thread of Hope*, 83–85; Collins, *Black Feminist Thought*, 48–52, 119–29; Wilson, "Context of the African American Family," 88–89; Billingsley and Giovannoni, *Children of the Storm*, 45–47; Askeland, "Informal Adoption," 10–13.
90. See Roberts, *Shattered Bonds*; and Billingsley and Giovannoni, *Children of the Storm*.
91. Billingsley and Giovannoni, *Children of the Storm*, 43.

92. Hacsi, *Second Home*, 26.
93. Booker T. Washington, "Destitute Colored Children of the South," *Proceedings of the Conference on the Care of Dependent Children*, 113–17.
94. Peebles-Wilkins, "Janie Porter Barrett," 137.
95. Rowe, "Good Girls and Useful Citizens."
96. Lindenmeyer, *"Right to Childhood,"* 20. See also Billingsley and Giovannoni, *Children of the Storm*, 73–74.
97. Peebles-Wilkins, "Janie Porter Barrett," 137, 139; Nelson Jackson to Lester Granger, January 23, 1947, 1947 Child Welfare Jan.–Aug., box 83, Records of the National Urban League, Library of Congress, Washington, D.C. (hereafter NUL records), part 4:A; Nelson Jackson, "Social Welfare Problems," December 23, 1946, 1946 Child Welfare, box 78, ibid.
98. Fox, *Three Worlds of Relief*, 73, 96.
99. Jacobs, *Generation Removed*, xxxiii, 17.
100. Nielsen, *Disability History of the United States*, 66–75.
101. Murphy, "Foster Care for Children," 164.
102. Agnes K. Hanna to Mr. Straten, February 25, 1935, 7-3-3-2 Foster Home Care, box 548, CB Central File 1933–1936. Other options did not disappear. In 1955, some states, such as Texas and Arkansas, were actually considering increasing the use of free homes. Mary Lois Pyles to Mrs. Florence A. Clark, December 13, 1955, 7-3-3-2 Jan. . . . 1957 Foster Home Care—Placing Out (Free Homes) 1953–1957, box 679, CB Central File 1953–57. By 1957, according to the Children's Bureau, there were still 8,000 children living in free, wage, or work homes (compared with 141,000 in boarding homes and 75,000 in institutions). CB, "Estimated Number of Children in Foster Care in the Continental United States and Territories," March 31, 1957, 7-3-3-2 Nov. 1961 Foster Home Care, Placing Out (Free Homes), box 886, CB Central File 1958–1962.
103. The following paragraphs describing the Costa case are based on the case record found in Complaint—Neglect, Folder #26656, box 18, Records of Minneapolis Family and Children's Services, Social Welfare History Archives, Minneapolis, Minn. All names from this case record have been changed.
104. U.S. Committee on Economic Security, *Social Security in America*, 527.
105. Trattner, *From Poor Law to Welfare State*, 4.

Chapter 2

1. "Report of the Committee on Economic Security," January 21, 1935, in U.S. Congress, House, Committee on Ways and Means, *Economic Security Act Hearings*, 47.
2. Boris and Klein, *Caring for America*, 21.
3. [Helen Davidson] to United States Information Service, October 1, 1941, and Fay Green to Mary Milburn, October 22, 1941, 7-3-1-4 Custody of Dependent Children 1941 September, box 166, CB Central File 1941–1944. On the Depression in Canton, see Gup, *Secret Gift*. The names of private citizens who wrote to the Children's Bureau have been changed. Pseudonyms are indicated by brackets.

4. Katharine Lenroot to Mildred Territt, October 16, 1934, 7-3-3-2 Foster Home Care, box 548, CB Central File 1933–1936. Figures for inflation-adjusted dollars, here and elsewhere, have been calculated at U.S. Department of Labor, Bureau of Labor Statistics, http://www.bls.gov/data/inflation_calculator.htm.

5. Mary E. Milbern to [Emery Brinkley], April 22, 1938, 7-3-3-2 Foster Home Care — Placing Out April 1938, box 820, CB Central File 1937–1940.

6. [Gladys Speck] to Agnes K. Hanna, July 19, 1934, 7-3-3-3 Boarding Homes, box 548, CB Central File 1933–1936.

7. Zelma J. Felten, "Report of Foster Care Study," May 6, 1960, folder 6, box 19, CWLA records.

8. U.S. Committee on Economic Security, *Report to the President*, 528.

9. Statement of Katharine Lenroot, January 30, 1935, in U.S. Congress, House, Committee on Ways and Means, *Economic Security Act Hearings*, 272.

10. White House Conference on Child Health and Protection, "Children's Charter."

11. Murphy, "Foster Care for Children," 164.

12. Creagh, "Science, Social Work, and Bureaucracy," 33.

13. The CWLA in 1933 defined "free homes" as those in which no money was given to the family and no payment was made by family to children except an allowance; "work homes" were those in which the child worked for the family in return for board and lodging; "wage homes" were homes in which the child received wages in exchange for services; and "boarding homes" were ones in which foster parents received some payment for costs associated with boarding. All of these types of homes were considered "foster homes." CWLA, *Standards for Children's Organizations Providing Foster Family Care* (1933), 16; Hacsi, "From Indenture to Family Foster Care," 166–67.

14. Carstens, "Child Welfare Services," 66–67.

15. Billingsley and Giovannoni, *Children of the Storm*, 77–79.

16. See, for example, Agnes K. Hanna to Miss E. Russell, July 14 [1939; erroneously dated 1949], and Regina M. Surprenant to Maud Morlock, November 28, 1939, folder 7-3-3-2 Foster Home Care — Placing Out [2], box 819, CB Central File 1937–1940; and Agnes K. Hanna to Martha Wood, May 6, 1940, folder 7-3-3-3 Boarding Homes, box 821, ibid.

17. Murphy, "Foster Care for Children," 162.

18. Agnes K. Hanna, "Memorandum on Supervision of Boarding Homes Caring for Children," May 24, 1938, 7-3-3-3 Boarding Homes, box 821, CB Central File 1937–1940; Agnes K. Hanna to Miss E. Russell, July 14 [1939; erroneously dated 1949], 7-3-3-2 Foster Home Care — Placing Out [2], box 819, CB Central File 1937–1940.

19. [Mrs. Earle Frisbie] to Children's Bureau, March 7, 1936, 7-3-3-3 Boarding Homes, box 548, CB Central File 1933–1936.

20. [Berta Washington] to Frances Perkins, August 7, 1933, ibid.

21. [Mrs. Henry Nickerson] to Children's Bureau, February 27, 1934, ibid.

22. [Mrs. J. T. Marschall] to Department of Agriculture, March 15, 1935, ibid.

23. [Frances Gaines] to Katharine Lenroot, February 16, 1940, 7-3-3-3 Boarding Homes, box 821, CB Central File 1937–1940.

24. [Mrs. A. S. Waugh] to President Roosevelt, September 23, 1937, 7-3-3-2 Foster Home Care — Placing Out January 1937, box 820, CB Central File 1937–1940.

25. Zelizer, *Pricing the Priceless Child*, 9–11.

26. In reading letters in the Records of the U.S. Children's Bureau from individuals hoping to board children, I found a few from men on behalf of their wives but only one from a man who himself hoped to become a boarding parent. This individual was a disabled veteran of World War I who needed extra income to support himself but who also felt that his disability gave him a perspective that would be helpful in "render[ing] the maximum amount of good to society in practically assisting these little ones." [Howard Stephens] to Katharine Lenroot, March 31, 1938, 7-3-3-3 Boarding Homes, box 821, CB Central File 1937–1940.

27. [Pauline Wagner] to President Roosevelt, June 5, 1938, ibid.

28. [Martha Dempster] to Frances Perkins, October 10, 1933, 7-3-3-3 Boarding Homes, box 548, CB Central File 1933–1936. Many agencies had religious matching policies for out-of-home placements, and indeed Delaware would pass a state law mandating a religious matching statute in 1935. Melosh, *Strangers and Kin*, 76.

29. [Walter Townes] to Mrs. Roosevelt, December 10, 1940, 7-3-1-4 Custody of Dependent Children July, box 814, CB Central File 1937–1940.

30. Regina M. Surprenant to Maud Morlock, November 28, 1939, 7-3-3-2 Foster Home Care — Placing Out [2], box 819, ibid.

31. Agnes K. Hanna to [Mrs. A. S. Waugh], September 1937, 7-3-3-2 Foster Home Care — Placing Out January 1937, box 820, ibid.

32. [Lois Bolinger] to Mrs. Roosevelt, March 14, 1940, 7-3-3-3 Boarding Homes, box 821, ibid.

33. [Mrs. James Oakley] to Mr. Franklin Roosevelt, January 29, 1940, ibid.

34. [Mrs. Katherine Turner] to Mrs. Franklin Roosevelt, May 13, 1935, 7-3-3-3 Boarding Homes, box 548, CB Central File 1933–1936.

35. George T. Swartzott to Katharine Lenroot, August 21, 1934, 7-3-3-2 Foster Home Care, box 548, CB Central File 1933–1936.

36. "Suggested Minimum Standards for Foster Homes," attached to Olive Bigger to Florence Sullivan, July 30, 1937, 7-3-3-2 Foster Home Care — Placing Out January 1937, box 820, CB Central File 1937–1940.

37. Ibid.

38. CWLA, *Standards for Children's Organizations Providing Foster Family Care* (1933).

39. Dorothy Hutchinson, notes on "Session V," undated, ca. 1940s, folder 121, Koppler, Peter and Mary, box 1, Dorothy Hutchinson Papers, Butler Rare Book and Manuscript Room, Columbia University, New York, N.Y. (hereafter Hutchinson Papers).

40. [Otto Hocker] to Mrs. Roosevelt, November 21, 1937, and Mary F. Godley to Agnes Hanna, December 28, 1937, 7-3-3-3 Boarding Homes, box 821, CB Central File 1937–1940.

41. McElvaine, *Great Depression*, 151.

42. Wisconsin Conference of Social Work, "The Children's Code in Wisconsin,

1929–1934," [draft], 1934, 104, folder 10, box 42, CWLA records; Murphy, "Foster Care for Children," 167.

43. Wisconsin Conference of Social Work, "The Children's Code in Wisconsin, 1929–1934," [draft], 1934, 104–5, 107, 109–12, folder 10, box 42, CWLA records.

44. Murphy, "Foster Care for Children," 166.

45. Agnes K. Hanna to Miss Jeannette Jenson, October 10, 1936, 7-3-3-3 Boarding Homes, box 548, CB Central File 1933–1936; Morris, *Limits of Volunteerism*, 17–18.

46. U.S. Committee on Economic Security, *Social Security in America*, 526.

47. Cornelia Hopkins Allen, Elda Kanally, Sophie Litsky, and Eleanor Morris Carr, "An Appraisal of the Facilities for the Care of Dependent, Neglected and Problem Children in New Haven, Connecticut," August 20, 1939, 17, 6, viii, folder 1, box 19, CWLA records.

48. Ibid., 8.

49. Hansan, "Philadelphia Training School for Social Work." See also Lenroot, "J. Prentice Murphy."

50. Murphy, "Foster Care for Children," 162.

51. Marie L. Ireland to Grace Abbott, January 24, 1934, 7-3-3-2 Foster Home Care, box 548, CB Central File 1933–1936.

52. Judith Hyams Douglas to Children's Bureau, May 27, 1933, ibid. All spelling in Douglas's quote is as it appears in the original letter.

53. Murphy, "Children in the New Deal," 121.

54. Agnes K. Hanna to Miss Jeannette Jenson, October 10, 1936, 7-3-3-3 Boarding Homes, box 548, CB Central File 1933–1936; Murphy, "Children in the New Deal," 123.

55. *Federal Emergency Relief Act of 1933*, 55–58.

56. Murphy, "Children in the New Deal," 122.

57. Ibid., 123–24; Morris, *Limits of Voluntarism*, 17.

58. Murphy, "Foster Care for Children," 166.

59. B. H. Robinson to Joseph P. Harris, May 21, 1935, 7-3-3-2 Foster Home Care, box 548, CB Central File 1933–1936.

60. Statement of E. E. Witt, January 21, 1935, in U.S. Congress, House, Committee on Ways and Means, *Economic Security Act Hearings*, 7.

61. Statement of Grace Abbott, January 30, 1935, in ibid., 493. See also "Report of the Committee on Economic Security," January 21, 1935, in ibid., 47.

62. Canaday, *Straight State*, 93.

63. "Report of the Committee on Economic Security," January 21, 1935, in U.S. Congress, House, Committee on Ways and Means, *Economic Security Act Hearings*, 19–20.

64. Johnson, "Lenroot, Katharine Fredrica," 488–89.

65. Katharine Lenroot, "Child-Welfare in State and Local Public Welfare Programs," presented at the Southeastern National Conference of the American Public Welfare Association, April 5, 1946, folder 8, box 5, series 1.1, Katharine Lenroot Papers, Butler Rare Book and Manuscript Room, Columbia University, New York, N.Y. (hereafter Lenroot Papers); Lindenmeyer, *"Right to Childhood,"* 185–86, 192, 195.

66. Katharine Lenroot, "Plans for Strengthening Child Health and Child Welfare

Services under the Social Security Program," September 22, 1935, folder 1, box 2, series I, Lenroot Papers; Lindenmeyer, *"Right to Childhood,"* 185–86, 251–52; Mittelstadt, *From Welfare to Workfare*, 24; Muncy, *Creating a Female Dominion*, 154.

67. See Willrich, "Home Slackers," 460–89; and Fraser and Gordon, "Genealogy of Dependency," 309–36.

68. Mink, *Wages of Motherhood*, 135–37.

69. Canaday, *Straight State*, 130.

70. Hoey, "Aid to Families with Dependent Children," 74–78.

71. Mittelstadt, *From Welfare to Workfare*, 46.

72. Fox, *Three Worlds of Relief*, 253. The image of the sieve comes from the NAACP and in its original expression referred only to African Americans. Fox, *Three Worlds of Relief*, 250. Fox argues, though, that the occupational exemptions and state implementation of certain Social Security programs meant similar disparate impacts on Mexicans and Mexican Americans as on African Americans.

73. Mink, *Wages of Motherhood*, 135–36.

74. Agnes K. Hanna to Mr. L. H. Atwell, August 7, 1935, 7-3-3-2 Foster Home Care, box 548, CB Central File 1933–1936; "Extent of Child Placing in the United States of America" [draft section of League of Nations report], undated, ca. 1938, 7-3-3-2 Foster Home Care — Placing Out April 1938, box 820, CB Central File 1937–1940.

75. Lucille N. Austin, "Trends in Differential Treatment in Social Casework," paper presented at the National Conference of Social Workers, April 1948, unlabeled folder, box 1, Hutchinson Papers.

76. CWLA, *Standards for Children's Organizations Providing Foster Family Care* (1941), 8.

77. Katharine Lenroot to Charles J. Bornman, April 26, 1937, 7-3-3-2 Foster Home Care — Placing Out January 1937, box 820, CB Central File 1937–1940.

78. U.S. Committee on Economic Security, *Social Security in America*, 613.

79. Arnold, "Federal Services for Children under Reorganization," 312.

80. Carstens, "Child Welfare Services," 69–71.

81. Atkinson, "Child Welfare Services," 618.

82. Hacsi, *Second Home*, 48.

83. U.S. Congress, House and Senate, *Social Security Act of 1935*, Title III — Grants to States for Unemployment Compensation, section 301; Title IV — Grants to States for Aid to Dependent Children, section 401; Title V — Grants to States for Maternal and Child Welfare, part 3 Child Welfare Services, section 521(a); Katharine Lenroot, "Plans for Strengthening Child Health and Child Welfare Services under the Social Security Program," September 22, 1935, folder 1, box 2, series 1, Lenroot Papers.

84. Testimony of Edwin Witte, January 25, 1935, in U.S. Congress, House, Committee on Ways and Means, *Economic Security Act Hearings*, 164.

85. Statement of Joseph Sweeney, January 30, 1935, in ibid., 546.

86. "Report of the Committee on Economic Security," January 21, 1935, in ibid., 48.

87. U.S. Committee on Economic Security, *Social Security in America*, 521; Lenroot, "Children's Titles in the Social Security Act," 131; U.S. Children's Bureau, *Public Social*

Services to Children, 12; Katharine Lenroot, "Child-Welfare in State and Local Public Welfare Programs," presented at the Southeastern National Conference of the American Public Welfare Association, April 5, 1946, folder 8, box 5, series 1.1, Lenroot Papers.

88. "States Having Laws Relating to Licensing of Boarding Homes," attached to Agnes K. Hanna to Ruby S. Perry, June 14, 1938, 7-3-3-3 Boarding Homes, box 821, CB Central File 1937–1940. States requiring no licensure for boarding homes at the time of the report were located primarily in the South and the West and included Arizona, Arkansas, Colorado, Georgia, Idaho, Kentucky, Louisiana, Mississippi, Montana, Nebraska, Nevada, New Mexico, Oklahoma, South Carolina, Tennessee, West Virginia, and Wyoming.

89. Miss Nutt to Mildred Arnold, April 25, 1944, 7-3-3-2 Foster Home Care—Placing Out, box 168, CB Central File 1941–1944.

90. Abbott, *Dependent and the Delinquent Child*, 20.

Chapter 3

1. Gardiner, *Children's War*, 83.

2. Leonard Mayo, "Plan of Organization and Function of the Child Care Division of the United States Committee," July 31, 1940; Leonard Mayo to Members and Associates of the Child Welfare League, July 1, 1940; and the United States Committee for the Care of European Children, "Bulletin No. 1," July 1, 1940, all in folder 6, box 18, CWLA records; "US Opens Its Homes and Hearts to Refugee Children of England," *Life*, July 22, 1940, 11; Lindenmeyer, *"Right to Childhood,"* 210–13.

3. Kathryn Close, "Transplanted Children," cited in Becker, *Marshall Field III*, 177.

4. Leonard Mayo to Members and Associates of the Child Welfare League, August 5, 1940, folder 6, box 18, CWLA records.

5. Obtaining precise figures on the number of stranger placements has proved a challenge. The numbers provided here are based on Kathryn Close's reports of the number of visas issued and the number of homes certified. Close, "When the Children Come," 132. For other discussions, see "Gratitude Due Our Guests," *New York Herald Tribune*, December 7, 1940; Becker, *Marshall Field III*, 185; Halstead, "'Dangers Behind, Pleasure Ahead,'" 164; and Gardiner, *Children's War*, 86.

6. Katharine F. Lenroot, "The United States Program for the Care of Refugee Children," June 5, 1941, folder 2, box 4, series 1.1, Lenroot Papers; Katharine F. Lenroot to Philip Levy, July 8, 1940, War Refugee Problems, box 32, series 1.4, ibid.; "Elsa Castendyck Dies, Child Welfare Expert," *Washington Evening Star*, January 6, 1970.

7. CWLA, *Standards for Children's Organizations Providing Foster Family Care* (1933); CWLA, *Standards for Children's Organizations Providing Foster Family Care* (1941); CWLA, "A Study of Board Rates," January 1942, folder 3, box 19, CWLA records.

8. "Gratitude Due Our Guests," *New York Herald Tribune*, December 7, 1940.

9. Howard Hopkirk, statement on F.W.A. Deficiency Appropriation Bill, Subcommittee on Deficiencies of the Senate Committee on Appropriations, March 22, 1944, folder 11, box 42, CWLA records.

10. Leonard Mayo, "Plan of Organization and Function of the Child Care Division of the United States Committee," July 31, 1940, folder 6, box 18, CWLA records.

11. Close, "When the Children Come," 132.

12. The United States Committee for the Care of European Children, "Bulletin No. 1," July 1, 1940, folder 6, box 18, CWLA records; Bradbury and Eliot, *Four Decades of Action for Children*, 61.

13. Becker, *Marshall Field III*, 182, 185.

14. On the sinking of the SS *City of Benares*, see Longden, *Blitz Kids*, 87–106.

15. Close, "When the Children Come," 136.

16. It was a catalyst for the development of adoption as well. Carp and Leon-Guerrero, "When in Doubt, Count." Some of the factors Carp and Leon-Guerrero point to, such as the dramatic rise in out-of-wedlock pregnancy and the growing practice of placing infants in an extended period of foster care before placement in a permanent adopted home, were also significant to the history of foster care, although the two practices were in the process of diverging.

17. Lebergott, "Annual Estimates of Unemployment in the United States," 215–16.

18. Mary Ruth Colby to [Mr. and Mrs. Robert Norman], August 27, 1942, 7-3-1-4 Custody of Dependent Children 1942 January, box 166, CB Central File 1941–1944.

19. Hanson, "Child Welfare" (1945), 79; Bradbury and Eliot, *Four Decades of Action for Children*, 50.

20. Elsa Castendyck to [Mrs. T. L. Roberts], October 7, 1942, 7-3-1-4 Custody of Dependent Children 1942 January, box 166, CB Central File 1941–1944.

21. Elsa Castendyck to [Mrs. James Mosby], January 26, 1943, 7-3-3-2 Foster Home Care—Placing Out March 12, 1942, box 168, CB Central File 1941–1944.

22. [Miss Gloria Jones] to Children's Bureau, January 6, 1945, 7-3-3-3 Boarding Homes 1945, box 157, CB Central File 1945–1948.

23. Elsa Castendyck to [Mrs. Evelyn Murphy], June 10, 1943, 7-3-3-3 Boarding Homes, box 168, CB Central File 1941–1944.

24. Tuttle, "Rosie the Riveter and Her Latchkey Children," 94.

25. Mary Ruth Colby to [Arlene Dearborn], August 27, 1942, 7-3-1-4 Custody of Dependent Children 1942 January, box 166, CB Central File 1941–1944.

26. Miss Rowe to Miss Castendyck, May 28, 1943, 7-3-3-3 Boarding Homes, box 168, CB Central File 1941–1944.

27. Mrs. Marguerite M. Gauchat to Mr. H. M. Bell, May 11, 1943, ibid.

28. Mary Ruth Colby to [Mrs. Arlene Dearborn], August 27, 1942, 7-3-1-4 Custody of Dependent Children 1942 January, box 166, ibid.

29. Ibid.

30. CWLA, *Standards for Children's Organizations Providing Foster Family Care* (1941), 40, 27. Louisiana and Mississippi allowed the boarding of six children at a time and Arizona allowed five (each of these states restricted the number to two if the children were under the age of two). Bernice E. Scroggie to Miss Arnold, January 18, 1945, 7-3-3-2 Foster Home Care Placing Out Jan. 1945 to June 1945, box 157, CB Central File 1945–1948.

31. Mary Ruth Colby to [Mrs. Arlene Dearborn], August 27, 1942, 7-3-1-4 Custody of Dependent Children 1942 January, box 166, CB Central File 1941–1944.

32. Extract from letter of Miss Gertrude L. Prack, March 2, 1945, 7-3-3-2 Foster Home Care Placing Out Jan. 1945 to June 1945, box 157, CB Central File 1945–1948.

33. Miss Stanton to Miss Shepperson and Miss Nutt, January 13, 1945, ibid.

34. Elsa Castendyck to Mrs. Louis V. Thompson, July 3, 1944, 7-3-3-2 Foster Home Care — Placing Out, box 168, CB Central File 1941–1944.

35. Miss Stanton to Miss Shepperson and Miss Nutt, January 13, 1945, and Miss Wood to Miss Arnold, January 29, 1945, 7-3-3-2 Foster Home Care Placing Out Jan. 1945 to June 1945, box 157, CB Central File 1945–1948.

36. Bernice E. Scroggie to Miss Arnold, January 18, 1945, ibid.

37. Hanson, "Child Welfare" (1945), 80.

38. CWLA, "A Study of Board Rates," January 1942, folder 3, box 19, CWLA records.

39. [Mrs. Peggy Crawford] to President Roosevelt, April 7, 1943, and [Mrs. Peggy Crawford] to Miss Frederickson, November 13, 1943, both in 7-3-3-2 Foster Home Care — Placing Out May 5, 1943, box 168, CB Central File 1941–1944.

40. Eleanor Hursh, "Foster Home Development for Emergency Shelter Care," Publication of District 10 Welfare Board, June–July 1945, 7-3-3-2 Foster Home Care, Placing Out July to Dec. 1945, box 156, CB Central File 1945–1948.

41. Bernice Scroggie to Miss Wood, July 9, 1945, ibid.

42. Hutchinson, *In Quest of Foster Parents*, 114.

43. Marshall Field, *The Relationship between Problems of Children and the Problems of Manpower*, November 18, 1942, CWLA Brochures, 1920–1950, box 83, CWLA records.

44. Mrs. Sara Smith to Miss Gwen Geach, February 18, 1944, 7-3-3-3 Boarding Homes, box 168, CB Central File 1941–1944.

45. Marshall Field, *The Relationship between Problems of Children and the Problems of Manpower*, November 18, 1942, CWLA Brochures, 1920–1950, box 83, CWLA records; Hanson, "Child Welfare" (1945), 78.

46. Cohen, "Brief History of Federal Financing for Child Care," 29.

47. CWLA, "A Study of Board Rates," January 1942, folder 3, box 19, CWLA records.

48. Stoltzfus, *Child Care*, 4.

49. Cohen, "Brief History of Federal Financing for Child Care," 29–30; Kathryn Close, "After Lanham Funds What?," undated, ca. 1945, folder 9, box 22, CWLA records; Stoltzfus, *Child Care*, 1–5.

50. See, for example, CWLA, "Children under Two in Foster Care," 1944, folder 4, box 19, CWLA records.

51. Winfred Allen, "Place of the Day Nursery in the Community Welfare Program," *National Association of Day Nurseries*, folder 9, box 21, CWLA records.

52. Howard Hopkirk, statement on F.W.A. Deficiency Appropriation Bill, Subcommittee on Deficiencies of the Senate Committee on Appropriations, March 22, 1944, folder 11, box 42, CWLA records.

53. CWLA, "Children under Two in Foster Care," 1944, folder 4, box 19, CWLA records.

54. Ibid.

55. For discussions of foster day care, see, for example, CWLA Committee on Day Care, Minutes, March 19, 1943, folder 8, box 21, CWLA records; and Hanson, "Child Welfare" (1945), 78–79.

56. Michel, *Children's Interests/Mothers' Rights*, 130.

57. Stoltzfus, *Child Care*, 4n5.

58. Howard Hopkirk, statement on F.W.A. Deficiency Appropriation Bill, Subcommittee on Deficiencies of the Senate Committee on Appropriations, March 22, 1944, box 42, CWLA records.

59. Kathryn Close, "After Lanham Funds What?," undated, ca. 1945, folder 9, box 22, CWLA records.

60. *Baltimore Morning Sun*, October 7, 1945.

61. CWLA, "Children under Two in Foster Care," 1944, folder 4, box 19, CWLA records.

62. *New Orleans Times Picayune*, December 17, 1944; *San Francisco Chronicle*, April 16, 1944.

63. Indiana Department of Public Welfare Children's Division, "Boarding Parents! Protect Yourselves with a License!," and "Mothers! Protect Your Children if They Must Live Away from Home," 1947, 7-3-3-2 Foster Home Care Placing Out 8/1948, box 157, CB Central File 1945–1948.

64. Herman, *Kinship by Design*, 134–47.

65. "Home Unlicensed Where 17 Died," *Daily Kennebec (Maine) Journal*, February 1, 1945.

66. Statement by Katharine F. Lenroot, February 26, 1945, folder 7, box 5, series 1.1, Lenroot Papers.

67. Hansan, "Hopkirk, Howard W."

68. Hopkirk acknowledged that he did not know exactly how many of the victims were children of servicemen. Of the three fathers whose occupations were listed in local newspaper coverage of the fire, however, two were serving in the navy and one in the army. Howard W. Hopkirk, *Did Sixteen Babies Have to Perish?*, CWLA pamphlet, undated, ca. 1945, CWLA Brochures, 1920–1950, box 83, CWLA records; "Home Unlicensed Where 17 Died," *Daily Kennebec (Maine) Journal*, February 1, 1945.

69. "Gratitude Due Our Guests," *New York Herald Tribune*, December 7, 1940.

70. Untitled clipping, May 15, 1943, 7-3-3-2 Foster Home Care—Placing Out May 5, 1943, box 168, CB Central File 1941–1944.

71. Louisiana Homefinding Campaign, "Save a Child for America," undated, ca. 1943, ibid.

72. Lenroot, "Child Welfare in the Reconversion Period," 4.

73. Miss Emma G. Puschner to Miss Marion White, October 17, 1945, 7-3-3-2 Foster Home Care, Placing Out July to Dec. 1945, box 156, CB Central File 1945–1948.

74. Hanson, "Child Welfare" (1945), 77. On inadequacy of servicemen's allowances, see Tuttle, "Rosie the Riveter and Her Latchkey Children," 94–95.

75. Howard Hopkirk, "War Hits Our Children," excerpted from *The Child Welfare League Bulletin* (September 1942), Reprints, 1939–1960s, box 84, CWLA records.

76. Hanson, "Child Welfare" (1943), 108.

77. Untitled clipping, May 15, 1943, 7-3-3-2 Foster Home Care — Placing Out May 5, 1943, box 168, CB Central File 1941–1944.

78. "A War Job for You in Your Own Home!," ca. 1943, ibid.

79. "Share Your Home with a Child," ca. 1943, ibid.

80. CWLA, "Children under Two in Foster Care," 1944, folder 4, box 19, CWLA records.

81. Lenroot, "Needed: Daytime Mothers."

82. Special Committee for Standards and Services of the Children's Bureau Conference on Day Care of Children of Working Mothers, "Preliminary Report on Standards for Day Care of Children of Working Mothers," February 1942, folder 1, box 22, CWLA records.

83. Katharine F. Lenroot, "Foster Home Care of Children an Essential Service in Wartime," box 4, folder 6, series 1.1, Lenroot Papers.

84. United Home Finding Campaign [Chicago], "*What* Can You Do?," ca. 1943, 7-3-3-2 Foster Home Care — Placing Out May 5, 1943, box 168, CB Central File 1941–1944.

85. "A War Job for You in Your Own Home!," ca. 1943, ibid.

86. "Share Your Home with a Child," ca. 1943, ibid.

87. United Home Finding Campaign [Chicago], "*Help Me* and You Help America!," ca. 1943, and New York City Committee on Child Welfare, "*Help Me* and You Help America," ca. 1943, both in ibid.

88. Foster Homes for Children Campaign [Connecticut], "*Won't You* Give Me a Home?," ca. 1943, ibid.

89. Louisiana Homefinding Campaign, "Save a Child for America," undated, ca. 1943, ibid.

90. "Share Your Home with a Child," ibid.

91. CWLA, "Children under Two in Foster Care," 1944, folder 4, box 19, CWLA records.

92. [Mrs. Bradbury Townes] to Woman's Bureau, November 12, 1940, 7-3-3-3 Boarding Homes, box 821, CB Central File 1937–1940.

93. [Mrs. Peggy Crawford] to President Roosevelt, April 7, 1943, 7-3-3-2 Foster Home Care — Placing Out May 5, 1943, box 168, CB Central File 1941–1944.

94. [Mrs. J. L. Vogt] to President Roosevelt, March 9, 1944, 7-3-3-3 Boarding Homes, ibid. Elsa Castendyck, who replied to Vogt, noted that there was no way to know precisely how many children were made homeless by the war, for there were many ways to interpret it. Castendyck to [Vogt], March 28, 1944, ibid.

95. [Miss Nora Hoyt] to President of the United States, October 17, 1942, 7-3-3-2 Foster Home Care — Placing Out March 12, 1942, box 168, CB Central File 1941–1944.

96. [Mrs. Mabel Gibson] to U.S. Information Bureau, November 2, 1942, ibid.

97. Warren E. Thompson, Director's Report, "United Home Finding Campaign," [1943], 7-3-3-2 Foster Home Care — Placing Out May 5, 1943, ibid.

98. Henrietta Gordon to Miss Gertrude L. Prack, March 19, 1945, 7-3-3-2 Foster Home Care Placing Out Jan. 1945 to June 1945, box 157, CB Central File 1945–1948.

99. Miss Helen H. Searl to Elsa Castendyck, August 25, 1943, and Elsa Castendyck to

Miss Helen H. Searl, September 7, 1943, 7-3-3-2 Foster Home Care — Placing Out May 5, 1943, box 168, CB Central File 1941–1944.

100. Cheney C. Jones to Katharine Lenroot, June 21, 1944, ibid.

101. Neumann, *Now That April's There*; Neumann, "Look! We're Home." This fictionalized story of children of a British university faculty member being hosted by a faculty family abroad reflects what Halstead found to be common in her work on British children evacuated to Canada. Halstead, "'Dangers Behind, Pleasure Ahead,'" 166–67.

102. "Gratitude Due Our Guests," *New York Herald Tribune*, December 7, 1940.

103. Close, "When the Children Come," 132; Gardiner, *Children's War*, 86; Becker *Marshall Field III*, 185.

Chapter 4

1. Blake, "They Call Her Aunt May." Quotations are from pp. 50 and 86.

2. The number of adoptions grew from seventeen thousand in 1937 to fifty thousand in 1945 and again to ninety-one thousand by 1957. Melosh, *Strangers and Kin*, 105.

3. Swartz, "Mothering for the State." Social work scholar Laura Curran has also explored the tensions within the midcentury constructions of foster motherhood; see Curran, "Feminine Women, Hard Workers."

4. Henrietta L. Gordon to Emily Mitchell Wires, January 3, 1945 Foster Care Homefinding Correspondence, 1954–1970, box 62, CWLA records; miscellaneous correspondence in 7-3-3-2 April 1955 Foster Home Care Placing Out (Free Homes) 1953–56, box 680, CB Central File, 1953–1957.

5. Herman, *Kinship by Design*, 85; Curran, "Social Work's Revised Maternalism," 119–20.

6. Foster Homes for Children Project [Philadelphia], "Sample Local Newspaper Material," undated, ca. 1948, 7-3-3-2 Foster Home Care, Placing Out July to Dec. 1945, box 156, CB Central File 1945–1948.

7. Quoted in Katz, "Foster Parents versus Agencies," 150.

8. On postwar adoption as the "best solution," see Melosh, *Strangers and Kin*, 105–57.

9. On the juvenile delinquency scare, see Mackert, "'But Recall the Kind of Parents,'" 196–219. The CB called a number of special conferences on juvenile delinquency in the 1950s. See Bradbury and Eliot, *Four Decades of Action for Children*, 78–79.

10. [Mrs. Mildred Woods] to President Truman, February 1950, 7-3-1-4 Custody of Dependent Children, box 442, CB Central File 1949–52.

11. Wolins, *Selecting Foster Parents*, 15.

12. Castendyck, review of *In Quest of Foster Parents*, 285.

13. Katharine Lenroot, comments on CWLA, "Preliminary Draft: Standards for Foster Family Care Service," September 1958, *Foster Family Care* revisions, box 62, CWLA records.

14. Haitch, *Orphans of the Living*, 10.

15. Wolins, *Selecting Foster Parents*, 17.

16. David Fanshel, "Dissertation Proposal: Toward More Understanding of Foster Parents," for presentation at dissertation seminar, April 14, 1959, folder 7, box 18, CWLA records.

17. Berkeley Social Welfare Department, "Martin Wolins, 1920–1985"; National Association of Social Workers, "David Fanshel."

18. Indeed, of the cities Maas and Engler investigated for their landmark 1959 study, *Children in Need of Parents*, one (referred to as "Centralia" in the study) had no provision for TPR whatsoever. Maas and Engler, *Children in Need of Parents*, 430.

19. On pre-adoptive placement, see Herman, *Kinship by Design*, 72–77. Due both to pressures from adoptive parents who preferred immediate placements of infants and to Bowlby's work on attachment, about half of adoption agencies were, by 1955, placing children less than one month old into permanent homes. The other half were, presumably, still using foster care for pre-adoptive placement. Melosh, *Strangers and Kin*, 75.

20. For background on this practice, sometimes known as concurrent planning, see D'Andrade, Frame, and Berrick, "Concurrent Planning in Public Child Welfare Agencies." Information on adopting through foster care is widely available today. For one example, see https://www.childwelfare.gov/topics/permanency/adoption/, accessed July 29, 2015.

21. [Rough draft of the manual on Foster Home Placements from the State of Vermont], June 1947, 7-3-3-2 Foster Home Care . . . Placing Out September 1, 1947, box 156, CB Central File 1945–1948.

22. [Mrs. Vernon Cook] to President Harry S. Truman, September 11, 1951, 7-3-1-4 Custody of Dependent Children 1949–1952 [2], box 445, CB Central File 1949–1952.

23. [Mr. and Mrs. Tom Yates] to President Truman, December 3, 1950, 7-3-1-4 Custody of Dependent Children 1949–1952, ibid.

24. I. Evelyn Smith to Orville Crays, January 18, 1949, 7-3-3-2 Foster Home Care Child Placing 1949–1952, box 157, ibid.

25. Dwight H. Ferguson to Orville Crays, April 9, 1959, 7-3-3-2 Nov. 1961 Foster Home Care, Placing Out (Free Homes), box 886, CB Central File 1958–1962.

26. Katz, "Foster Parents versus Agencies," 146–47. See also Court of Appeals of New York, *In the Matter of Jewish Child Care Association of New York*.

27. Katz, "Foster Parents versus Agencies," 149; Court of Appeals of New York, *In the Matter of Jewish Child Care Association of New York*, 226; "L. I. Custody Fight Centers on Girl," *New York Times*, December 20, 1957; Wolins, *Selecting Foster Parents*, 31–32. As Katz notes, Laura's case indicates the conflict between several legal principles. Even if "the best interests of the child" were served by allowing her to remain with the Sanderses, to do so would have meant "reward[ing] persons who had failed to fulfill their promises and who had undermined the Agency's decision" (152).

28. Haitch, *Orphans of the Living*, 10.

29. David Fanshel, "Dissertation Proposal: Toward More Understanding of Foster Parents," for presentation at dissertation seminar, April 14, 1959, folder 7, box 18, CWLA records.

30. On kinship and foster parenting, see, for example, Fonseca, "Circulation of Children"; and Alber, "'Real Parents Are the Foster Parents.'"

31. Wilson, "Context of the African American Family," 86–89; Jacobs, *Generation Removed*, xxxiii.

32. "Cheaper by the Score"; "Mom Whyte's Home Closed, 117 Kids Removed," *Ottawa Citizen*, August 1, 1959; Canadian Welfare Council, "Editorial," *Canadian Welfare*, December 15, 1956, 7-3-3-2 Jan. . . . 1957 Foster Home Care — Placing Out (Free Homes) 1953-1957, box 679, CB Central File 1953–57.

33. "Suggested Minimum Standards for Foster Homes," attached to Olive Bigger to Florence Sullivan, July 30, 1937, 7-3-3-2 Foster Home Care — Placing Out January 1937, box 820, CB Central File 1937–1940.

34. Herman, *Kinship by Design*, 101.

35. Henrietta L. Gordon to Israel Smith, September 13, 1945, Foster Care Homefinding Correspondence, 1954–1970, box 62, CWLA records.

36. Charnley, *Art of Child Placement*, 146.

37. "E. H.," comments attached to CWLA, "Preliminary Draft: Standards for Foster Family Care Service," September 1958, *Foster Family Care* revisions, box 62, CWLA records.

38. Zitha Turitz, "The Growth and Development of Standards for Adoption Service," February 15, 1958, Material on Standards Development, box 54, CWLA records.

39. "Use of Child Welfare League of America Standards," May 1963, CWLA Standards — Sections re: Definitions, Principles, Responsibilities, Problems, ibid.

40. Hutchinson, *In Quest of Foster Parents*, 51–52.

41. Wolins, *Selecting Foster Parents*, 47–48.

42. Foster Homes for Children Project [Philadelphia], "Sample Local Newspaper Material," undated, ca. 1948, 7-3-3-2 Foster Home Care, Placing Out July to Dec. 1945, box 156, CB Central File 1945–1948.

43. Meier, *Care of Foster Children with Psychotic Mothers*, 7.

44. Fanshel, *Foster Parenthood*, 11.

45. Herman, *Kinship by Design*, 98–99, 114–15; Solinger, *Wake Up Little Susie*, 86–102; May, *Barren in the Promised Land*, 151–79.

46. Kunzel, *Fallen Women, Problem Girls*, 148–49; Herman, *Kinship by Design*, 85, 88; Curran, "Social Work's Revised Maternalism," 119.

47. Kline and Overstreet, *Casework with Foster Parents*, 6, 10.

48. Josselyn, "Evaluating Motives of Foster Parents," 5.

49. National Association of Social Workers, "David Fanshel"; Columbia School of Social Work, "Professor Emeritus David Fanshel, World Expert on Foster Care, Dies."

50. David Fanshel, "Instructions for Use of Foster Parent Appraisal Form," undated, ca. 1958, folder 7, box 20, CWLA records.

51. Fanshel, *Foster Parenthood*, 32–33, 74, 76.

52. Ibid., 62.

53. K. Doyle, *Homes for Foster Children*, 15.

54. Fanshel, *Foster Parenthood*, 47.

55. Hutchinson, *In Quest of Foster Parents*; Fanshel, *Foster Parenthood*; Wolins, *Selecting Foster Parents*.

56. CWLA, *Standards for Foster Family Care Service*, 1965, 35; Department of Re-

search and Statistics, Amherst H. Wilder Charity, "The Foster Home Problem in St. Paul," November 8, 1946, 7-3-3-2 Foster Home Care, Placing Out Jan. to April 1946, box 156, CB Central File 1945–1948; Stroud, *An Introduction to the Child Care Service*, 89.

57. CWLA, *Standards for Foster Family Care Service*, 1965, 35.

58. Monroe County Department of Public Welfare and Oregon State Public Welfare Commission, comments on CWLA, "Preliminary Draft: Standards for Foster Family Care Service," September 1958, Foster Family Care revisions, box 62, CWLA records.

59. Hutchinson, *In Quest of Foster Parents*.

60. Helen R. Hagan to Leonard Mayo, January 20, 1959, folder 1, box 42, CWLA records.

61. David Fanshel, "Instructions for Use of Foster Parent Appraisal Form," undated, ca. 1958, folder 7, box 20, CWLA records.

62. Wolins, *Selecting Foster Parents*, 51. See also CWLA, "Form D-2: Outline for the Study of a Foster Home," folder 6, box 18, CWLA records.

63. Josselyn, "Cultural Forces," 267–68.

64. May, *Homeward Bound*, 129, 132.

65. Ibid., 130–31.

66. Griswold, *Fatherhood in America*, 194. Griswold and others have identified the postwar period as the moment when the new conceptions of fatherhood took off. Ralph LaRossa, however, has shown that many of the ideas associated with the "new" fatherhood (engaged fathering, for example) could be found earlier (in the twenties and thirties), even though they were not yet as ubiquitous as they would become. LaRossa, *Modernization of Fatherhood*.

67. Quoted in "Latest Need: Less of Mom, More of Pop," *Spartanburg (S.C.) Herald-Journal*, March 26, 1957.

68. "Foster Parent Educational Aids," undated, ca. 1972, Foster Parent Educational Loan Packet, ca. 1972, box 61, CWLA records.

69. For example, see, Elsa Castendyck to Helen H. Searl, September 7, 1943, folder 7-3-3-2 Foster Home Care — Placing Out May 5, 1943, box 168, CB Central File 1941–1944.

70. Department of Research and Statistics, Amherst H. Wilder Charity, "The Foster Home Problem in St. Paul," November 8, 1946, 7-3-3-2 Foster Home Care, Placing Out Jan. to April 1946, box 156, CB Central File 1945–1948; Fanshel, *Foster Parenthood*, 54–57.

71. May, *Barren in the Promised Land*, 137.

72. Griswold, *Fatherhood in America*, 183–86.

73. Wolins, *Selecting Foster Parents*, 50.

74. May, *Homeward Bound*, 130.

75. K. Doyle, *Homes for Foster Children*, 14.

76. Fanshel, *Foster Parenthood*, 10. The description of foster mothers as the "dominating figure in homes offered to the placement agency" was reflected in professional standards at least as early as 1941. CWLA, *Standards for Children's Organizations Providing Foster Family Care* (1941), 41.

77. Herman, *Kinship by Design*, 111.

78. Hutchinson, *In Quest of Foster Parents*, 8.
79. Charnley, *Art of Child Placement*, 174–75.
80. Fanshel, *Foster Parenthood*, 10.
81. Hutchinson, *In Quest of Foster Parents*, 12.
82. Collins, *Black Feminist Thought*, 73.
83. Apple, *Perfect Motherhood*, 107, 117–19; Spock, *Common Sense Book of Baby and Child Care*.
84. Wolins, *Selecting Foster Parents*, 97; Fanshel, *Foster Parenthood*, 80.
85. Hutchinson, *In Quest of Foster Parents*, 12; Wolins, *Selecting Foster Parents*, 99.
86. Melosh, *Strangers and Kin*, 127.
87. Lundberg and Farnham, *Modern Woman*, especially 298–321.
88. Fanshel, *Foster Parenthood*, 5, 19, 45–46.
89. Ibid., 46–48.
90. Kathleen Jackson to Miss Arnold, March 11, 1960, 7-3-3-2 January 1960 Foster Home Care, Placing Out (Free Homes), box 887, CB Central File 1958–1962.
91. Katharine Lenroot, comments on CWLA, "Preliminary Draft: Standards for Foster Family Care Service," September 1958, *Foster Family Care* revisions, box 62, CWLA records.
92. Modell, *Sealed and Secret Kinship*, 92.

Chapter 5

1. K. Doyle, *Homes for Foster Children*, 1; Bowlby, *Maternal Care and Mental Health*, especially 109–28.
2. Lindsey, *Welfare of Children*, 37–38.
3. "Child Welfare Services: Report of the Advisory Council," 9.
4. Cornelia Hopkins Allen, Elda Kanally, Sophie Litsky, and Eleanor Morris Carr, "An Appraisal of the Facilities for the Care of Dependent, Neglected and Problem Children in New Haven, Connecticut," August 20, 1939, folder 1, box 19, CWLA records. In another example, the Child Welfare League's 1937 *Standards* had noted that "even a home which is characterized by grave defects and dangers can seldom be broken without shock both to children and adults." CWLA, *Standards for Child Protective Organizations*, 15.
5. The number of orphans had dropped in the same period from not quite 17 percent of children under eighteen in 1920 to 5 percent in 1954. The number of full orphans also dropped in the same period from about 750,000 in 1920 to 60,000 in 1954, or from 2.0 to 0.1 percent of the nation's population under age eighteen. Shudde and Epstein, "Orphanhood," 639.
6. Rev. Wm. T. Swaim Jr., "The Care of Dependent Children in Pennsylvania," undated, ca. 1945, 7-3-3-2 Foster Home Care, Placing Out July to Dec. 1945, box 156, CB Central File 1945–1948.
7. CWLA, *The Haunted Child*, undated, ca. 1959, CWLA Brochures, 1951–1964, box 83, CWLA records.

8. In one example, Martin Wolins wrote that "the growth of social insurances and public assistance coverage has resulted in a marked reduction of the number of children who come under care of an agency due to economic inadequacy of their homes." Martin Wolins, "Research Proposal," September 6, 1957, folder 4, box 20, CWLA records. See also Agnes K. Hanna to L. H. Atwell, August 7, 1935, 7-3-3-2 Foster Home Care, box 548, CB Central File 1933–1936.

9. Rev. Wm. T. Swaim Jr., "The Care of Dependent Children in Pennsylvania," undated, ca. 1945, 7-3-3-2 Foster Home Care, Placing Out July to Dec. 1945, box 156, CB Central File 1945–1948.

10. In 1965, there were only about seventy-nine thousand dependent children living in institutions, a decrease of about 45 percent since 1933. In 1965, 78 percent of children in foster family care were under the care of publicly funded agencies. Low, "Foster Care of Children," 643–45.

11. "Let's Get Together," undated, ca. 1943, and "Share Your Home with a Child," undated, ca. 1943, 7-3-3-2 Foster Home Care — Placing Out, May 5, 1943, box 168, CB Central File 1941–1944.

12. Meier, *Care of Foster Children with Psychotic Mothers*, 1–2.

13. Mary Taylor to Mildred Arnold, April 18, 1955, 7-3-3-2 April 1955 Foster Home Care Placing Out (Free Homes) 1953–1956, box 680, CB Central File 1953–57.

14. Maas and Engler, *Children in Need of Parents*, 137.

15. Quoted in CWLA, "Board Rates — 1949," folder 3, box 19, CWLA records.

16. CWLA, *The Haunted Child*, undated, ca. 1959, CWLA Brochures, 1951–1964, box 83, CWLA records. See also Martin Wolins, "Research Proposal," September 6, 1957, folder 4, box 20, CWLA records; and Meier, *Care of Foster Children with Psychotic Mothers*, 2–3.

17. Meier, *Care of Foster Children with Psychotic Mothers*, 2–3.

18. Lindsey, *Welfare of Children*, 31–35.

19. Ibid., 27.

20. For an example of how this idea is used to train foster parents in more recent times, see Pasztor et al., *STARS Trainer's Guide*, 3.17–3.24.

21. Gordon, *Heroes of Their Own Lives*, 5.

22. [Miss Virginia Dixon] to President Truman, May 1947, and Judge Frank H. Bicek to Mildred Arnold, June 17, 1947, 7-3-1-4 Custody of Dependent Children 1945–August 1947, box 155, CB Central File 1945–1948.

23. [Ruth Parker] to Welfare Bureau, Children's Agency, November 31 [sic], 1947; [Ruth Parker] to Dear Madam, December 8, 1947; [Ruth Parker] to Dear Madam, January 16, 1948; [Ruth Parker] to Children's Welfare Bureau, November 30, 1949; [Ruth Parker] to President Truman, March 3, 1950, all in 7-3-1-4 Custody of Dependent Children, box 442, CB Central File 1949–1952.

24. Kunzel, *Fallen Women, Problem Girls*, 148–53. Quotation is from 152.

25. [Bessie Clay] to Dear Sur [sic], August 5, 1947; Miss Loretta Chappell to Mildred Arnold, May 6, 1947; Miss Loretta Chappell to Mildred Arnold, April 29, 1947, all in 7-3-1-4 Custody of Dependent Children 1945–August 1947, box 155, CB Central File 1945–1948. The Milledgeville facility is described in Cranford, *But for the Grace of God*.

26. Michel, *Children's Interests/Mothers' Rights*, 5.

27. [Jimmy Hendrickson] to Agnes K. Hanna, July 14, 1940, and Olive O'Brien to Agnes Hanna, August 19. 1940, 7-3-1-4 Custody of Dependent Children July, box 814, CB Central File, 1937–1940.

28. Olive O'Brien to Agnes Hanna, August 19, 1940, ibid.

29. Children's and Family Services of Portland, typed comments attached to CWLA, "Preliminary Draft: Standards for Foster Family Care Service," September 1958, *Foster Family Care* revisions, box 62, CWLA records.

30. CWLA, "Board Rates — 1949," folder 3, box 19, CWLA records.

31. There was a similar concept in the adoption field, referring to those children for whom it was difficult to find permanent adoptive homes, because of the desire by most adopters for young, healthy white children. Herman, *Kinship by Design*, 196–200. The earliest use of the term "hard-to-place" in foster care literature that I have found comes from the 1946 board rate study in the CWLA's discussion of variations from the basic board rate for certain types of children, whom the author describes as "hard to place." CWLA, "Board Rates — 1946," folder 3, box 19, CWLA records.

32. CWLA, "A Study of Board Rates," 1942, folder 3, box 19, CWLA records.

33. Ibid.; CWLA, *Board Rates in December 1954*, 9.

34. CWLA, "Board Rates — 1946," folder 3, box 19, CWLA records; Gordon, *Board Rates in 1951*, 21–29.

35. Henrietta Gordon, "Board Rates," *Child Welfare*, March 1959, reprint in folder 3, box 19, CWLA records.

36. For an example of one such program, see Virginia State Department of Health, "A New Crippled Children's Service."

37. Gordon, *Board Rates in 1951*, 35.

38. Ibid., 26–27. See also CWLA, "A Study of Board Rates," 1942, folder 3, box 19, CWLA records; CWLA, *Board Rates in December 1954*.

39. CWLA, "A Study of Board Rates," 1942, folder 3, box 19, CWLA records (emphasis added).

40. CWLA, "Board Rates — 1946," ibid.

41. Gordon, *Board Rates in 1951*, 29.

42. Ibid., 26.

43. CWLA, "A Study of Board Rates," 1942, folder 3, box 19, CWLA records.

44. Gordon, *Board Rates in 1951*, 25.

45. CWLA, *Board Rates in December 1954*, 10.

46. "CWLA Board Rates — 1946," folder 3, box 19, CWLA records.

47. CWLA, "Board Rates — 1949," ibid. See also CWLA, "Board Rates — 1946," ibid.

48. Gordon, *Board Rates in 1951*, 8. This report later notes that one agency paid a different rate based on race for subsidized homes (foster homes in which the family was paid a subsidy to keep beds available, even if no child was placed there). It paid a fifty-dollar subsidy for a home for African American children but a seventy-five-dollar subsidy for a white home. Ibid., 30.

49. Annie Lee Sandusky, "Comments Preliminary Draft II Standards for Protective Service," October 3, 1958, Protective Standards, box 72, CWLA records.

50. Nelson Jackson to Lester Granger, revision of "Program to Improve Foster Home and Adoptive Services for Negro Children," November 26, 1954, Adoption Program Correspondence and Memoranda (general), box 19, NUL records, part 1:B.

51. Roberts, *Shattered Bonds*, 6.

52. On the shift from the exclusion of African American children from child welfare services to their "overinclusion," see Peebles-Wilkins, "Janie Porter Barrett," 135–53 (quotation is from 149).

53. Nelson Jackson to Lester Granger, revision of "Program to Improve Foster Home and Adoptive Services for Negro Children," November 26, 1954, Adoption Program Correspondence and Memoranda (general), box 19, NUL records, part 1:B.

54. Explanatory statement of Nelson C. Jackson, Southern Field Director National Urban League on "Protective Services for Children," March 18, 1947, 1947 Child Welfare Jan.–Aug., box 83, NUL records, part 4:A.

55. Nelson Jackson to Lester Granger, January 23, 1947, ibid.; Nelson Jackson to Executives of Southern Affiliates, December 23, 1946, 1946 Child Welfare, box 78, NUL records, part 4:A.

56. Billingsley and Giovannoni, *Children of the Storm*, 86, 102.

57. David Fanshel to CWLA staff, January 8, 1962, folder 8, box 18, CWLA records; Billingsley and Giovannoni, *Children of the Storm*, 107–11, 132.

58. Nelson C. Jackson, "The National Urban League's Project in Foster Home and Adoption Services" [preliminary draft for discussion], undated, ca. February 1954, Adoption Program Reports 1953–55, box 19, NUL records, part 1:B.

59. Ougheltree, *Finding Foster Homes*, 9.

60. Jacobs, *Generation Removed*, 135.

61. Nelson Jackson to Lester Granger, revision of "Program to Improve Foster Home and Adoptive Services for Negro Children," November 26, 1954, Adoption Program Correspondence and Memoranda (general), box 19, NUL records, part 1:B; Nelson Jackson to Mrs. Mollie Moon, September 21, 1959, Child Welfare League of America 1958–61, box 2, NUL records, part 1:B.

62. Leonard Lavis, "Educational Recruitment—A Method of Home Finding," November 11, 1955, attached to Leonard Lavis to Miss Sarah L. Doran, March 1, 1956, 7-3-3-2 Sept. 1957 Foster Home Care [2], box 679, CB Central File 1953–57.

63. Ougheltree, *Finding Foster Homes*.

64. Billingsley and Giovannoni, *Children of the Storm*, 143, 167–70.

65. Jacobs, *Generation Removed*, 259.

66. Ibid., 39.

67. Leonard Lavis, "Educational Recruitment—A Method of Home Finding," November 11, 1955, attached to Leonard Lavis to Miss Sarah L. Doran, March 1, 1956, 7-3-3-2 Sept. 1957 Foster Home Care [2], box 679, CB Central File 1953–57.

68. Ibid. See also Ougheltree, *Finding Foster Homes*, 9.

69. Introduction [overview of National Urban League home-finding project in Michigan], undated, ca. 1955, 1955 Foster Home Placement, box 167, NUL records, part 6:A.

70. See for example, Negro Foster Home Finding Committee of the Community Welfare Council of Milwaukee County, "Every Child's Right...A Home of His Own,"

undated, ca. April 1955, attached to Leonard Lavis to Miss Sarah L. Doran, March 1, 1956, 7-3-3-2 Sept. 1957 Foster Home Care [2], box 679, CB Central File 1953–57; Solomon, "Publicity Methods in Finding Foster Homes," 15.

71. Jeweldean Jones to Miss Margie J. Friend, December 15, 1961, Health and Welfare—Adoptions, box 13, NUL records, part 2:D.

72. Billingsley and Giovannoni, *Children of the Storm*, 142–43.

73. NUL, Community Resources for Services to Unmarried Mothers [draft proposal], undated, ca. 1960, Child Welfare League of America 1958–61, box 2, NUL records, part 1:B.

74. Billingsley and Giovannoni, *Children of the Storm*, 108–11.

75. CWLA, "Proposal for a Coordinated Research Program in Foster Care," April 1964, folder 8, box 20, CWLA records.

76. Ibid.; Jeter, *Children, Problems, and Services in Child Welfare Programs*.

77. Jacobs, *Generation Removed*, 17.

78. Bernice Boehm, "Children in Need of Adoption," September 5, 1957, folder 6, box 19, CWLA records.

79. "New Mexico Inventory of Foster Care Needs of Children," January 18, 1956, 7-3-3-2 April 1955 Foster Home Care Placing Out (Free Homes) 1953–56, box 680, CB Central File 1953–57.

80. Katherine Oettinger to Fred C. Schenk, February 10, 1961, 7-3-3-2 Jan. 1961 Foster Home Care, Placing Out (Free Homes), box 886, CB Central File 1958–1962.

81. Joseph R. Reid, "Current Social Concepts in Placement of Handicapped Children," in *Governor's Conference on Finding Families for Handicapped Children* (September 15, 1970), 12–13, copy in Special Needs (Non-CWLA), box 61, CWLA records.

82. Balogh, *Associational State*, 7.

83. Shudde and Epstein, "Orphanhood," 638. See also Jack Wiener to Martha M. Eliot, September 28, 1955, 7-3-3-2 July 1956 Foster Home Care—Place Out (Free Homes) 1953–1957, box 679, CB Central File 1953–57.

84. Holcomb, "When Husbands Run Away," 24–25.

85. Alling and Leisy, "Aid to Dependent Children in a Postwar Year," 7.

86. CWLA, *Standards for Homemaker Service for Children*, 5–6.

87. Boris and Klein, *Caring for America*, 36, 47.

88. Child Welfare League of America, *Standards for Homemaker Service for Children*, 2.

89. Katherine Oettinger to Charles B. Lawrence Jr., February 21, 1958, 7-3-3-2 Foster Home Care, Placing Out (Free Homes), box 887, CB Central File 1958–1962; K. Doyle, *Homes for Foster Children*, 1.

Chapter 6

1. See Zelizer, *Pricing the Priceless Child*, 6.

2. UK and British Commonwealth nations now use the term "foster carers" rather than "foster parents," a term that implies a bit of distance from the parenting analogy. See, for example, Colton and Williams, *World of Foster Care*, a book published in the United Kingdom, which uses this term throughout.

3. [Mrs. Henry Jacobs] to My Most Beloved Eleanor [Roosevelt], April 2, 1940, 7-3-3-2 Foster Home Care — Placing Out [2], box 819, CB Central File 1937–1940.

4. Agnes K. Hanna to [Mrs. Henry Jacobs], April 1940, ibid.

5. This phrase was part of the standard responses sent to those indicating interest in earning money through boarding children. For example, see Agnes K. Hanna to [Mrs. Clyde Rowden], November 1938, 7-3-3-3 Boarding Homes, box 821, CB Central File 1937–1940.

6. CWLA, "A Study of Board Rates," 1942, folder 3, box 19, CWLA records.

7. Katharine Lenroot to Grover Deillman, February 18, 1935, 7-3-3-3 Boarding Homes, box 548, CB Central File 1933–1936.

8. [Mr. and Mrs. Carlo Accurso] to President Truman, undated, ca. May 1951, 7-3-1-4 Custody of Dependent Children 1949–1952, box 1949–1952, CB Central File.

9. Buck, "Interview with My Adopted Daughter," 5.

10. The qualms about payments are reflected in a number of studies of board rates conducted by the CWLA. CWLA, "A Study of Board Rates," 1942; Marjorie Herzig, "Board Rates — 1946"; Henrietta L. Gordon, "Board Rates — 1949," all in folder 3, box 19, CWLA records; Gordon, *Board Rates in 1951*; CWLA, *Board Rates in December 1954*; Henrietta Gordon, "Board Rates," *Child Welfare*, March 1959, reprint in folder 3, box 19, CWLA records.

11. Zelizer, *Pricing the Priceless Child*, 72.

12. Henrietta Gordon to Miss Gertrude L. Prack, March 19, 1945, 7-3-3-2 Foster Home Care Placing Out Jan. 1945 to June 1945, box 157, CB Central File 1945–1948.

13. Viviana Zelizer discusses this process for an earlier period, although this "rehabilitation" was still ongoing well into the twentieth century. Zelizer, *Pricing the Priceless Child*, 188.

14. Hutchinson, *In Quest of Foster Parents*, 136.

15. Agnes Hanna to [Mrs. A. S. Waugh], October 1937, 7-3-3-2 Foster Home Care — Placing Out January 1937, box 820, CB Central File 1937–1940.

16. Ripple, review of *Standards for Foster Family Care Service*, 184.

17. Herman, *Kinship by Design*, 122–34, 95. Quotation is from 95.

18. Ibid., 134–39; Melosh, *Strangers and Kin*, 53–54; Berebitsky, *Like Our Very Own*, 138.

19. CWLA, *Standards for Foster Family Care Service*, 35. The concern about grandparents is found in Minutes of Staff Meeting, March 16, 1956, attached to Bess Craig to Miss Louise Noble, December 17, 1956, 7-3-3-2 Sept. 1957 Foster Home Care, box 678, CB Central File 1953–57.

20. On relative family size between rural and urban families, see Glick, "Family Trends in the United States."

21. [Mrs. Annette Alderink] to President Truman, February 6, 1947, and Mildred Arnold to [Mrs. Annette Alderink], April 2, 1947, 7-3-3-3 Boarding Homes 1945, box 157, CB Central File 1945–1948.

22. CWLA, "A Study of Board Rates," 1942, folder 3, box 19, CWLA records; CWLA, *Standards for Children's Organizations Providing Foster Family Care* (1941), 40; CWLA, *Standards for Foster Family Care Service*, 36.

23. For example, see Elsa Casatendyck to Helen H. Searl, September 7, 1943, 7-3-3-2 Foster Home Care — Placing Out May 5, 1943, box 168, CB Central File 1941–1944; and CWLA, "A Study of Board Rates," 1942, folder 3, box 19, CWLA records.

24. Department of Research and Statistics, Amherst H. Wilder Charity, "The Foster Home Problem in St. Paul," November 8, 1946, 7-3-3-2 Foster Home Care, Placing Out Jan. to April 1946, box 156, CB Central File 1945–1948. Victoria Strong-Boag noted a similar lack of interest in fostering among middle-class Canadians at midcentury. Strong-Boag, *Fostering Nation?*, 8, 73.

25. David Fanshel, "Dissertation Proposal: Toward More Understanding of Foster Parents" [for presentation at dissertation seminar], April 14, 1959, folder 7, box 18, CWLA records.

26. K. Doyle, *Homes for Foster Children*, 25.

27. Felker, *Foster Parenting Young Children*, 81.

28. Eleanor P. Sheldon, "Cost Plus Service," excerpt from Child Welfare League of America, *Bulletin — Child Welfare League of America, Inc.*, March 1945, 7-3-3-3 Boarding Homes 1945, box 157, CB Central File 1945–1948.

29. Charnley, *Art of Child Placement*, 147.

30. Josselyn, "Evaluating Motives of Foster Parents," 7.

31. K. Doyle, *Homes for Foster Children*, 16–17.

32. Rosen, *World Split Open*, 19.

33. CWLA, *Standards for Homemaker Service for Children*, 8, 11. See also "Homemaker Service as a Child Welfare Service."

34. CWLA, *Standards for Homemaker Service for Children*, 23.

35. Boris and Klein, *Caring for America*, 48–49.

36. Ibid., 19, 22–23, 49. Quotation is from 49.

37. Lindenmeyer, *"Right to Childhood,"* 221.

38. On this transition, see Boris and Klein, *Caring for America*, especially chapter 2.

39. Meier, *Care of Foster Children with Psychotic Mothers*, 18.

40. Helen H. Erdman, "A Foster Mother in Honolulu," *Family Letter* [Child and Family Services of Honolulu], reproduced by the Louisiana Department of Public Welfare for the State Staff, 7-3-3-2 Foster Home Care . . . Placing Out January 1, 1947–August 30, 1947, box 156, CB Central File 1945–1948.

41. Margaret Emery to Regional Directors, April 7, 1947, ibid.

42. CWLA, "More Urgent Than Uranium," undated, ca. 1949, Pamphlets, box 83, CWLA records. See also Gertrude Layden, "Some Comments on Board Rates, Service Fees and Salaries for Foster Parents," January 1968, CWLA — Historical Source of Information, box 98, CWLA records.

43. CWLA, *Standards for Foster Family Care Service* (1959), 53. For an earlier discussion (from 1952), see Buran, "Foster Mother's Service Fee in League Member Agencies," 8.

44. C. Maxwell (S.C.), comments on CWLA, "Preliminary Draft: Standards for Foster Family Care Service," September 1958, *Foster Family Care* revisions, box 62, CWLA records.

45. Helen R. Hagan to General Files with copies to staff, April 15, 1961, folder 8, box 18, CWLA records.

46. Kennedy, "Foster Parent Looks at Foster Care," 247. In 1972, foster parents in Watts complained about intimidation. Donna M. Cicco to Bruce Mallott, February 24, 1972, National Foster Parent Assoc. [4], box 62, CWLA records.

47. [Questionnaire for Coordinated Research Program in Foster Care study], August 1966, folder 8, box 20, CWLA records.

48. CWLA, "More Urgent Than Uranium," undated, ca. 1949, Pamphlets, box 83, CWLA records. For a similar statement from almost twenty years later, see Gertrude Layden, "Some Comments on Board Rates, Service Fees and Salaries for Foster Parents," January 1968, CWLA—Historical Source of Information, box 98, CWLA records.

49. Jeanette Harris to Barbara C. Coughlan, July 30, 1958, 7-3-3-2 June 1958 Foster Home Care, Placing Out (Free Homes), box 887, CB Central File 1958–1962. See also Friendship House (Scranton, Penn.), comments on CWLA, "Preliminary Draft: Standards for Foster Family Care Service," September 1958, *Foster Family Care* revisions, box 62, CWLA records.

50. Gertrude Layden, "Some Comments on Board Rates, Service Fees and Salaries for Foster Parents," January 1968, CWLA—Historical Source of Information, box 98, CWLA records.

51. See, for example, Radinsky, Free, and Rubenstein, "Recruiting and Serving Foster Parents," 38; and Haitch, *Orphans of the Living*, 12.

52. Curran, "Social Work's Revised Maternalism," 114.

53. EEG, fragment of typescript (1964), 26, Source Material—Foster Care—to 1970, box 70, CWLA records.

54. CWLA, *Standards for Foster Family Care Services*, 35.

55. Melosh, *Strangers and Kin*, 114–15.

56. [Barbara Fillmore] to Honorable John W. Gardner, December 21, 1965; Beatrice Garrett to [Barbara Fillmore], January 6, 1966, 7-3-3-2 January '66 Foster Home Care Placing Out (Free Homes), box 1034, CB Central File 1963–66.

57. Comments on a draft of the 1958 revision to the CWLA's foster care standards indicate that a number of agencies wanted the standards on a mother's employment to be relaxed and suggest that they or agencies they knew about were already making exceptions. See, for example, Maryland Children's Aid Society, Maryland State Department, and Katharine Lenroot, comments attached to CWLA, "Preliminary Draft: Standards for Foster Family Care Service," September 1958, *Foster Family Care* revisions, box 62, CWLA records.

58. Community Council of Greater New York, comments attached to ibid. See also Fred C. Schenk to Mrs. Katherine B. Oettinger, December 15, 1960, 7-3-3-2 Jan. 1961 Foster Home Care, Placing Out (Free Homes), box 886, CB Central File 1958–1962.

59. Stone, *Reflections on Foster Care*, 30. See also Ougheltree, *Finding Foster Homes*, 9.

60. "E. H.," comments on CWLA, "Preliminary Draft: Standards for Foster Family Care Service," September 1958, *Foster Family Care* revisions, box 62, CWLA records.

61. Mary Daly, "Responsibility for Care and Service" [draft copy], folder 12, box 20, CWLA records.

62. Stone, *Foster Care in Question*, iv–vi.

63. Examples of newspaper coverage of the case of the "bright" child, Alice Marie, in-

clude "Foster Pair May Lose Bright Girl," *New York Times*, March 7, 1960; and "Couple Win Battle for Bright Child, 4," ibid., March 16, 1960. On the case of the Italian American couple, the Liunis, see Family Court, Ulster County, New York, *Mtr. of Fitszimmons v. Liuni*. The Child Welfare League did not support the decision to remove Elizabeth from the Liunis. See Myron R. Chevlin to Professional Staff RE: CWLA Position on Liuni Adoption Case and Surrounding Controversy, January 10, 1967, folder 1, box 43, CWLA records.

64. Clare Golden to Mrs. Kate Helms, September 15, 1958, 7-3-3-2 June 1962 Foster Home Care, Placing Out (Free Homes), box 886, CB Central File 1958–1962.

65. CWLA, *A Concern for Children: Child Welfare League of America, Inc. Progress Report, 1974*, Programs and Services Brochures, box 83, CWLA records. On origins of CATHY, see Mrs. Ruby Kennedy, "Foster Parents and Child Care Workers Look at Foster Care: A Panel Presentation," October 29–November 1, 1967, Conference on Foster Care of Children, box 61, CWLA records. On origins of the Christopher Street Society, see Child Welfare League of America Foster Parent Project Staff, "The National Foster Parents Association: The Beginning Years," September 1974, NFPA [6], box 62, CWLA records.

66. Nadasen, *Welfare Warriors*, 231–32.

67. Kennedy, "Foster Parent Looks at Foster Care," 241–43, 246.

68. Mrs. Ruby Kennedy, "Foster Parents and Child Care Workers Look at Foster Care: A Panel Presentation," and JoAnn LeBaron, "Foster Parents and Child Care Workers Look at Foster Care: A Panel Presentation," October 29–November 1, 1967, Conference on Foster Care of Children, box 61, CWLA records.

69. Mrs. Ruby Kennedy, "Foster Parents and Child Care Workers Look at Foster Care: A Panel Presentation," ibid.

70. Child Welfare League of America Foster Parent Project Staff, "The National Foster Parents Association: The Beginning Years," September 1974, NFPA [6], box 62, CWLA records.

71. Hunzeker, *New Partnership*, 18; SPB to JHR, February 25, 1970, 1st National Conference of Foster Parents, box 62, CWLA records.

72. Saul R. Rosoff to Joseph Reid, July 1, 1974, National Foster Parent Assoc., ibid.

73. "Happenings" [summary of General Session of the First National Conference of Foster Parents], May 9, 1971, National Foster Parent Assoc. [2], ibid.

74. "Insurance Protection—What Coverage Do You Need?," 1974, 4th National Conference of Foster Parents, 1974; and Resolutions Presented at the General Membership Meeting, April 29, 1973, attached to National Foster Parent Association Board of Directors Minutes, April 26, 1973, both in ibid.

75. National Foster Parent Association Board of Directors Minutes, November 18–19, 1972, ibid.

76. NFPA General Business Meeting Minutes, April 29, 1973, 3rd National Conference of Foster Parents, 1973, ibid.

77. "Surprise Your Husband with a Child That Isn't His," undated, ca. 1975, NFPA [5], ibid.

78. See, for example, Revised Position Statement of the National Foster Parent As-

sociation on the Education and Training of Foster Parents, undated, ca. summer 1973, National Foster Parent Assoc., ibid.

79. David T. Evans to Members, Board of Directors, May 17, 1976, 6th National Conference of Foster Parents, 1976, ibid.; Foster Parent Education Aids, undated, ca. 1972, Foster Parent Educational Loan Packet, ca. 1972, box 61, CWLA records.

80. David T. Evans to Members, Board of Directors, May 17, 1976, 6th National Conference of Foster Parents, 1976, box 62, ibid.; CWLA, "What's New... in Foster Care Education?," May 8, 1975, folder 5, box 21, ibid.

81. CWLA, "Prospectus to the Department of Health, Education, and Welfare for New Recruitment Approaches and Techniques Upgrading Current Foster Care Practices," November 20, 1973, National Foster Parent Association [3], box 62, ibid.; Bruce L. Warren, "Survey of the States: Mandatory Training Requirements," 1981, Permanent Homes for Children Project 1981, box 72, ibid.; Children's Bureau, "Home Study Requirements for Prospective Foster Parents."

82. CWLA report to National Foster Parent Association Board, October 13, 1973, National Foster Parent Assoc., box 62, CWLA records.

83. National Foster Parent Association Board of Directors Minutes, November 18–19, 1972, National Foster Parent Assoc. [2], box 62, CWLA records.

84. National Foster Parent Association Board of Directors Minutes, April 26, 1973, National Foster Parent Assoc., ibid.

85. Sidney Rosendorn, "Joining Together to Help Foster Children," May 30, 1972, National Foster Parent Assoc. [4], ibid.

86. *National Foster Parent Association* [brochure], undated, National Foster Parent Association [3], ibid.

87. Joseph H. Reid, "Patterns of Partnership," address to First Annual Foster Parents Conference, November 8, 1969, folder 5, box 21, ibid.

88. *Smith v. Organization of Foster Families for Equality and Reform*, 430–31.

89. Ann W. Shyne to Miss Kathryn Close, January 5, 1971, Foster Care — Board Rate Study, 1970–1973, box 62, CWLA records.

Chapter 7

1. Toward the end of World War II, Arizona conducted a study of children who had been in foster home care for more than six months. A representative from the state social services agency thought the survey pointed to a need for a national study that would provide information on the number of children placed who returned home and the number who did not. He also suggested that it might also be useful to collect data on the age and race of foster children, on the marital status of parents, reasons for referral, and the reasons for continued need of foster care. Edward E. Schwartz to Miss Martha Wood, October 21, 1945, 7-3-3-2 Foster Home Care, Placing Out July to Dec. 1945, box 156, CB Central File, 1945–1948.

2. Zelma Felten, "Children in Need of Adoption (A Proposal for Study)," January 30, 1957, folder 12, and Zelma Felten to Members of the New Haven Adoption Study

Advisory Committee, February 14, 1957, both in folder 2, box 16, CWLA records. Biographical material is found in "What the League Did Last Year, 1982," box 84, ibid.

3. Maas and Engler, *Children in Need of Parents*, vii–viii.

4. "Proposal for a Coordinated Research Program in Foster Care," April 1964, folder 8, box 20, CWLA records.

5. For example, the CB journal—called *The Child* from 1936 to 1954 and then renamed *Children*—published twenty-eight articles related to American foster family care from 1936 to 1958, an average of 1.21 articles per year. In the years 1959 through 1971, fifty-seven such articles appeared or 4.38 articles per year.

6. Zelma J. Felten, "Foster Care Project," May 28, 1957, folder 6, box 19, CWLA records.

7. Maas and Engler, *Children in Need of Parents*, 1, 389.

8. Bernice Boehm, "Children in Need of Adoption," September 5, 1957, folder 6, box 19, CWLA records.

9. Maas and Engler, *Children in Need of Parents*, 1.

10. National Survey of Child and Adolescent Well-Being, "Risk of Long-Term Foster Care Placement."

11. Zelma J. Felten, "Report of Foster Care Study," May 6, 1960, folder 6, box 19, CWLA records; Zelma Felten to Mildred Arnold, May 3, 1960, 7-3-3-2 Jan. 1961 Foster Home Care, Placing Out (Free Homes), box 886, CB Central File 1958–1962. Another study, conducted in the Twin Cities, found that of children placed due to "neglect," about two-thirds were from families on public assistance and/or in "severe financial difficulties." Boehm, "Child in Foster Care," 222.

12. Connie Maxwell Home, comments attached to CWLA, "Preliminary Draft: Standards for Foster Family Care Service," September 1958, *Foster Family Care* revisions, box 62, CWLA records.

13. Zelma Felten to Mildred Arnold, May 3, 1960, 7-3-3-2 Jan. 1961 Foster Home Care, Placing Out (Free Homes), box 886, CB Central File 1958–1962.

14. Arnold, "Growth of Public Child Welfare Services," 625.

15. Gerstle, *Liberty and Coercion*, 299.

16. "Child Welfare Services: Report of the Advisory Council," 8–9.

17. Edna Hughes to Social Service Staff, July 3, 1959, folder 2, box 42, CWLA records.

18. "Statement by Chief of Children's Bureau on Grants to States for Maternal and Child Welfare, Children's Bureau, 1962 Estimate," April 1962, Legislative Children's Bureau, box 77, ibid.

19. Kendrick, Review of *Standards for Child Protective Service*, 185.

20. Arnold, "Growth of Public Child Welfare Services," 625.

21. Low, "Foster Care of Children," 644.

22. See, for example, Martha M. Eliot to Charles Schottland, April 4, 1955, 7-3-3-2 Dec. 1955 Foster Home Care Placing Out (Free Homes), box 680, CB Central File 1953–57; Joseph H. Reid, "Summary of Child-Health and Welfare Amendments of 1956," attached to Joseph H. Reid to Member Agencies, February 21, 1956, folder 2, box 42, CWLA records; Schottland, "Social Security Amendments of 1956"; Katharine Len-

root to Emma C. Pushner, June 29, 1945, 7-3-3-2 Foster Home Care Placing Out Jan. 1945 to June 1945, box 157, CB Central File 1945–1948.

23. Katharine Lenroot, "Child-Welfare in State and Local Public Welfare Programs," presented at the Southeastern National Conference of the American Public Welfare Association, April 5, 1946, folder 8, box 5, series 1.1, Lenroot Papers.

24. Lindenmeyer, *"Right to Childhood,"* 250–52; Lenroot, "United States Children's Bureau in Its New Home," 78.

25. Mittelstadt, *From Welfare to Workfare*, 46.

26. Ibid., 86, 88.

27. Nadasen, *Welfare Warriors*, 10.

28. Bent-Goodley, "Regulating the Lives of Children," 34.

29. Katharine Lenroot, "Comments on 'Suggestions for Possible Family and Child Welfare Aid Program,' and Alternative Suggestions," December 27, 1960, folder 2, box 42, CWLA records.

30. "Child Welfare Services: Report of the Advisory Council," 3; Kidneigh, "Look to the Future in Child Welfare Services," 66–67.

31. "Child Welfare Services: Report of the Advisory Council," 3–4.

32. Ibid., 4.

33. "Public Assistance: Report of the Advisory Council," 11.

34. Wilbur J. Cohen, "Summary of 1961 Public Assistance Amendments to the Social Security Act," undated, 1961, Legislative HEW, box 77, CWLA records; Davies, *From Opportunity to Entitlement*, 160–61. For more on AFDC–Unemployed Parent, see Mittelstadt, *From Welfare to Workfare*, 109–19.

35. Mitteldstadt, *From Welfare to Workfare*, 121.

36. Mrs. O. Donald Oldson to Senator Harry S. Byrd, March 24, 1961, Legislative HEW, box 77, CWLA records.

37. Joseph Reid, "Comments on 'Suggestions for Possible Family and Child Welfare Aid Program' and an Alternative Plan," January 11, 1961, folder 4, box 43, ibid.

38. Atkinson, "Child Welfare Services," 618. As Mrs. O. Donald Oldson of the Advisory Committee to the Colorado Child Welfare Division noted, while her committee supported AFDC–Unemployed Parent, it "strongly oppose[d]" the proposals under AFDC–Foster Care to transfer administration of Title V, part 3, from the CB and to public assistance. Mrs. O. Donald Oldson to Senator Harry S. Byrd, March 24, 1961, Legislative HEW, box 77, CWLA records.

39. Margaret Emery to Miss Trout, June 10, 1948, 7-3-3-2 Foster Home Care—Placing Out, box 156, CB Central File, 1945–1948. See also Katharine Lenroot, "Comments on 'Suggestions for Possible Family and Child Welfare Aid Program,' and Alternative Suggestions," December 27, 1960, folder 2, box 42, CWLA records.

40. Joseph R. Reid, "Statement for Sub-committee of the Advisory Council on Public Welfare," February 18, 1965, Testimony 1965–1977, box 77, CWLA records.

41. Lindsey, *Welfare of Children*, 23n7.

42. Joseph Reid, testimony given before House Ways and Means Committee, February 13, 1962, folder 11, box 42, CWLA records.

43. Michel, *Children's Interests/Mothers' Rights*, 5.
44. CB, "Workshop for Foster Care Consultants," 7-3-3-2 Foster Home Care Placing Out (Free Homes), box 1034, CB Central File 1963–1966.
45. Jean Rubin to Executive Directors of League Member Agencies and Affiliates, April 2, 1969, folder 5, box 42, CWLA records.
46. Winford Oliphant, "A Study of Policies Pertaining to AFDC Foster Care," undated [December 1973], folder 6, box 21, ibid. See also Winford Oliphant, "AFDC Foster Care: Problems and Recommendations," 1973, Foster Care AFDC, box 63, ibid.
47. On subsequent amendments to AFDC–Foster Care, see U.S. Congress, Senate, Committee on Finance, *Staff Data and Materials Related to Foster Care, Adoption Assistance, and Child Welfare Services under the Social Security Act*, 2.
48. Summary of the Public Policy Committee Meeting, June 7, 1967, folder 14, box 43, CWLA records.
49. Winford Oliphant, "A Study of Policies Pertaining to AFDC Foster Care," undated [December 1973], folder 6, box 21, ibid. See also Winford Oliphant, "AFDC Foster Care: Problems and Recommendations," 1973, Foster Care AFDC, box 63, ibid.
50. Albert, *Law and Social Work Practice*, 40; Wilbur J. Cohen, "Summary of 1961 Public Assistance Amendments to the Social Security Act," undated, 1961, Legislative HEW, box 77, CWLA records.
51. Joseph Reid, "Comments on 'Suggestions for Possible Family and Child Welfare Aid Program' and an Alternative Plan," January 11, 1961, folder 4, box 43, CWLA records; Katharine F. Lenroot, "Comments on 'Suggestions for Possible Family and Child Welfare Aid Program,' and Alternative Suggestions," December 27, 1960, ibid.
52. CWLA, "CWLA Standards: Definition of Service," ca. May 1963, CWLA Standards Sections re: Definitions, Principles, Responsibilities, Problems, box 54, ibid.
53. Maas and Engler, *Children in Need of Parents*, appendix D: Legal Data, 424–37.
54. Zelma J. Felten, "Report of Foster Care Study," May 6, 1960, folder 6, box 19, CWLA records; CWLA, *Children in Need of Parents*, undated pamphlet (ca. 1959), 7, folder 6, box 19, CWLA records.
55. Annie Lee Sandusky to Zitha R. Turitz, September 26, 1958, Protective Standards, box 72, CWLA records. See also Annie Lee Sandusky, "Comments on Preliminary Draft II Standards for Protective Service," October 1958, ibid.
56. Lucille J. Grow, "Requests for Child Welfare Services: A Five-Day Census," undated [December 1969], Requests for Child Welfare Services, 1969–1975, box 70, ibid.
57. Gordon, *Heroes of Their Own Lives*, 295.
58. Staff Committee, "An Analysis of a State Child Welfare Program That Has Been Limited to Foster Care with a Large Part of Intake through Court Commitment," February 1957, 7-3-3-2 Jan. 1957 Foster Home Care — Placing Out (Free Homes) 1953–1957, box 679, CB Central File 1953–57.
59. Zelma J. Felten, "Report of Foster Care Study," May 6, 1960, folder 6, box 19, CWLA records; Maas and Engler, *Children in Need of Parents*, 361.
60. CWLA, *Standards for Foster Family Care Service*, 15.
61. Missouri Division of Welfare, comments on CWLA, "Preliminary Draft: Stan-

dards for Foster Family Care Service," September 1958, *Foster Family Care* revisions, box 62, CWLA records; Zelma J. Felten, "Report of Foster Care Study," May 6, 1960, folder 6, box 19, ibid.

62. Miss Camille Killian to Katharine Lenroot, February 13, 1942, 7-3-3-2 Foster Home Care — Placing Out May 5, 1943, box 168, CB Central File 1941–1944.

63. Joseph R. Reid, "Statement for Sub-committee of the Advisory Council on Public Welfare," February 18, 1965, Testimony 1965–1977, box 77, CWLA records.

64. Joseph Reid, "Comments on 'Suggestions for Possible Family and Child Welfare Aid Program and an Alternative Plan,'" January 11, 1961, folder 4, box 43, 4, CWLA records.

65. Winford Oliphant, "A Study of Policies Pertaining to AFDC Foster Care," undated [December 1973], folder 6, box 21, ibid.; Elizabeth Wickenden, "Note on the WIN Program," June 10, 1968, Public Assistance Corres. for Use in Standards Development, box 77, ibid.

66. Winford Oliphant, "A Study of Policies Pertaining to AFDC Foster Care," undated [December 1973], folder 6, box 21, ibid.; Winford Oliphant, "Report on Minnesota, August 20–22, 1973," October 15, 1973, folder 6, box 21, ibid.; Winford Oliphant to Zelma J. Felten, August 21, 1973, folder 10, box 42, ibid.

67. Maas and Engler, *Children in Need of Parents*, 380–83.

68. Winford Oliphant, "A Study of Policies Pertaining to AFDC Foster Care," undated, [December 1973], folder 6, box 21, CWLA records. See also Winford Oliphant, "AFDC Foster Care: Problems and Recommendations," 1973, Foster Care AFDC, box 63, ibid.

69. Children's Defense Fund, *Children without Homes*, 123.

70. Billingsley and Giovannoni, *Children of the Storm*, vii, 17.

71. On the National Welfare Rights Organization, see Nadasen, *Welfare Warriors*.

72. National Association of Black Social Workers, "History"; Billingsley and Giovannoni, *Children of the Storm*, 217.

73. National Association of Black Social Workers, "Position Statement on Transracial Adoption."

74. Eve Erdstrom, "Radicals' Demands Stun and Polarize Welfare Leaders," *Washington Post*, June 1, 1969.

75. Katharine Lenroot to Leo Porlis, June 20, 1969, Cohen, Wilbur, box 28, series 1.4, Lenroot Papers.

76. Jacobs, *Generation Removed*, 114.

77. *Indian Child Welfare Act*. On the transition from a policy promoting adoption of Indian children by white families to one of discouraging it, see Palmiste, "From the Indian Adoption Project to the Indian Child Welfare Act."

78. Black Administrators in Child Welfare, Inc., "History: 1971–1981," Black Administrators in Child Welfare 1980–1985, unattributed notes re: black administrators in child welfare, ca. 1980s, Black Administrators in Child Welfare, box 102, CWLA records.

79. NUL, "Statement to the Ad Hoc Committee on Revision of the Adoption Law, Pennsylvania Department of Public Welfare," September 25, 1962, Health and

Welfare — Adoptions, box 13, NUL records, part 2:D; "Informal Adoption among Black Families" [grant application], February 1, 1973, Adoptions, Feb. 1973–June 1978, H. D. (1 of 3), box 164, ibid., part 3.

80. Membership Committee to Board of Directors, December 4, 1968, Affirmative Action 1961–1973, box 100, CWLA records.

81. "Have a Black Perspective: An Additional Set of Standards for Foster Family Care for Black Children and Young Adults," January 7, 1974, Minorities — Black Concerns, box 71, ibid.; [excerpted pages from minutes of meeting about standards revision], undated, ca. 1970s, ibid.

82. Minutes of CWLA's ad hoc committee on *Policies in Respect to Race in Child Welfare*, November 15, 1965, folder 8, box 12, ibid.

83. *Civil Rights Act of 1964*, 252.

84. Minutes of CWLA's ad hoc committee on *Policies in Respect to Race in Child Welfare*, November 15, 1965, folder 8, box 12, CWLA records; excerpts from A[merican] P[ublic] W[elfare] A[association] letter to members, March 26, 1965, Affirmative Action 1961–1973, box 100, ibid.

85. [Excerpted pages from minutes of meeting about standards revision], undated, ca. 1970s, Minorities — Black Concerns, box 71, ibid.; "Have a Black Perspective: An Additional Set of Standards for Foster Family Care for Black Children and Young Adults," January 7, 1974, ibid.

86. [Excerpted pages from minutes of meeting about standards revision], undated, ca. 1970s, Minorities — Black Concerns, box 71, ibid.; "Have a Black Perspective: An Additional Set of Standards for Foster Family Care for Black Children and Young Adults," January 7, 1974, ibid.

87. Minutes of CWLA's ad hoc committee on *Policies in Respect to Race in Child Welfare*, November 15, 1965, folder 8, box 12, ibid.

88. CWLA, Inc. to Child Welfare Agencies, State Departments of Public Welfare, Welfare Planning Councils, State Associations of Child Welfare Agencies RE: Title XX, April 22, 1975, folder 9, box 42, ibid.; CWLA, "Hecht Institute for State Child Welfare Planning," September 26, 1975, Child Welfare Goals and Strategy Project of the Children's Bureau (1975–1976 [1]), box 100, ibid.

89. Boehm, "Child in Foster Care," 222.

90. Richard J. Clendenen to Wilbur J. Cohen, February 3, 1961, 7-3-3-2 Jan. 1961 Foster Home Care, Placing Out (Free Homes), box 886, CB Central File 1958–1962.

Conclusion

1. Modell, *Sealed and Secret Kinship*, 86.
2. Ibid., 83.
3. Victoria Strong-Boag makes a similar observation about foster parents in Canada in *Fostering Nation?*, 84.
4. T. M. Jim Parham [to Honorable Charles A. Weltner], January 3, 1966, 7-3-3-2 March '66 Foster Home Care Placing Out, box 1034, CB Central File 1963–66.

5. CWLA, "More Urgent Than Uranium," undated, ca. 1949, Pamphlets, box 83, CWLA records.

6. Gertrude Layden, "Some Comments on Board Rates, Service Fees and Salaries for Foster Parents," January 1968, CWLA — Historical Source of Information, box 98, ibid. Similarly, a draft of a handbook produced by the Public Assistance Administration noted that "when foster parents specifically ask to contribute some part of the cost of care, this should be recognized both as service to the child and contribution to the welfare of the community." Draft Handbook of Public Assistance Administration Part IV, Section 3452, September 17, 1962, 7-3-3-2 June 1962 Foster Home Care, Placing Out (Free Homes), box 886, CB Central File 1958–1962.

7. Kathleen Jackson to Mildred Arnold, March 11, 1960, 7-3-3-2 January 1960 Foster Home Care, Placing Out (Free Homes), box 887, CB Central File 1958–1962.

8. See J. Nelson, "Of Markets and Martyrs"; and England, Budig, and Folbre, "Wages of Virtue." Few of these scholars include foster care providers in their studies. For one who does, see Swartz, *Parenting for the State*.

9. Boris and Klein, *Caring for America*, 9.

10. Herman, *Kinship by Design*, 73.

11. In 2004, a National Association of Social Workers study of its members working in child welfare found that 84 percent were female and 77 percent were white (more heavily female and more racially diverse than the social work profession as a whole). They earned an average salary of $33,000 at public and $27,000 at private agencies. National Association of Social Workers, "'If You're Right for the Job, It's the Best in the World,'" 11, 14. A 2006 study on turnover in the child welfare workforce noted that child welfare workers earn about $9,000 less than employees in fields requiring similar education and skills such as teaching or probation. Strolin, McCarthy, and Caringi, "Causes and Effects of Child Welfare Workforce Turnover."

12. Sribnick, "Rehabilitating Child Welfare," 15.

13. Lindsey, *Welfare of Children*, 60, 90, 109.

14. Modell, *Sealed and Secret Kinship*, 18–19.

15. Wantingtobond, "just got a fost-adopt placement," posting to the Adoptive Breastfeeding Resource website, August 8, 2005, www.fourfriends.com/abrw/forum/index.php?, accessed November 14, 2005.

16. Joseph Reid, "Press Release from CWLA," September 9, 1957, folder 6, box 19, CWLA records. Reid cited the New York City study to which he referred as Community Council of Greater New York, *Fact Book on Children in New York City* (1957). He did not provide further information about the Los Angeles study.

17. Joseph Reid, "Press Release from CWLA," September 23, 1957, folder 6, box 19, CWLA records.

18. Zelma J. Felten, "Report of Foster Care Study," May 6, 1960, ibid.

19. Elizabeth Cole, "Permanency Planning Defined," undated, ca. 1981, Permanent Families for Children Project 1981, box 72, ibid.

20. Lindsey, *Welfare of Children*, 54, 57.

21. Bartholet, *Nobody's Children*, 41.

22. Spaulding for Children, Testimony before the Senate Subcommittee on Children and Youth, July 14, 1975, Testimony 1971–1977, box 77, CWLA records; Elizabeth Cole to the National Commission for Children in Need of Permanent Parents, October 12, 1977, Testimony 1973–1977, ibid.

23. Spaulding for Children, Testimony before the Senate Subcommittee on Children and Youth, July 14, 1975, Testimony 1971–1977, ibid.

24. Testimony of Abe Lavine to Subcommittee on Public Assistance, U.S. Senate Committee on Finance, July 19, 1977, ibid.

25. U.S. Congress, Senate, Committee on Finance, *Staff Data and Materials Related to Foster Care, Adoption Assistance, and Child Welfare Services under the Social Security Act*, 7.

26. Testimony of Abe Lavine to Subcommittee on Public Assistance, U.S. Senate Committee on Finance, July 19, 1977, Testimony 1971–1977, box 77, CWLA records; U.S. Congress, Senate, Committee on Finance, *Staff Data and Materials Related to Foster Care, Adoption Assistance, and Child Welfare Services under the Social Security Act*, 5–6.

27. *Adoption Assistance and Child Welfare Act of 1980*.

28. Maas and Engler, *Children in Need of Parents*, 401–2, 425–35; CWLA, *Children in Need of Parents*, undated pamphlet (ca. 1959), 11–13, folder 6, box 19, CWLA records.

29. Zelma J. Felten, "Report of Foster Care Study," May 6, 1960, folder 6, box 19, CWLA records.

30. Quotation is from Principle 6, Declaration of the Rights of the Child, United Nations General Assembly Resolution 1386 (XIV), November 20, 1959.

31. Maas and Engler, *Children in Need of Parents*, 383.

32. *Orphans of the Living*, September 1960, CWLA Brochures, 1951–1964, box 83, CWLA records.

33. *The Multiethnic Placement Act of 1994*; *Adoption and Safe Families Act of 1997* (amended Title IV-E of the *Social Security Act*).

34. Bartholet, *Nobody's Children*, 23–24.

35. See Roberts, *Shattered Bonds*, 104–13; CWLA, *Impact of ASFA on Children and Families of Color*; and Modell, *Sealed and Secret Kinship*, 118.

36. U.S. Congress, House and Senate, *Personal Responsibility and Work Opportunity Act*; Smith, "Bring Back the Orphanages?," 108–09; London, "1994 Orphanage Debate," 84–87.

37. Modell, *Sealed and Secret Kinship*, 82–83.

Appendix

1. Katz, "Foster Parents versus Agencies," 146n2.

2. "Child Placement Contract between the Tennessee Department of Public Welfare and Foster Parents Approved to Provide Temporary Care," undated, ca. 1959, 7-3-3-2 Nov. 1961 Foster Home Care, Placing Out (Free Homes), box 886, CB Central File 1958–1962.

BIBLIOGRAPHY

Primary Sources

MANUSCRIPT COLLECTIONS

College Park, Md.
   National Archives
      Records of the U.S. Children's Bureau
Minneapolis, Minn.
   Social Welfare History Archives
      Records of Minneapolis Family and Children's Services
      Records of the Child Welfare League of America
New York, N.Y.
   Columbia University, Butler Rare Book and Manuscript Room
      Dorothy Hutchinson Papers
      Katharine Lenroot Papers
Washington, D.C.
   Georgetown University, Lauenger Library, Special Collections Research Center
      Robert F. Wagner Papers
   Library of Congress
      Records of the National Urban League

GOVERNMENT PUBLICATIONS

Bradbury, Dorothy E., and Martha M. Eliot. *Four Decades of Action for Children; A Short History of the Children's Bureau.* Washington, D.C.: Department of Health, Education, and Welfare, 1956.

Conference on the Care of Dependent Children. *Proceedings of the Conference on the Care of Dependent Children.* Washington, D.C.: Government Printing Office, 1909.

Kutz, Gregory D. *HHS Guidance Could Help State Improve Oversight of Psychotropic Prescriptions: Testimony before the Subcommittee on Federal Financial Management, Government Information, Federal Services, and International Security, Committee on Homeland Security and Governmental Affairs.* Washington, D.C.: U.S. Government Accountability Office, 2011. http://www.gao.gov/assets/590/586570.pdf. Accessed October 26, 2016.

"Social Security Act Amendments." In *CQ Almanac 1946*, 2nd ed., 04-666-04-671. Washington, D.C.: Congressional Quarterly, 1947. http://library.cqpress.com/cqalmanac/cqal46-1410787. Accessed November 8, 2016.

Stoltzfus, Emilie. *Child Care: The Federal Role during World War II.* Congressional

Research Service Report for Congress. June 29, 2000. https://file.wikileaks.org/file/crs/RS20615.pdf. Accessed 9 March 2017.

U.S. Committee on Economic Security. *Report to the President*. Washington, D.C., 1935. Reprinted in *Children and Youth in America: A Documentary History; Volume III, 1933–1973, Parts 1–4*, edited by Robert H. Bremner, 527–29. Cambridge, Mass.: Harvard University Press, 1974.

———. *Social Security in America: The Factual Background of the Social Security Act as Summarized from Staff Reports to the Committee on Economic Security*. Social Security Board Pub. No. 20, Washington, D.C., 1937. Reprinted in Robert H. Bremner, ed. *Children and Youth in America: A Documentary History; Volume III, 1933–1973, Parts 1–4*. Cambridge, Mass.: Harvard University Press, 1974.

U.S. Congress. House. Committee on Ways and Means. *Economic Security Act Hearings on H.R. 4120*. 74th Cong., 1st sess., 1935.

———. Senate. Committee on Finance. *Staff Data and Materials Related to Foster Care, Adoption Assistance, and Child Welfare Services under the Social Security Act*. Washington, D.C.: Government Printing Office, 1985. http://files.eric.ed.gov/fulltext/ED264939.pdf. Accessed November 8, 2016.

———. Public Assistance. *Report to the Senate of the Advisory Council on Public Assistance Containing Findings and Recommendations Dated January 1960*. Washington, D.C.: Government Printing Office, 1960.

U.S. Department of Health and Human Services. *The AFCARS Report*. 18 September 2015. http://www.acf.hhs.gov/cb/resource/afcars-report-22. Accessed November 1, 2016.

U.S. Department of Labor, Children's Bureau. *Foster-Home Care for Dependent Children*. Washington, D.C.: Government Printing Office, 1924.

U.S. Government Accountability Office. *African American Children in Foster Care: Additional HHS Assistance Needed to Help States Reduce the Proportion in Care*. July 2007. http://www.gao.gov/new.items/d07816.pdf. Accessed May 29, 2013.

LEGAL DOCUMENTS

"An Act to Provide for the Adoption of Children." *Acts and Resolves Passed by the General Court of Massachusetts*. Boston: Secretary of the Commonwealth, 1851.

Adoption Assistance and Child Welfare Act of 1980: [An Act to Establish a Program of Adoption Assistance...]. Public Law 96-72. June 17, 1980.

Adoption and Safe Families Act of 1997. Public Law 105-89. November 19, 1997.

Civil Rights Act of 1964. Public Law 88-352. 78 Stat. 241. July 2, 1964.

Court of Appeals of New York. *In the Matter of Jewish Child Care Association of New York*. 4 N.Y. 2d 1036 (1958). Decided: January 23, 1959.

Family Court, Ulster County, New York. *Mtr. of Fitzsimmons v. Liuni*. 51 Misc. 2d 96 (1966). http://www.leagle.com/decision/196614751Misc2d96_1122.xml/MTR.%20OF%20FITZSIMMONS%20v.%20LIUNI. Accessed November 14, 2016.

Federal Emergency Relief Act of 1933. Public Law 73-15. 73rd Cong., 1st Sess., 1933.

Indian Child Welfare Act. Public Law 95-608. November 8, 1978.

Massachusetts Court of Assistants. *The Colonial Laws of Massachusetts: Reprinted from the Edition of 1672, with Supplements through 1686.* Boston: Rockwell and Churchill, City Printers, 1890.
The Multiethnic Placement Act of 1994. Public Law 103-382. October 20, 1994.
Smith v. Organization of Foster Families for Equality and Reform. 431 U.S. 816, 97 S. Ct. 2094, 53 L. Ed. 2d 14 (1977).
U.S. Congress. House and Senate. *Personal Responsibility and Work Opportunity Reconciliation Act of 1996.* Public Law 104-193. 104th Cong., 2nd Sess. 1996, H.R. 3734, August 22, 1996.
———. *Social Security Act of 1935.* August 14, 1935.

NEWSPAPERS

Amarillo (Tex.) Globe-News
Daily Kennebec (Maine) Journal
Los Angeles Times
New York Herald Tribune
New York Times
Ottawa Citizen
Spartanburg (S.C.) Herald-Journal

PUBLISHED PRIMARY SOURCES

Abbott, Grace. *The Dependent and the Delinquent Child: The Child of Unmarried Parents.* Vol. 2 of *The Child and the State.* Chicago: University of Chicago Press, 1938.
———. *Legal Status in the Family Apprenticeship and Child Labor.* Vol. 1 of *The Child and the State.* Chicago: University of Chicago Press, 1938.
Alling, Elizabeth, and Agnes Leisy. "Aid to Dependent Children in a Postwar Year." *Social Security Bulletin* 13, no. 8 (August 1950): 3–12.
Arnold, Mildred. "Federal Services for Children under Reorganization." *Social Service Review* 11, no. 3 (September 1947): 309–15.
———."The Growth of Public Child Welfare Services." *Children* 7 (1960): 131–35. Reprinted in *Children and Youth in America: A Documentary History; Volume III, 1933–1973, Parts 1–4,* edited by Robert H. Bremner, 621–26. Cambridge, Mass.: Harvard University Press, 1974.
Atkinson, Mary Irene. "Child Welfare Services." *The Annals of the American Academy of Political and Social Sciences* (1939), 82. Reprinted in *Children and Youth in America: A Documentary History; Volume III, 1933–1973, Parts 1–4,* edited by Robert H. Bremner, 616–20. Cambridge, Mass.: Harvard University Press, 1974.
Berkeley Social Welfare Department. "Martin Wolins, 1920–1985." http://socialwelfare.berkeley.edu/faculty/martin-wolins-1920–1985. Accessed November 8, 2016.
Blake, Dorothy. "They Call Her Aunt May." *Woman's Day,* May 1945, 50–51, 85–87.
Boehm, Bernice. "The Child in Foster Care." In *Foster Care in Question: A National Reassessment by Twenty-One Experts,* edited by Helen D. Stone, 220–27. New York: Child Welfare League of America, 1970.

Bowlby, John. *Maternal Care and Mental Health: A Report Prepared on Behalf of the World Health Organization as a Contribution to the United Nations Programme for the Welfare of Homeless Children.* Geneva: World Health Organization, 1952.

Brace, Charles L. "'Placing Out' Plan for Homeless and Vagrant Children." *Proceedings of the National Conference of Charities and Correction*, 1876, 135–50.

Bremner, Robert H., ed. *Children and Youth in America: A Documentary History; Volume III, 1933–1973, Parts 1–4.* Cambridge, Mass.: Harvard University Press, 1974.

Buck, Pearl S. "An Interview with My Adopted Daughter." *Reader's Digest*, June 1946, 4–8.

Buran, Lucy. "The Foster Mother's Service Fee in League Member Agencies." *Child Welfare* 31, no. 10 (December 1952): 8–9.

Carstens, C. C. "Child Welfare Services." In *Social Work Yearbook 1937*, edited by Russel H. Kurtz, 64–72. New York: Russell Sage Foundation, 1937.

Castendyck, Elsa. Review of *In Quest of Foster Parents*, by Dorothy Hutchinson. *Survey Midmonthly: Journal of Social Work* 79 (1943): 285.

Charnley, Jean. *The Art of Child Placement.* Minneapolis: University of Minnesota Press, 1955.

Children's Bureau. "Home Study Requirements for Prospective Foster Parents." March 2014. https://www.childwelfare.gov/pubPDFs/homestudyreqs.pdf. Accessed September 12, 2016.

Children's Defense Fund. *Children without Homes: An Examination of Public Responsibility to Children in Out-of-Home Care.* Washington, D.C.: Children's Defense Fund, 1978.

Child Welfare League of America. *Board Rates in December 1954: A Study Based on the Participation of League Member Agencies.* New York: Child Welfare League of America, 1956.

———. *The Impact of ASFA on Children and Families of Color: Proceedings of a Forum November 2000.* Washington, D.C.: Child Welfare League of America, 2002.

———. *Standards for Adoption Service.* New York: Child Welfare League of America, 1958.

———. *Standards for Child Protective Organizations.* New York: Child Welfare League of America 1937.

———. *Standards for Child Protective Service.* New York: Child Welfare League of America, 1960.

———. *Standards for Children's Organizations Providing Foster Family Care.* New York: Child Welfare League of America, 1933.

———. *Standards for Children's Organizations Providing Foster Family Care.* New York: Child Welfare League of America, 1941.

———. *Standards for Foster Family Care Service.* 1959; repr., New York: Child Welfare League of America, 1965.

———. *Standards for Homemaker Service for Children.* 1959; repr., New York: Child Welfare League of America, 1965.

———. "Youth after Foster Care Statistics." http://66.227.70.18/programs/housing/youthfostercarestats.htm. Accessed November 8, 2016.

"Child Welfare Services: Report of the Advisory Council." *Social Security Bulletin* 23, no. 22 (February 1960): 3–10.

Close, Kathryn. *Transplanted Children: A History.* New York: U.S. Committee for the Care of European Children, 1953.

———. "When the Children Come." *Survey Midmonthly,* 1940, 283–86. Reprinted in *Children and Youth in America: A Documentary History; Volume III, 1933–1973, Parts 1–4,* edited by Robert H. Bremner, 131–36. Cambridge, Mass.: Harvard University Press, 1974.

Colorado State University–Pueblo Continuing Education. *Foster Parent Core Training: Participant Workbook.* 2008. http://coned.colostate-pueblo.edu/SiteCollection Documents/Participant%20Workbook%20Rev%205-14-08CSUP.pdf. Accessed June 12, 2012.

Columbia School of Social Work. "Professor Emeritus David Fanshel, World Expert on Foster Care, Dies." January 10, 2013. http://socialwork.columbia.edu/news /professor-emeritus-david-fanshel-world-expert-on-foster-care-dies/. November 1, 2016.

Doyle, Kathleen Cassidy. *Homes for Foster Children: Public Affairs Pamphlet No. 223.* New York: Public Affairs Committee, 1955.

Falconer, Douglas P. "Child and Youth Protection." In *Social Work Yearbook 1935,* edited by Fred S. Hall, 63–66. New York: Russell Sage Foundation, 1935.

Fanshel, David. *Foster Parenthood; A Role Analysis.* Minneapolis: University of Minnesota Press, 1966.

Felker, Evelyn H. *Foster Parenting Young Children: Guidelines from a Foster Parent.* New York: Child Welfare League of America, 1974.

Fessler, Pam. "Report: Foster Kids Face Tough Times after Age 18." *NPR Morning Edition,* April 7, 2010.

Geddes, Anne E. "Children and the Assistance and Insurance Programs." *Children* 2, no. 4 (July–August 1955): 154–59.

Glick, Paul C. "Family Trends in the United States." *American Sociological Review* 7, no. 4 (August 1942): 505–14.

Gordon, Henrietta. *Board Rates in 1951: A Study Based on the Participation of League Member Agencies.* New York: Child Welfare League of America, 1952.

Grossman, Harry. "Administration of the Servicemen's Dependents Allowance Act of 1942." *Social Security Bulletin* 6, no. 7 (July 1943): 21–24.

Haitch, Richard. *Orphans of the Living: The Foster Care Crisis.* New York: Public Affairs Committee in Cooperation with the Child Welfare League of America, 1968.

Hanson, Charlotte Leeper. "Child Welfare." In *Social Work Yearbook 1943,* edited by Russell H. Kurtz, 103–15. New York: Russell Sage Foundation, 1943.

———. "Child Welfare." In *Social Work Yearbook, 1945,* edited by Russell H. Kurtz, 73–84. New York: Russell Sage Foundation, 1945.

Hart, Hastings. "The Development of Child Placing in the United States." In *Foster-Home Care for Dependent Children,* edited by Grace Abbott, 1–15. Washington, D.C.: Government Printing Office, 1926.

Hoey, Jane M. "Aid to Families with Dependent Children." *Annals of the American Academy of Political and Social Science* 202 (March 1939): 74–81.

Holcomb, Claire. "When Husbands Run Away." *Rotarian*, June 1952, 24–26.

"Homemaker Service as a Child Welfare Service." *Child Welfare* 30, no. 4 (April 1951): 14–15.

Hunzeker, Jeanne M. *A New Partnership: Foster Parent Associations and Liaison Social Workers.* New York: Foster Parent Project, Child Welfare League of America, 1973.

Hutchinson, Dorothy. *In Quest of Foster Parents: A Point of View on Homefinding.* New York: Columbia University Press, 1943.

Jeter, Helen Rankin. *Children, Problems, and Services in Child Welfare Programs.* Washington, D.C.: U.S. Department of Health Education and Welfare, 1963.

Josselyn, Irene M. "Cultural Forces, Motherliness and Fatherliness." *American Journal of Orthopsychiatry* 26, no. 2 (July 1956): 264–71.

———. "Evaluating Motives of Foster Parents." *Child Welfare* 31, no. 2 (February 1952): 3–14.

Katz, Sanford N. "Foster Parents versus Agencies: A Case Study in the Judicial Application of 'The Best Interests of the Child' Doctrine." *Michigan Law Review* 65, no. 1 (November 1966): 145–70.

Kendrick, Roberta. Review of *Standards for Child Protective Service*, by Child Welfare League of America. *Public Welfare*, July 1960, 185–86.

Kennedy, Ruby. "A Foster Parent Looks at Foster Care." In *Foster Care in Question: A National Reassessment by Twenty-one Experts*, edited by Helen D. Stone, 241–49. New York: Child Welfare League of America, 1970.

Kidneigh, John C. "A Look to the Future in Child Welfare Services." *Children* 7, no. 2 (March–April 1960): 66–70.

Kline, Draza, and Helen Mary Overstreet. *Casework with Foster Parents: A Discussion of the Characteristics of the Caseworker-Foster-Parent Relationship, Some of the Psychological Aspects of Foster Parenthood, and the Adaptation of Treatment Skills to Casework Practice with Foster Parents.* New York: Child Welfare League of America, 1956.

Knitzer, Jane, and Mary Lee Allen. *Children without Homes: An Examination of Public Responsibility to Children in Out-of-Home Care.* Washington, D.C.: Children's Defense Fund, 1978.

Lacrosse County [Wisc.] Human Services Department. "Connections." May 2006. http://www.co.la-crosse.wi.us/humanservices/fc/docs/fostercare/Connections/2006/May%202006%20Connections.pdf. Accessed April 2, 2013.

Lebergott, Stanley. "Annual Estimates of Unemployment in the United States, 1900–1954." In *The Measurement and Behavior of Unemployment: A Conference of the Universities–National Bureau Committee for Economic Research*, 211–42. Princeton, N.J.: Princeton University Press, 1957.

Lenroot, Katharine F. "The Children's Titles in the Social Security Act: Origins of the Social Welfare Provision." *Children*, July–August 1960, 127–31.

———. "Child Welfare in the Reconversion Period." *Georgia Welfare*, 1946, 3–4, 8.

———. "J. Prentice Murphy—Child Welfare Leader." *Child Welfare League of America Bulletin*, February 1936, 1, 6–7.

———. "Needed: Daytime Mothers." *New York Times Magazine*, December 13, 1942, 18–19, 25.

———. "United States Children's Bureau in Its New Home." *World's Children*, 1947, 78–80.

Low, Seth. "Foster Care of Children: Major National Trends and Prospects." *Welfare in Review*, October 1966, 12–21. Reprinted in *Children and Youth in America: A Documentary History; Volume III, 1933–1973, Parts 1–4*, edited by Robert H. Bremner, 643–45. Cambridge, Mass.: Harvard University Press, 1974.

Lundberg, Emma Octavia. "C. C. Carstens: Interpreter of the Needs of Dependent Children (1865–1939)." *The Social Welfare History Project*. Virginia Commonwealth University Libraries. http://socialwelfare.library.vcu.edu/programs/child-welfare child-labor/c-c-carstens-interpreter-of-the-needs-of-dependent-children. Accessed November 17, 2016.

———. *Unto the Least of These: Social Services of Children*. New York: D. Appleton-Century, 1947.

Lundberg, Ferdinand, and Myrynia Farnham. *Modern Woman: The Lost Sex*. New York: Harper, 1947.

Maas, Henry S., and Richard E. Engler Jr., in collaboration with Zelma J. Felten and Margaret Purvine. *Children in Need of Parents*. New York: Columbia University Press, 1959.

Meier, Elizabeth G. *The Care of Foster Children with Psychotic Mothers*. New York: Child Welfare League of America, 1955.

Mitchell, Max. "Remarks." In *Proceedings of the Conference on the Care of Dependent Children*, 49–50. Washington, D.C.: Government Printing Office, 1909.

Murphy, J. Prentice. "Children in the New Deal." *Annals of the Academy of Political and Social Science*, November 1934, 121–30.

———. "Conserving the Child's Parental Home." In *Foster-Home Care for Dependent Children*, edited by Grace Abbott, 17–31. Washington, D.C.: Government Printing Office, 1926.

———. "Foster Care for Children." In *Social Work Yearbook 1935: A Description of Organized Activities in Social Work and in Related Fields*, edited by Fred S. Hall, 159–68. New York: Russell Sage Foundation, 1935.

National Association of Black Social Workers. "History." http://nabsw.org/?page =History. Accessed November 8, 2016.

———. "Position Statement on Trans-racial Adoption." September 1972. http://c.ymcdn .com/sites/nabsw.org/resource/collection/E1582D77-E4CD-4104-996A-D42D08 F9CA7D/NABSW_Trans-Racial_Adoption_1972_Position_(b).pdf. Accessed November 8, 2016.

National Association of Social Workers. "'If You're Right for the Job, It's the Best Job in the World': The National Association of Social Workers' Child Welfare Specialty Practice Section Members Describe Their Experiences In Child Welfare."

National Association of Social Workers, June 2004. http://www.naswdc.org/practice/children/NASWChildWelfareRpt062004.pdf. Accessed November 8, 2016.

———. "NASW Social Work Pioneers: David Fanshel." *National Association of Social Workers Foundation*. 2004. http://www.naswfoundation.org/pioneers/f/fanshel.html. Accessed November 8, 2016.

National Survey of Child and Adolescent Well-Being. "Risk of Long-Term Foster Care Placement among Children Involved with the Child Welfare System." *Research Brief* 19 (September 2013). http://www.acf.hhs.gov/sites/default/files/opre/nscaw_ltfc_research_brief_19_revised_for_acf_9_12_13_edit_clean.pdf. Accessed November 8, 2016.

Neumann, Daisy. "Look! We're Home." *New Yorker*, May 20, 1944, 66–70.

———. *Now That April's There*. Chicago: Consolidated Book Publishers, 1945.

Ougheltree, Cornelia M. *Finding Foster Homes; A Report on the Homefinding Program*. New York: Child Welfare League of America, 1957.

Pasztor, Eileen Mayers, et al. *STARS Trainer's Guide: Pre-service Training for Foster Parents and Adoptive Parents*. Washington, D.C.: CWLA Press, 2003.

"Philadelphia Training School for Social Work—1908." *The Social Welfare History Project*. Virginia Commonwealth University Libraries. http://socialwelfare.library.vcu.edu/organizations/philadelphia-training-school-for-social-work-1908/. Accessed November 8, 2016.

"Pilgrim Village Families Sketch: Francis Eaton." *The Great Migration Begins: Immigrants to New England 1620–1633*. Vol. 1. http://www.americanancestors.org/StaticContent/articles?ssearchb=topic&subquery=Mayflower%20Research&id=79. Accessed November 10, 2016.

"Public Assistance: Report of the Advisory Council." February 1960, 10–22, 36. https://www.ssa.gov/policy/docs/ssb/v23n2/v23n2p10.pdf. Accessed November 20, 2016.

Radinsky, Elizabeth K., Bessie Schick Free, and Helen Rubenstein. "Recruiting and Serving Foster Parents." In *Today's Child and Foster Care*, edited by the Child Welfare League of America, 37–41. New York: Child Welfare League of America, 1963.

Riis, Jacob. *How the Other Half Lives*. 1890; repr., New York: Dover, 1971.

Ripple, Helen E. Review of *Standards for Foster Family Care Service*, by Child Welfare League of America. *Public Welfare*, July 1960, 184.

Schottland, Charles I. "Social Security Amendments of 1956: A Summary and Legislative History." *Social Security Bulletin* 19, no. 9 (1956): 3–15.

Shudde, Louis, and Lenore Epstein. "Orphanhood—A Diminishing Problem." *Social Security Bulletin* 18, no. 3 (1955): 17–18. Reprinted in *Children and Youth in America: A Documentary History; Volume III, 1933–1973, Parts 1–4*, edited by Robert H. Bremner, 637–39. Cambridge, Mass.: Harvard University Press, 1974.

Shurtleff, Nathanial B., ed. *Records of the Colony of New Plymouth, in New England*. Volume 1, *Court Orders 1633–1640*. Boston: Press of William White, 1855; New York: AMS Press, 1968.

Solomon, Albert. "Publicity Methods in Finding Foster Homes." *Child Welfare* 31, no. 5 (May 1952): 7–9, 14–16.

Spock, Benjamin. *The Common Sense Book of Baby and Child Care*. New York: Duell, Sloan, and Pearce, 1946.
Stone, Helen D. *Reflections on Foster Care: A Report of a National Survey of Attitudes and Practices*. New York: Child Welfare League of America, 1969.
———, ed. *Foster Care in Question: A National Reassessment by Twenty-One Experts*. New York: Child Welfare League of America, 1970.
Strolin, Jessica S., Mary McCarthy, and Jim Caringi. "Causes and Effects of Child Welfare Workforce Turnover: Current State of Knowledge and Future Directions." *Journal of Public Child Welfare* 1, no. 2 (2006): 29–52.
Stroud, John. *An Introduction to the Child Care Service*. London: Longmans, 1965.
U.S. Children's Bureau. *Public Social Services to Children: A Decade of Progress—1935–1945*. Washington, D.C.: U.S. Children's Bureau, 1946. https://books.google.com/books/about/Public_Social_Services_to_Children.html?id=rNBRnQEACAAJ. Accessed November 19, 2016.
Virginia State Department of Health. "A New Crippled Children's Service . . . Boarding Home Care." *Virginia Health Bulletin* 7, no. 2 (June 1954): 2–12.
White House Conference on Child Health and Protection. "The Children's Charter [Government Document]." In *Children and Youth in History*, annotated by Kriste Lindenmeyer, item #124. http://chnm.gmu.edu/cyh/case-studies/124. Accessed November 8, 2016.
Wolins, Martin. *Selecting Foster Parents: The Ideal and the Reality*. New York: Columbia University Press, 1963.

Secondary Sources

Alber, Erdmute. "'The Real Parents Are the Foster Parents': Social Parenthood among the Baatombu in Northern Benin." In *Cross-Cultural Approaches to Adoption*, edited by Fiona Bowie, 33–47. New York: Routledge, 2004.
Albert, Raymond. *Law and Social Work Practice: A Legal Systems Approach*. 2nd ed. New York: Springer, 2000.
Apple, Rima D. *Perfect Motherhood: Science and Childrearing in America*. New Brunswick, N.J.: Rutgers University Press, 2006.
Ashby, LeRoy. *Endangered Children: Dependency, Neglect, and Abuse in American History*. New York: Twayne, 1997.
Askeland, Lori. "Informal Adoption, Apprentices, and Indentured Children in the Colonial Era and the New Republic, 1605–1850." In *Children and Youth in Adoption, Orphanages, and Foster Care: A Historical Handbook and Guide*, edited by Lori Askeland, 3–16. Westport, Conn.: Greenwood Press, 2006.
Balcom, Karen. *The Traffic in Babies: Cross-Border Adoption and Baby-Selling between the United States and Canada, 1930–1972*. Toronto: University of Toronto Press, 2011.
Balogh, Brian. *The Associational State: American Governance in the Twentieth Century*. Philadelphia: University of Pennsylvania Press, 2015.
Bartholet, Elizabeth. *Nobody's Children: Abuse and Neglect, Foster Drift, and the Adoption Alternative*. Boston: Beacon Press, 1999.

Beam, Cris. *To the End of June: The Intimate Life of American Foster Care*. New York: Houghton Mifflin Harcourt, 2013.
Becker, Stephen D. *Marshall Field III: A Biography*. New York: Simon and Schuster, 1964.
Bent-Goodley, Tricia B. "Regulating the Lives of Children: Kinship Care as a Cultivated Resistance Strategy of the African American Community." In *Social Welfare Policy: Regulation and Resistance among People of Color*, edited by Jerome H. Schiele, 25–42. New York: Sage, 2011.
Berebitsky, Julie. *Like Our Very Own: Adoption and the Changing Culture of Motherhood, 1851–1950*. Lawrence: University of Kansas Press, 2000.
Bernstein, Nina. *The Lost Children of Wilder: The Epic Struggle to Change Foster Care*. New York: Pantheon, 2001.
Billingsley, Andrew, and Jeanne M. Giovannoni. *Children of the Storm: Black Children and American Child Welfare*. New York: Harcourt Brace Jovanovich, 1972.
Birk, Megan. *Fostering on the Farm: Child Placement in the Rural Midwest*. Urbana: University of Illinois Press, 2015.
Boris, Eileen. *Home to Work: Motherhood and the Politics of Industrial Homework in the United States*. New York: Cambridge University Press, 1994.
———. "On the Importance of Naming: Gender, Race, and the Writing of Policy History." *Journal of Policy History* 17, no. 1 (2005): 72–92.
Boris, Eileen, and Jennifer Klein. *Caring for America: Home Health Workers in the Shadow of the Welfare State*. New York: Oxford University Press, 2012.
Briggs, Laura. "Orphaning the Children of Welfare: 'Crack Babies,' Race, and Adoption Reform." In *Outsiders Within: Writing on Transracial Adoption*, edited by Jane Jeong Trencka, Julia Chinyere Oparah, and Sun Yung Shin, 75–88. Cambridge, Mass.: South End Press, 2006.
———. *Somebody's Children: The Politics of Transracial and Transnational Adoption*. Durham, N.C.: Duke University Press, 2012.
Canaday, Margot. *The Straight State: Sexuality and Citizenship in Twentieth Century America*. Princeton, N.J.: Princeton University Press, 2009.
Carp, E. Wayne. *Family Matters: Secrecy and Disclosure in the History of Adoption*. Cambridge, Mass.: Harvard, 1998.
———. "Orphanages vs. Adoption: The Triumph of Biological Kinship, 1800–1933." In *With Us Always: A History of Private Charity and Public Welfare*, edited by Donald T. Critchlow and Charles H. Parker, 123–44. Lanham, Md.: Rowman and Littlefield, 1998.
Carp, E. Wayne, and Anna Leon-Guerrero. "When in Doubt, Count: World War II as a Watershed in the History of Adoption." In *Adoption in America: Historical Perspectives*, edited by E. Wayne Carp, 181–217. Ann Arbor: University of Michigan Press, 2002.
Chappell, Marisa. *The War on Welfare: Family, Poverty, and Politics in Modern America*. Philadelphia: University of Pennsylvania Press, 2010.
Cmiel, Kenneth. *A Home of Another Kind: One Chicago Orphanage and the Tangle of Child Welfare*. Chicago: University of Chicago Press, 1995.

Cohen, Abby J. "A Brief History of Federal Financing for Child Care in the United States." *Future of Children* 6, no. 2 (Summer–Autumn 1996): 26–40.

Collins, Patricia Hill. *Black Feminist Thought: Knowledge, Consciousness, and the Politics of Empowerment*. New York: Routledge, 1991.

Colton, Matthew, and Margaret Williams, eds. *The World of Foster Care: An International Sourcebook on Foster Family Care Systems*. Brookfield, Vt.: Arena, 1997.

Cranford, Peter G. *But for the Grace of God: Milledgeville! The Inside Story of the World's Largest Insane Asylum*. Savannah: Georgia Consumer Council, 1998.

Creagh, Dianne. "Science, Social Work, and Bureaucracy: Cautious Development in Adoption and Foster Care." In *Children and Youth in Adoption, Orphanages, and Foster Care: A Historical Handbook and Guide*, edited by Lori Askeland, 31–44. Westport, Conn.: Greenwood Press, 2006.

Curran, Laura. "Feminine Women, Hard Workers: Foster Motherhood in Midcentury America (1946–1963)." *Journal of Family History* 31, no. 4 (2006): 386–412.

———. "Social Work's Revised Maternalism: Mothers, Workers, and Welfare in Early Cold War America, 1946–1963." *Journal of Women's History* 17, no. 1 (Spring 2005): 112–36.

D'Andrade, Amy, Laura Frame, and Jill Duerr Berrick. "Concurrent Planning in Public Child Welfare Agencies: Oxymoron or Work in Progress?" *Children and Youth Services Review* 28, no. 1 (2006): 78–95.

Davies, Gareth. *From Opportunity to Entitlement: The Transformation and Decline of Great Society Liberalism*. Lawrence: University of Kansas Press, 1996.

Doyle, Joseph J., Jr. "Child Protection and Adult Crime: Using Investigator Assignment to Estimate Causal Effects of Foster Care." *Journal of Political Economy* 116, no. 4 (August 2008): 746–70.

England, Paula, Michelle Budig, and Nancy Folbre. "Wages of Virtue: The Relative Pay of Care Work." *Social Problems* 49, no. 4 (November 2002): 455–73.

Fonseca, Claudia. "The Circulation of Children in a Brazilian Working-Class Neighbourhood: A Local Practice in a Globalized World." In *Cross-Cultural Approaches to Adoption*, edited by Fiona Bowie, 165–81. New York: Routledge, 2004.

Fox, Cybelle. *Three Worlds of Relief: Race, Immigration and the American Welfare State from the Progressive Era to the New Deal*. Princeton, N.J.: Princeton University Press, 2012.

Fraser, Nancy, and Linda Gordon. "A Genealogy of Dependency: Tracing a Keyword in the U.S. Welfare State." *Signs* 19, no. 2 (January 1994): 309–36.

Freundlich, Madelyn. *The Market Forces in Adoption*. Washington, D.C.: Child Welfare League of America, 2000.

Gardiner, Juliet. *The Children's War: The Second World War through the Eyes of the Children of Britain*. London: Piatkus Books, 2005.

Geiser, Robert L. *The Illusion of Caring: Children in Foster Care*. Boston: Beacon Press, 1973.

Gerstle, Gary. *Liberty and Coercion: The Paradox of American Government from the Founding to the Present*. Princeton, N.J.: Princeton University Press, 2015.

Gordon, Linda. *The Great Arizona Orphan Abduction*. Cambridge, Mass.: Harvard University Press, 1999.

———. *Heroes of Their Own Lives: The Politics and History of Family Violence; Boston, 1880–1960*. New York: Viking, 1988.

———. *Pitied but Not Entitled: Single Mothers and the History of Welfare, 1890–1935*. New York: Free Press, 1994.

———, ed. *Women, the State, and Welfare*. Madison: University of Wisconsin Press, 1990.

Griswold, Robert L. *Fatherhood in America: A History*. New York: Basic Books, 1993.

Grossberg, Michael. *Governing the Hearth: Law and the Family in Nineteenth-Century America*. Chapel Hill: University of North Carolina Press, 1985.

Gup, Ted. *A Secret Gift: How One Man's Kindness—and a Trove of Letters—Revealed the Hidden History of the Great Depression*. New York: Penguin Press, 2010.

Hacsi, Tim. "From Indenture to Family Foster Care: A Brief History of Child Placing." In *A History of Child Welfare*, edited by Eve P. Smith and Lisa A. Merkel-Holguin, 155–74. New Brunswick, N.J.: Transaction, 1996.

———. *Second Home: Orphan Asylums and Poor Families in America*. Cambridge, Mass.: Harvard University Press, 1997.

Halstead, Claire. "'Dangers Behind, Pleasure Ahead': British-Canadian Identity and the Evacuation of British Children to Canada during the Second World War." *British Journal of Canadian Studies* 27, no. 2 (2014): 163–79.

Hansan, John E. "Hopkirk, Howard W." *The Social Welfare History Project*. Virginia Commonwealth University Libraries. http://socialwelfare.library.vcu.edu/people/hopkirk-howard-w/. Accessed October 24, 2016.

———. "Philadelphia Training School for Social Work—1908." *The Social Welfare History Project*. Virginia Commonwealth University Libraries. http://socialwelfare.library.vcu.edu/organizations/philadelphia-training-school-for-social-work-1908/. Accessed October 24, 2016.

Harrison, Kathy. *Another Place at the Table: A Story of Shattered Childhoods Redeemed of Love*. Repr. ed. New York: TarcherPerigee, 2004.

Heinemann, Isabel, ed. *Inventing the Modern American Family: Family Values and Social Change in 20th Century United States*. Frankfurt and New York: Campus Verlag, 2012.

Herman, Ellen. *Kinship by Design: A History of Adoption in the Modern United States*. Chicago: University of Chicago Press, 2008.

Hine, Darlene Clark. *A Shining Thread of Hope: The History of Black Women in America*. New York: Broadway Books, 1998.

Holt, Marilyn Irvin. "Adoption Reform, Orphan Trains, and Child-Saving, 1851–1929." In *Children and Youth in Adoption, Orphanages, and Foster Care: A Historical Handbook and Guide*, edited by Lori Askeland, 17–30. Westport, Conn.: Greenwood Press, 2006.

———. *The Orphan Trains: Placing Out in America*. Lincoln: University of Nebraska Press, 1992.

Jacobs, Margaret D. *A Generation Removed: The Fostering and Adoption of Indigenous Children in the Postwar World*. Lincoln: University of Nebraska Press, 2014.

Johnson, James E. "Lenroot, Katharine Fredrica." In *Biographical Dictionary of Social Welfare*, edited by Walter I. Trattner, 488–91. Westport, Conn.: Greenwood Press, 1986.

Kessler-Harris, Alice. *In Pursuit of Equity: Women, Men, and the Quest for Economic Citizenship in Twentieth-Century America*. New York: Oxford University Press, 2001.

Kingan, Ruth. "Barriers to Recruitment and Retention of Foster Homes." *Kentucky Center for Health and Family Services*. http://chfs.ky.gov/nr/rdonlyres/2d555642 -6848-4c07-bdd6-425304867df2/0/2005fsfosterparents_adoptiveparentskingan _ruth.pdf. Accessed April 2, 2013.

Kunzel, Regina. *Fallen Women, Problem Girls: Unmarried Mothers and the Professionalization of Social Work, 1890–1945*. New Haven, Conn.: Yale University Press, 1993.

Ladd-Taylor, Molly. *Mother-Work: Women, Child Welfare, and the State, 1890–1930*. Urbana: University of Illinois Press, 1994.

LaRossa, Ralph. *The Modernization of Fatherhood: A Social and Political History*. Chicago: University of Chicago Press, 1997.

Lindenmeyer, Kriste. *"A Right to Childhood": The U.S. Children's Bureau and Child Welfare, 1912–46*. Urbana: University of Illinois Press, 1997.

Lindsey, Duncan. *The Welfare of Children*. 1994; repr., New York: Oxford University Press, 2003.

London, Ross D. "The 1994 Orphanage Debate: A Study in the Politics of Annihilation." In *Rethinking Orphanages for the 21st Century*, edited by Richard B. McKenzie, 79–102. Thousand Oaks, Calif.: Sage, 1999.

Longden, Sean. *Blitz Kids: The Children's War against Hitler*. London: Constable, 2012.

Mackert, Nina. "'But Recall the Kind of Parents We Have to Deal With': Juvenile Delinquency, Interdependent Masculinity and the Government of Families in the Postwar U.S." In *Inventing the Modern American Family: Family Values and Social Change in 20th Century United States*, edited by Isabel Heinemann, 196–222. New York: Campus Verlag, 2012.

May, Elaine Tyler. *Barren in the Promised Land: Childless Americans and the Pursuit of Happiness*. New York: Basic Books, 1995.

———. *Homeward Bound: American Families in the Cold War Era*. 1988; repr., New York: Basic Books, 2008.

McElvaine, Robert. *The Great Depression: America, 1929–1941*. 1984; repr., New York: Times Books, 2009.

Melosh, Barbara. *Strangers and Kin: The American Way of Adoption*. Cambridge, Mass.: Harvard University Press, 2002.

Meyer, Madonna Harrington, ed. *Care Work: Gender, Class, and the Welfare State*. New York: Routledge, 2000.

Michel, Sonya. *Children's Interests/Mothers' Rights: The Shaping of America's Child Care Policy*. New Haven, Conn.: Yale University Press, 1999.

Mink, Gwendolyn. *The Wages of Motherhood: Inequality in the Welfare State, 1917–1942*. Ithaca: Cornell University Press, 1995.
Mittelstadt, Jennifer. *From Welfare to Workfare: The Unintended Consequences of Liberal Reform, 1945–1965*. Chapel Hill: University of North Carolina Press, 2005.
Modell, Judith Schachter. *A Sealed and Secret Kinship: The Culture of Policies and Practices in American Adoption*. New York: Berghahn, 2002.
Morris, Andrew J. F. *The Limits of Voluntarism: Charity and Welfare from the New Deal through the Great Society*. New York: Cambridge University Press, 2009.
Muncy, Robyn. *Creating a Female Dominion in American Reform, 1890–1935*. New York: Oxford University Press, 1991.
Nadasen, Premilla. *Welfare Warriors: The Welfare Rights Movement in the United States*. New York: Routledge, 2005.
Nelson, Barbara J. "The Origins of the Two-Channel Welfare State: Workmen's Compensation and Mothers' Aid." In *Women, the State, and Welfare*, edited by Linda Gordon, 123–51. Madison: University of Wisconsin Press, 1990.
Nelson, Julie A. "Of Markets and Martyrs: Is It OK to Pay Well for Care?" *Feminist Economics* 5, no. 3 (November 1999): 43–59.
Nielsen, Kim E. *A Disability History of the United States*. Boston: Beacon, 2012.
O'Connor, Stephen. *Orphan Trains: The Story of Charles Loring Brace and the Children He Saved and Failed*. Boston: Houghton Mifflin, 2001.
Oh, Arissa H. *To Save the Children of Korea: The Cold War Origins of International Adoption*. Stanford: Stanford University Press, 2015.
Palmiste, Claire. "From the Indian Adoption Project to the Indian Child Welfare Act." *Indigenous Policy Journal* 22, no. 1 (Summer 2011): 1–10.
Pasztor, Eileen Mayers, and Kathy Barbell. "United States of America." In *The World of Foster Care: An International Sourcebook on Foster Family Care Systems*, edited by Matthew Colton and Margaret Williams, 249–66. Brookfield, Vt.: Arena, 1997.
Peebles-Wilkins, Wilma. "Janie Porter Barrett and the Virginia Industrial School for Colored Girls: Community Response to the Needs of African American Children." In *A History of Child Welfare*, edited by Eve P. Smith and Lisa A. Merkel-Holguin, 135–54. New Brunswick, N.J.: Transaction, 1996.
Quadagno, Jill S. *The Color of Poverty: How Racism Undermined the War on Poverty*. New York: Oxford University Press, 1995.
Ramsey, Sarah H., and Douglas E. Abrams. *Children and the Law in a Nutshell*. St. Paul, Minn.: West, 2003.
Roberts, Dorothy. *Shattered Bonds: The Color of Child Welfare*. New York: Basic Books, 2002.
Rosen, Ruth. *The World Split Open: How the Modern Women's Movement Changed America*. New York: Penguin Books, 2000.
Rowe, LeRoy. "Becoming Good Girls and Useful Citizens: Growing Up Poor, Black, and Female in Jim Crow Era Missouri, 1909–1944." Ph.D. diss., University of Missouri, 2012.
Rymph, Catherine E. "From 'Economic Want' to 'Family Pathology': Foster Family

Care, the New Deal, and the Emergence of a Public Child Welfare System." *Journal of Policy History* 24, no. 1 (January 2012): 7–25.

———. "Looking for Fathers in the Postwar U.S. Foster Care System." In *Inventing the Modern American Family: Family Values and Social Change in 20th Century United States*, edited by Isabel Heinemann, 177–95. Chicago: Campus Verlag, 2012.

Smith, Eve P. "Bring Back the Orphanages? What Policymakers of Today Can Learn from the Past." In *A History of Child Welfare*, edited by Eve P. Smith and Lisa A. Merkel-Holguin, 107–34. New Brunswick, N.J.: Transaction, 1996.

———, and Lisa A. Merkel-Holguin, eds. *A History of Child Welfare*. New Brunswick, N.J.: Transaction, 1996.

Solinger, Rickie. *Beggars and Choosers: How the Politics of Choice Shapes Adoption, Abortion, and Welfare in the United States*. New York: Hill and Wang, 2001.

———. *Wake Up Little Susie: Single Pregnancy and Race before "Roe v. Wade"*. 1992; repr., New York: Routledge, 2000.

Sommer, Cristina Dugger. "Empowering Children: Granting Foster Children the Right to Initiate Parental Rights Termination Proceedings." *Cornell Law Review* 79, no. 5 (July 1994): 1200–1262.

Sribnick, Ethan G. "Rehabilitating Child Welfare: Children and Public Policy, 1945–1980." Ph.D. diss., University of Virginia, 2007.

Strong-Boag, Veronica. *Fostering Nation? Canada Confronts Its History of Childhood Disadvantage*. Waterloo, Ont.: Wilfred Laurier University Press, 2011.

Swartz, Teresa Toguchi. "Mothering for the State: Foster Parenting and the Challenges of Government-Contracted Carework." *Gender and Society* 18, no. 5 (October 2004): 567–87.

———. *Parenting for the State: An Ethnographic Analysis of Non-profit Foster Care*. New York: Routledge, 2005.

Swift, Karen J. "An Outrage to Common Decency: Historical Perspectives on Child Neglect." *Child Welfare* 74, no. 1 (January 1995): 71–91.

Tiffin, Susan. *In Whose Best Interest? Child Welfare Reform in the Progressive Era*. Westport, Conn.: Greenwood Press, 1982.

Toth, Jennifer. *Orphans of the Living: Stories of America's Children in Foster Care*. New York: Simon and Schuster, 1997.

Trattner, Walter I. *From Poor Law to Welfare State: A History of Social Welfare in America*. 6th ed. New York: Free Press, 1999.

Tuttle, William M., Jr. "Rosie the Riveter and Her Latchkey Children: What Americans Can Learn about Child Day Care from the Second World War." In *A History of Child Welfare*, edited by Eve P. Smith and Lisa A. Merkel-Holguin, 83–106. New Brunswick, N.J.: Transaction, 1996.

Wexler, Richard. "Take the Child and Run: Tales from the Age of ASFA." *New England Law Review* 36, no. 1 (Fall 2001): 129–52.

———. *Wounded Innocents: The Real Victims of the War against Child Abuse*. Buffalo, N.Y.: Prometheus Books, 1995.

Willrich, Michael. "Home Slackers: Men, the State, and Welfare in Modern America." *Journal of American History* 87, no. 2 (September 2000): 460–89.

Wilson, Melvin W. "The Context of the African American Family." In *Child Welfare: An Africentric Perspective*, edited by Joyce E. Everett, Sandra P. Chipungu, and Bogart R. Leashore, 85–118. New Brunwsick, N.J.: Rutgers University Press, 1991.

Zelizer, Viviana A. *Pricing the Priceless Child: The Changing Social Value of Children*. New York: Basic Books, 1985.

INDEX

Abbott, Grace, 32, 56, 58, 65

Adoption, 3, 6–7, 205n2; agency-supervised practice of, 79; associated with child rescue or welfare, 26, 127, 185; class and racial dynamics of, 12, 26–27, 35, 46, 62, 93, 109, 127, 148, 173–74, 182, 184–85; as distinct from foster care, 6–7, 22, 27, 37–38, 95–97, 112, 137–39, 140, 147, 159, 180, 183; foster parenting as a path to, 181–85; independent practice of, 79, 139; as means of designing kinship, 27, 140; promotion of after foster care, 7, 95, 159, 182–83; psychology and psychiatry influence on, 101–2; and race, 147–48; scholarship on, 11–12; sentimental understanding of, 27; standards for, 92, 100; subsidies for, 183; and World War II, 201n16. *See also* Adoption experts; Adoptive homes; Adoptive parents

Adoption and Safe Families Act (ASFA), 184–85

Adoption Assistance and Child Welfare Act, 183

Adoption experts, 27, 79, 127, 140, 182. *See also* Case workers

Adoptive homes, 3, 7, 130, 138, 158–59, 174, 181, 185

Adoptive parents: consideration of foster parents for, 95–99, 148, 150; and foster parents, 7, 11, 12, 98–99, 108–09, 139, 181–83

Advisory Council on Child Welfare Services, 164–65

African Americans: and adoption, 182; child welfare activists, 127–28, 130, 150, 172–75; dependent children, 29, 34–36, 124–25; and effects of slavery on child rearing methods, 34–35; exclusion from child welfare and family security services, 28, 60–61, 130–34, 163; families, 29, 34–36, 99, 169, 124, 174–75; and female heads of household, 60–61, 128, 133–34, 145, 148; and foster care, 1, 12–13, 118–19, 124–28, 131, 156, 175–76, 185; foster care recruitment material targeted toward, 13, 84–85, 148; foster parents, 13, 47, 85, 103, 130, 150; and orphanages, 19, 20, 34–36, 46; racialized images of families, 61, 108; and segregated childcare services, 34, 99, 126–28; and working homes, 34

Aid to Dependent Children (ADC), 6, 11, 37; eligibility for, 59–60, 81–82, 93, 160, 163–65, 179; and gender, 60–61, 117, 133, 160, 163, 179; and race, 11, 131, 133–34, 163; Title IV of Social Security Act of 1935, 9, 10, 44, 59–60, 63, 115, 133–34, 160–62. *See also* Aid to Families with Dependent Children

Aid to Families with Dependent Children (AFDC), 10, 179, 185; AFDC–Unemployed Parent, 165; and African American families, 171; Child Welfare League concerns about, 162–67, 170–72; and single mothers, 163, 165, 168, 170. *See also* Aid to Families with Dependent Children–Foster Care

Aid to Families with Dependent Children–Foster Care (AFDC-FC), 161, 164–65; problems with, 161–63,

165–68, 170–72, 183; and single mothers, 163, 168
Almshouses, 19, 20, 34, 37, 46, 192n17
American Legion's Child Welfare Division, 73, 81
Arnold, Mildred, 49, 141, 142, 160
Art of Child Placement (Charnley), 100
Association of American Indian and Alaskan Native Social Workers, 173
Atkinson, Mary Irene, 60, 63
Attachment theory, 113, 206n19. *See also* Bowlby, John

Baby and Child Care (Spock), 108
Baby farmers, 24
Bartholet, Elizabeth, 182, 185
Billingsley, Andrew, and Jeanne Giovannoni, 20, 34, 46, 127, 129, 172; *Children of the Storm*, 172
Biological parents of foster children, 3, 7, 8, 11, 13, 45, 63, 94, 97, 113, 139; legal rights of, 95, 175, 185; seen as "pathological," 93, 116–17, 119–20, 132; and "psychotic mother," 116; and single mothers, 29, 59, 71, 73, 119
Black Administrators in Child Welfare, 130, 173–75
Board rates: criticism of, 178; and disability, 122; efforts to raise, 138, 142, 145–46, 152, 156; and hard-to-place children, 120–24, 126; increase of during the war and postwar period, 121, 138, 146–47, 150; low, 49, 73–74, 86, 161; and race, 156
Boarding fathers, 197n26. *See also* Foster fathers
Boarding mothers, 49, 50, 138; emotional attachment of to wards, 25; and needed income, 23, 43, 50–51, 87; state subsidies to, 24; suspicion of, 135, 138; as widows, 106. *See also* Foster mothers
Boarding homes, 3, 23–25, 196n13; boarding out, 12, 23, 24, 41, 47, 161; during Depression, 37–38, 41, 46, 50–51, 69, 87; independent or private systems of, 54, 70, 76, 79, 197n28; running, as a job, 106, 137; lack of, 73, 142; licensing of, 52, 64, 78, 200n88; and race, 46; resistance to, 29; shift from, to foster family care, 37, 78, 138, 141, 166; shift from free homes to, 25, 38, 46, 53–54, 137
Board of Public Welfare (Washington, D.C.), 75
Boehm, Bernice, 149, 176
Boston Council of Social Agencies, Children's Department, 85–86
Boston Federated Jewish Charities, 29
Bowlby, John, 113, 114, 206n19. *See also* Attachment theory
Brace, Charles Loring, 20, 22, 24–25, 159. *See also* Children's Aid Society; Orphan trains
Buck, Pearl S., 137
Bulletin (Child Welfare League of America), 143
Bureau of Indian Affairs, 36, 127, 131
Bureau of Public Assistance, 166

Canaday, Margot, 4, 60
Canadian Child Welfare Agencies, 5
Care work: as performed by foster mothers, 7, 12, 65, 92, 138, 178–79; undervaluing of, 14, 65, 179
Carstens, C. C., 32, 33, 34, 37, 76
Caseworkers in child welfare: in adoption field, 79; expectations of for foster parents, 98, 101, 103, 148, 171; in foster care field, 123, 140, 168; foster day care field, 77; inadequate number of, 161; and race, 119, 130, 175; resistance to by foster parents, 150–51, 171; and view of family pathology, 117, 119. *See also* Casework for child welfare
Casework for child welfare, 2, 14, 77–78,

94, 123, 139, 162, 166, 182; and foster fathers, 155; origins of, 30–32, 47, 52–53; and New Deal, 61–62; and "problem children," 116–17; and race, 130, 169; and "whole child" approach, 59. *See also* Caseworkers in child welfare; Professionalization; Richmond, Mary
Castendyck, Ella, 67, 73, 88, 94
Charnley, Jean, 100, 108, 143
Child abuse, 1, 9, 10, 24, 154, 180: by parents, 63, 116; physical, 9, 10; and poverty, 8, 9, 27, 165; sexual, 2, 9. *See also* Child neglect
Child neglect, 4, 9, 24, 39–40, 119, 120, 164; and AFDC–Foster Care, 170–71; during Depression, 46, 50, 54; and foster care, 1, 9, 34, 94, 153, 155–56, 160, 165, 168–69; and New Deal, 56–57, 62–64; and poverty, 8, 21, 27; and race, 124, 175; and single motherhood, 117; during World War II, 73. *See also* Child abuse; Dependent and neglected children
Child placement, 3, 13, 17, 41, 49, 55, 92; in boarding homes, 37–38; and family pathology, 115–17; free, 22, 24, 53; and hard-to-place child, 113, 181; independent or private, 25, 78; influence of poverty and poverty-related neglect on, 21, 43, 45, 94, 131, 134, 179; pre-adoptive, 97, 184; and race, 34, 37, 41, 52, 125–28, 131, 173–74, 184; rural and farm, 22, 24, 34, 47; science and professionalization of, 7, 11, 30–33, 79, 104; social workers in, 7, 12, 41, 59, 64, 67, 93, 104, 180; standards for, 52, 68, 140, 162, 166; subsidies for, 21, 62, 161, 183; as temporary, 20–21, 95, 97, 138, 159, 181; voluntary nature of, 45, 63, 119, 168–70; and working mothers, 148; and World War II, 9, 71–74, 81, 86
Child protective services, 9, 28, 41; association with foster care, 171, 176; and child welfare services, 168–69, 171
Child removal, 170, 182; for neglect or poverty, 120, 131; for transgressive parenting, 169; from foster home, 98; Native Americans and, 36–37, 131; suspicion of, 28, 114, 180
Children of the Storm (Billingsley and Giovannoni), 172
Children in Need of Parents (Maas and Engler), 158, 160; and "foster care drift," 159; and permanency movement, 159, 181
Children's Aid Society, 21, 22. *See also* Brace, Charles Loring
Children's Bureau, 4; during Depression, 45; formation of, 28, 31–32; and foster care, 54, 56, 77–78, 92, 94–95, 97, 111, 131, 139, 141, 158, 165–66, 178; and gender, 32, 60, 148, 162; letters to, 13, 47, 49, 56, 64, 71, 97, 119, 136; marginalized status of, 160–63, 166; and New Deal, 44, 58–63, 162; promotion of research on child welfare services, 149, 154, 164; and race, 111, 124, 126–27; and "whole child" philosophy, 31, 59, 162; and World War II, 66–67, 81, 83, 88
Children's Charter, 46
Children's Defense Fund, 172
Children's Overseas Reception Board (CORB), 66, 89
Child rescue, 26–27, 50, 185; association with adoption, 27; and *Delineator* campaign, 26; and Native Americans, 127; of war orphans, 80, 88–89
Child welfare, 3, 6, 9, 22, 26, 34; and dependent children, 56, 61–62, 89; and Depression, 40–41, 43, 54–55; development as profession, 2, 11, 25–28, 30–34, 53, 65, 100, 156; during postwar era, 92–93, 113–16, 134, 139; and family pathology, 104–5, 117, 119; and foster care, 1, 5, 14, 17, 55, 69, 92, 99, 138, 144;

246 | Index

and race, 12–13, 20, 34–37, 46, 119, 124–30, 172–75, 177; shift from private to public, 20, 24, 27, 44, 53–54, 64, 136, 157; and views of foster parents, 108, 110, 112; women leadership in, 28; and World War II, 68–69, 75–76, 80–81, 89
Child Welfare (Child Welfare League of America), 121
Child Welfare League of America, 4, 5, 114, 184; and board rate studies, 74, 121, 138; concerns about AFDC–Foster Care, 161–62, 164–67, 171–72; creation of, 31–34; during Depression, 44, 52, 55; and foster care, 73–74, 77–78, 80–81, 86–87, 92, 99, 137, 144–47, 149–50, 152, 154–55, 158, 176, 178, 181; and Native Americans, 127, 131; and race, 124–31, 173–75, 182; special needs adoption project (ARENA), 182; and *Standards* for foster care, 34, 52, 67, 72, 92, 100, 105, 139–43, 146–48, 170, 175; and World War II, 66–70, 73–74, 76, 78, 80–83, 86. See also *Bulletin*; *Child Welfare*; Indian Adoption Project; National Foster Parent Association
Child welfare services, 17, 37, 164; during Depression, 43–44, 53, 55–56; expansion of, 44, 57; and foster care, 63, 73, 146, 149, 158, 162, 166–70, 176, 183; public and private funding for, 20–21, 53–54; and race, 20, 46, 125–26, 129–30, 163–64, 172, 175; role of private families in, 7; and Title V of Social Security Act of 1935, 59–60, 62–64, 132; voluntary nature of, 63, 119
Christopher Street Society (Michigan), 150, 151
Churchill, Winston, 68
Civil Rights Act (1964): Title VI, 175
Clerc, Laurent, 37
Cole, Betsy, 182
Columbia School of Social Work, 95. See also New York School of Social Work

Community Assistance to Homeless Youngsters (CATHY) (Los Angeles), 150, 151
Connecticut Child Welfare Association, 84
Crippled children. See Disabled children

Daly, Mary, 149
Day care, 6; and New Deal, 10, 62; opposition to, 166–67, 177–78; and race, 131, 133–34; and single and/or working mothers, 119, 177; and World War II, 69, 75–77, 83, 133, 138. See also Day nurseries; Foster day care
Delinquent children, 34, 43, 62, 126. See also Juvenile delinquency
Department of Health, Education and Welfare (HEW), 152, 163, 166, 171
Dependent and neglected children, 6, 8–9, 25, 34, 156, 165, 190n25; and boarding homes, 38, 49; and Depression, 44, 46–47, 54–55; and foster care, 1, 3, 5, 8–9, 12, 14, 34, 37, 68, 93–94, 111, 121, 134, 137, 145, 158, 171; and indenture, 18; meaning of term "neglected children", 8, 9, 24, 27, 39, 40, 54, 62, 73, 116, 117, 119, 153, 160, 169, 170, 171, 180; and New Deal, 8–9, 10–11, 56–57, 59, 61–62, 115, 160–61, 179; and orphanages, 20; and race, 34–36, 124–26, 175; studies on, 219n11; views of during Progressive Era, 28, 30; and World War II, 68–69, 73, 80, 82, 86–87, 89. See also Aid to Dependent Children
Dependent children. See Dependent and neglected children
Depression, the: boarding during, 50, 69, 87; child welfare services during, 38–41, 44, 46, 52–54; and foster care, 43, 46, 55, 69; impact on families, 44–46
Developmental disabilities, 37, 105, 122, 123
Disabled children, 43, 60, 132; board rates for, 121–22; and foster care, 34,

41, 86, 122, 154; nineteenth-century institutions for, 19–20, 37; and race, 182; and Social Security Act of 1935, 59, 62–63. *See also* Developmental disabilities
Douglas, Judith, 56

Eaton, Benjamin, 18, 191n3
Eliot, Martha, 58, 78
Engler, Richard E., 158–59, 169, 181, 183–84. See also *Children in Need of Parents*
European immigrants: children, 26, 28, 31, 88; Costa family, 17, 38–41; families, 21, 27–29, 36

Fair Labor Standards Act, 58, 135
"Family pathology," 113, 115–17, 120, 132, 145, 147; and race, 172, 175
Family preservation, 4, 28, 29, 181–82, 184–85
Family security: and foster care, 64–65, 160, 180; and gender, 58, 133; and New Deal, 8, 10, 56, 59–60, 69, 114, 133, 157–58, 160; and race, 61, 131
Fanshel, David, 95, 149; study of foster care, 103–5, 107–10, 142
Federal Emergency Relief Act (FERA), 56, 57
Federal Housing Authority (FHA), 74
Federal Transient Program, 60
Federal Works Administration, 78
Felten, Zelma "Buzz," 158, 160
Field, Marshall, III, 66, 75
Flemming, Arthur, 163, 164, 173; and "Flemming Rule," 163, 168, 171. *See also* Department of Health, Education and Welfare
Fordham School of Social Work, 82
Post-adopt programs, 95, 184, 186
Foster care: and adoption, 6–7, 11, 26–27, 92, 96, 98, 100, 122, 138, 147, 159, 181–83, 185; and AFDC–Foster Care, 161–63,

167–68, 170–72, 183; association with welfare, 6–8, 13–14, 27, 42, 55, 65, 133, 157, 166, 168, 176, 178; and board rates, 122, 126, 138, 161, 165; and class, 8, 12, 43, 106, 112–13, 131, 134, 157, 159–60, 166; colonial practices of, 18–19; as a component of household economy, 5; and day care, 6, 77, 138, 166–67; during Depression, 43, 55; and family pathology, 115, 120, 145; system of, 1–2, 6, 15, 22, 41–42, 63, 130, 168; and gender, 8, 11, 14, 105–7, 109–10, 112, 133, 144, 155, 168, 178; negative view of, 113, 115, 120, 178, 180; and New Deal, 10, 32, 44, 55, 58–65, 114–15, 131–33, 160–61, 176, 179; origins of, 3–5, 14, 17–18, 22, 27, 31–34, 42; and orphanages, 20, 22; overrepresentation of black children in, 185; payment to parents for, 136, 138, 142–47, 161, 178; professionalization of, 31, 134, 150; as public obligation, 5, 178; public and private extension of, 6, 11, 54, 63; as a punitive system, 8, 15, 158, 168, 170–71, 176, 180; and race, 12–13, 34–35, 112–13, 118, 124–27, 129–31, 155, 163, 172, 174–76, 185, 189n2, 211n48; sentimental understanding of, 27; as service, 12, 34, 130, 143, 166, 168; standards for, 72, 104, 130, 139–40, 142, 159, 170, 216n57; studies on, 2, 92, 113, 116, 131, 149, 158, 218n1, 219n11; as temporary, rehabilitative practice, 92–95, 102, 109, 140, 159, 168, 180, 186; as therapeutic service, 93, 105, 116, 119, 157, 159, 168, 185–86; as type of family, 5, 93, 99; and voluntarism, 45, 119, 168, 170, 183; and work homes, 3, 27, 37; and World War II, 14, 69, 75, 77, 80–86, 137–38, 201n16

—as synonym for: adoptive homes, 3, 6, 27; boarding homes, 3, 54, 138; free homes, 3; indenture, 3, 19; orphanages, 3, 27

See also Foster children; Foster family care; Foster homes
Foster care drift, 41, 159, 172, 185. See also *Children in Need of Parents*
Foster children, 2, 13, 91, 107; abuse of, 1, 2, 9, 10, 24, 145–46, 153–54, 164–65; and adoption, 7, 12, 95, 150, 180; and class, 115, 134, 142–43, 146, 157, 179; and convalescence, 122; and "foster care drift," 159; negative view of, 6–7, 12, 93, 112–16, 120–21, 134, 146, 157, 179; and race, 2, 12, 28–29, 131, 144, 156, 172, 175; rates for boarding, 73–74, 156; relationship with foster parents, 7, 49, 51, 92, 98, 104, 108, 136, 139, 156, 182–84; voluntary placement of, 169; and World War II, 80–82, 85, 87, 89. *See also* Dependent and neglected children; Hard-to-place children
Foster day care: as a synonym for day care, 6; and World War II, 77–78, 86
Foster family care, 1, 10, 17, 94, 115, 168, 177; and adoption, 27, 37; and day care, 76; development of, 3–7, 22–23, 41; definition of homes of, 189n13; and poverty, 14; public funding of, 11, 32, 37, 62, 65, 161; and race, 41; shift from boarding homes to, 37, 41, 141; standards for, 34, 140, 146; as a therapeutic service, 14, 140. *See also* Foster care
Foster fathers, 7, 11, 65, 105–11, 154–55; as boarding fathers, 197n26; and class, 107, 110–12, 116; and conceptions of fatherhood, 106–7, 110, 112, 208n66; as "passive," 108–10; and race, 111, 154
Foster mothers: and attachment to foster children, 98, 101, 136, 139; as care workers, 7, 12, 65, 92, 138, 178–79; and class, 143, 148, 179; and professional homemakers, 133, 144–45; expectation of maternal instincts among, 93, 98–99, 101, 134, 139; board payments to, 48, 54, 65, 86, 123, 137–38, 144–47, 151,

178–79; professionalization of, 77, 145; and race, 103, 128, 144, 148, 155; and single women, 73, 104; stereotypes and suspicions of, 101–3, 108, 137, 139, 142, 178–79, 208n76; and undervaluing of care work, 14, 65, 179; and World War II, 69, 80, 82–83, 86, 138. *See also* Boarding mothers

Foster parents: activism among, 97, 149–57, 173; and adoption, 7, 12, 95–97, 181–86; and class, 12, 106–7, 109, 111–12, 134, 138, 142, 155, 182–83; contracts signed by, 187–88; as workers, 86, 112, 135–36; negative views of, 7, 24, 93, 95–96, 100–102, 109, 111–13, 137, 146, 148–49, 182; as parents, 91, 94, 99, 144, 181, 185, 213n2; payments to, 8, 12, 38, 49, 51, 123–24, 133–34, 137, 142, 144, 146–47, 151, 156, 177–78, 183; professionalization of, 8, 14, 52, 136, 140, 144–45, 148, 153, 185; and race, 12–13, 85, 109, 111, 124, 126–29, 150, 173; screening of, 98, 112, 140, 143; as sentimental role, 49, 136, 151; as service providers, 103, 138, 143, 146, 224n6; standards and expectations for, 72, 91–93, 95–96, 100, 107, 134, 140–42, 148; as temporary role, 94–95, 97–98, 181, 186; training for, 7, 92, 106, 151–54, 184; and World War II, 14, 72, 80–81, 83–84, 86–87, 89, 92. *See also* Foster care; Foster fathers; Foster mothers

Free homes, 195n102; compared to foster homes, 120–21, 145–46; criticism or rejection of, 28, 52, 135; definition of, 196n13; during Depression, 46, 54–55; shift to boarding homes from, 25, 38; as synonym for foster care, 3
Friend, Margie, 129

Gallaudet, Thomas Hopkins, 37
Georgia State Department of Child Welfare, 118

Gingrich, Newt, 185
Giovannoni, Jeanne. *See* Billingsley, Andrew, and Jeanne Giovannoni
Glynn, Eugene, 151
Gordon, Henrietta, 87, 99, 121–23, 138
Gordon, Linda, 8, 10, 27, 30, 117
Group homes, 1

Hacsi, Tim, 9, 11, 17, 19
Handicapped children. *See* Disabled children; Hard-to-place children
Hanna, Agnes, 49, 136, 139
Hard-to-place children, 15, 113, 120–21, 123–24, 126, 132, 159, 211n31
Harris, Jeanette, 147
Herman, Ellen, 99, 140, 179
Homemaker services, 133, 144; called mother's aid, 6, 133; as child welfare service, 62, 131, 133, 161; contrasted with foster care, 133, 144–45; and foster care, 37, 131, 144; and home health care workers, 145; inadequate funds for, 46, 161; performed by trained homemakers, 133, 144–45; standards for, 92; as work relief, 133, 144–45
Hoover, Herbert, 56
Hopkins, Harry, 37, 56, 57
Hopkirk, Howard, 76, 78, 80, 82, 125
Howe, Samuel Gridley, 37
Hutchinson, Dorothy, 52, 73, 105, 108, 139

Illinois Children's Home in Chicago, 102
Immigrants. *See* European immigrants; Mexican Americans
Indenture, 12; colonial practices of, 18–19; contrasted with foster care, 19, 37; indenture laws, 3; and placing-out system, 21–22; and race, 35
Indian Adoption Project (IAP), 127, 173
Indian Child Welfare Act, 173
Indigenous Americans. *See* Native Americans

In Quest of Foster Parents (Hutchinson), 104
Ittleson Foundation, 100

Jackson, Nelson, 125
Jeter, Helen, 130
Jones, Cheney, 88
Jones, Jeweldean, 129
Josselyn, Irene, 102, 103, 105, 106, 143
Juvenile court, 25, 40, 72, 120; and foster care, 57, 170; and race, 34
Juvenile delinquency, 62, 94, 106–7

Kelley, Florence, 31
Kensington, Meredith, 1, 2
Kentucky Department of Child Welfare, 129
Kinship care, 27, 35, 55, 99, 140

Lanham Act, 76, 78, 167
Lathrop, Julia, 32
Layden, Gertrude, 147
League of Nations, 5, 67
Lenroot, Katharine, 162, 173; expectations of foster parents, 94–95, 111; promotion of foster care during World War II, 80–81, 83, 88; work on Social Security Act of 1935, 58–59
Lindsey, Duncan, 117, 166, 180
Liuini case, 216–17n63
Louisiana Children's Home Society, 56
Lundberg, Emma, 9, 59
Lundberg, Ferdinand, 109

Maas, Henry S., and Richard E. Engler, 158–59, 169, 181, 183–84. *See also Children in Need of Parents*
Massachusetts Child Council, 86
Massachusetts School for Idiotic Children and Youth, 37
Massachusetts Society for the Prevention of Cruelty to Children, 32
Mental illness: of foster children, 37,

62, 114, 115, 122, 123, 131; of parents as reason for child placement, 93, 101, 116, 117, 118, 119
Mexican Americans: children, 29, 39; families, 13, 28, 29, 61
Milwaukee Negro Foster Home Finding Committee, 128
Minneapolis Children's Protective Society, 38, 39, 40
Missouri Social Security Commission, 73
Mitchell, Max, 29
Modell, Judith, 111, 177–78, 180
Montgomery County Public Welfare Department, 150
Mothers' pensions, 11, 29, 32, 37, 44, 45, 58, 59, 60, 65, 114, 179. *See also* Aid to Dependent Children
Multiethnic Placement Act (MEPA), 184
Murphy, J. Prentice, 55

National Association of Black Social Workers (NABSW), 173, 174
National Association of Day Nurseries, 76
National Association of Social Workers, 125
National Conference on Foster Care, 149
National Conference on Social Work, 173
National Foster Parent Association (NFPA), 18, 152–55
National Urban League, 124–27, 174
National Welfare Rights Organization, 173
Native Americans: activists, 173; boarding schools for, 36; and child welfare, 131, 173; children, 13, 18, 29, 34, 36–37, 124, 127, 131; families, 99, 126–27, 131; foster parents, 13, 126, 173. *See also* Indian Adoption Project; Indian Child Welfare Act
Neglected children. *See* Dependent and neglected children

New Deal, 2, 4, 8, 32; and child welfare, 10, 44, 61, 93, 116, 132, 176, 179; and family security, 58, 60–61, 65, 69, 92–93, 114–16, 131–33, 157, 160; and foster care, 10, 14, 132, 179; and gender, 58; limits of, 132, 160; and race, 131; reformers, 32, 171, 176. *See also specific programs and legislation*
New England Homes for Little Wanderers, 88
New York Federation of Protestant Welfare Agencies, 127
New York Jewish Child Care Association, 97, 98, 187, 187–88
New York School of Social Work, 52, 73, 80, 92, 95, 105. *See also* Columbia School of Social Work
New York State Department of Social Welfare, 52, 171
Neuberger, Laura, case. *See* Sanders, Mr. and Mrs. Seymour
North Carolina Foster Home Services, 140
Now That April's There (Neumann), 88
Nurse mothers, 23

Oettinger, Katherine, 131
Old Age and Survivors Insurance (OASI), 6, 10, 59, 60
Oliphant, Winford, 171–72
Oregon State Public Welfare Department, 105
Orphanages, 3, 185; criticism of, 28–29; decreasing numbers of, 209n5; during Depression, 38, 46, 57; and foster care, 37, 41, 46, 54, 94, 114–15, 141, 177; foster care as a synonym for, 3, 27; in nineteenth century, 19–24, 34; as precursor to foster care, 20, 22–24; private or religious, 19–20, 46, 53, 57, 64; and race, 19, 34–36, 46; state subsidies of, 20, 24

Orphan trains, 21, 22, 34, 66, 192n25. *See also* Brace, Charles Loring; Placing out
Ougheltree, Cornelia, 127, 128

Parens patriae, 18
Pennsylvania School of Social Work, 55
Perkins, Frances, 47, 56–57
Permanency movement, 159, 181–82, 184–86
Personal Responsibility and Work Opportunity Act, 185
Placing out, 21–22, 159. *See also* Orphan trains
Poverty: and adoption, 26, 185; and boarding homes, 23, 48, 51; and child neglect, 8–9, 27, 43, 165; and family pathology, 116–17, 119, 132, 145; and foster care, 8, 10, 14, 17, 43, 51, 93–94, 115–16, 120, 131, 134, 145, 157–59, 162, 165–67, 170, 176, 180–81; ideas about among welfare experts, 29–31, 44, 114–16, 164; and immigration, 21, 24–29; and indenture, 12, 18, 35; and New Deal, 8–10, 44, 57–61, 65, 93, 114–16, 132, 158, 160, 163, 176, 179; and orphanages, 19, 23; and race, 20, 35, 112, 125, 129–30, 150, 185; and unmarried mothers, 118, 170, 179–80; and World War II, 76, 81, 87–88, 90
Prack, Gertrude, 73
Professionalization: and foster care, 11, 150, 156; scientific method applied to, 31; of social work and child welfare, 17, 26–27, 30–31, 43–44, 46–47, 65–66, 134, 136, 140. *See also* Casework for child welfare
Progressive Era: and gender, 6, 138; ideas on child welfare during, 27, 28, 30, 43–44, 58, 60, 114
"Psychotic mother," 116
Puschner, Emma, 81

Reconstruction Finance Corporation (RFC), 56
Reid, Joseph, 132, 155, 164, 166, 181
Restrictive zoning, 146
Richmond, Mary, 31, 32
Riis, Jacob, 24–25
Ripple, Helen, 140
Roberts, Dorothy, 125, 185
Robinson, B. H., 57
Robinson, Halbert B., 149
Roosevelt, Eleanor, 48–49, 66, 135
Roosevelt, Franklin D., 55–57
Roosevelt, Theodore, 28

Sanders, Mr. and Mrs. Seymour, 97–98, 101, 150, 206n27
Sandusky, Annie Lee, 124, 169
Simmons School of Social Work, 100
Single fathers, 60, 105, 133, 160
Single mothers, 45, 62–63, 179; and Aid to Dependent Children (ADC), 11, 59–60, 64–65, 163; and Aid to Families with Dependent Children (AFDC) and AFDC–Foster Care, 165, 168, 185; and boarding, 71, 87; and foster parenting, 73, 94, 104–5; and mothers' pensions, 29, 59; psychiatric explanations for, 101–2, 106, 118–19; punitive measures against, 117, 177; and race, 119, 133–34; and World War II, 71, 73, 81–82, 88
Smith v. OFFER, 156
Social Security Act of 1935, 4; Committee on Economic Security, 43, 57; and gender, 58, 60; 1962 Public Assistance Amendments to, 161, 165, 170; and race, 61, 176, 199n72; Title IV of, 9–10, 59–61, 162, 175, 179, 183; Title V of, 59, 62–64, 67, 132, 161, 164
Social Security Board, 60, 81
Social work: and child welfare, 27–28, 41, 46–47, 52, 62, 64, 66–67, 100, 109, 116–17, 120, 144, 158–59, 177; and foster

parents, 148–155, 169; and gender, 30, 32, 109–10, 118; professionalization of, 11, 30–34, 47, 52, 63–64; psychology and psychiatry influence on, 102–3, 114, 116–18, 134, 139, 149; and race, 28, 36, 41, 118, 125–30, 172–75; research in, 100, 114, 158; schools of, 4, 30, 34, 52, 55, 73, 80, 82, 92, 95, 100, 105, 125, 149, 158, 171, 173. *See also* Social workers; Casework for child welfare
Social workers: as child welfare experts, 6, 14, 30–31, 47, 62–64, 123–24; and foster care, 2, 4, 54, 120, 149, 155, 158–59, 169, 177; and gender, 32, 224n11; negative views of, 13, 32; and the New Deal, 56; professionalization of, 11, 52; and race, 28, 36, 41, 125, 127, 129, 173, 175, 224n11; view of foster parents by, 103–04, 109–10; and World War II, 67. *See also* Caseworkers in child welfare; Social work
Societies for the Prevention of Cruelty to Children, 27
Special needs. *See* Hard-to-place child; Disabled children
Spock, Benjamin: *Baby and Child Care*, 108
Standards for foster care. *See* Child Welfare League of America: and *Standards* for foster care
St. Louis Children's Aid Society, 51
Swaim, Rev. William, 114–15, 131, 132

Tennessee Welfare Department, 97
Termination of Parental Rights (TPR), 95, 183, 184
Travelers Aid Society (Washington, D.C.), 73
Truman, Harry S., 15, 94, 96, 117
Turitz, Zitha, 100

United Home Finding Campaign, 84, 87
United Nations, 5; and Declaration on Rights of the Child, 184

University of Washington, Child Development Laboratory, 149
Unwed mothers. *See* Single mothers
U.S. Children's Bureau. *See* Children's Bureau
U.S. Committee for the Care of European Children (USCOM), 66–68

Wagner-Rogers Bill, 89
Wald, Lillian, 31
War orphans, 80–81, 83, 120
Washington, Booker T., 35–36
Welfare state: foster care in, 6–7, 13, 42, 55, 134, 155–57; and gender, 11, 65, 155; and New Deal, 2, 4, 14, 32, 115, 132–33; public child welfare in, 17, 43–44, 55–59, 132–33; and race, 11, 61, 155; White House Conference on the Care of Dependent Children and, 28–31, 176, 183–84
White House Conference on Child Health and Protection: 1930 Children's Charter, 46
Wickenden, Elizabeth, 171
Wolins, Martin, 94–95, 105
Workman's Compensation, 65, 115
Work or wage homes, 3, 27, 37–38, 46, 196n13
World War II: British children during, 66, 80–82, 88–89; and conceptions of fatherhood, 107; day care during, 75–78, 83, 86, 138; effect on board rates, 73, 74, 86, 121, 138; family disruption during, 70–71, 204n94; and foster care, 14, 68–69, 77–78, 80–82, 84–85, 87, 89, 129, 132–33, 136–38, 167, 201n16; Jewish children from Reich during, 89; shortage of foster homes during, 72–75, 86, 92, 121; single parenthood during, 71, 73, 82; war orphans during, 80–81, 83, 120; and working mothers, 75–76

Zelizer, Viviana, 19, 48, 137, 139

www.ingramcontent.com/pod-product-compliance
Lightning Source LLC
Chambersburg PA
CBHW020644230426
43665CB00008B/307